D1338662

SONGS OF THE TROUBADOURS

SONGS OF THE TROUBADOURS

Edited and translated by
Anthony Bonner

London
GEORGE ALLEN & UNWIN LTD
RUSKIN HOUSE   MUSEUM STREET

A N'Eva

La genser etz c'om posc' el mon chauzir,
o no i vei clar dels olhs ab que us remir.

CONTENTS

Introduction

Who Were the Troubadours?

To the average English-speaking reader the word "troubadour" conjures up little more than an image of a fellow dressed in a Robin Hood costume singing under his lady's window and accompanying himself with a lute. This was the notion implanted by Sir Walter Scott and since propagated by Hollywood. That the troubadours wrote great poetry and are therefore worthy of our literary consideration was an idea that, to my knowledge, was only suggested to the English-speaking public by two critics, Chaytor and Ezra Pound, who wrote in the years immediately preceding and following the First World War. Before and since, the silence has been all but deafening,[1] so the average reader shouldn't feel guilty for knowing so little. But it does make it necessary for us to begin by defining our terms.

The troubadours were men who wrote lyric poetry in a language called Provençal during the two centuries between 1095 and 1295. It was a poetry written almost exclusively under the patronage of the greater noblemen of the day and is therefore predominantly aristocratic or courtly. Furthermore—and this is of great importance—it was the first lyric poetry in any modern European language, and all other lyric poetry in Europe either descends from it or was at one time tremendously influenced by it. Although much of it is love poetry, the troubadours did in fact write on almost every topic conceivable, from politics to the most scatological humor. Lastly, in addition to being a poet, the troubadour was also a musician, and as far as we know, his poetry was sung, not recited.

* Notes accompanying this section begin on p. 238.

This culture, although it grew up and flourished in the South of France—in the area which scholars have named Occitania, comprising Aquitaine, Languedoc, Auvergne and Provence—soon spread south into Spain and east into Italy. But the heart of this culture was always Occitania, and in order to understand it, to begin to feel what kind of a society gave birth to this poetry, and in what kind of an environment the troubadours lived and wrote, we must give some historical background.

A Brief History of the Period

When in 987 the Carolingian dynasty came to an end and the first Capetian took the throne of France, centuries of chaos and unrelenting war had reduced the country to a pitiable state. The population was so scant that there were no cities or even towns of any size, many villages were either partly or totally deserted, and large tracts of land remained uncultivated. Life was almost completely rural and closed in upon itself, each feudal community living on what it could itself produce. Since the Roman roads had gone into disuse because of the dangers of traveling, and since that great artery of Roman trade, the Mediterranean, had been closed off to the West by the Moslems, commerce had all but ceased to exist.

Such tremendous and all-consuming insecurity was, however, on its way to finding a solution: a specialization of labor called feudalism, with a peasant class (the serfs) deriving protection from—in return for feeding—a warrior class (the nobility), and this warrior class in turn divided into a hierarchy of the lesser nobility deriving protection from—in return for providing troops for—the higher nobility. This was the nucleus around which society slowly reorganized itself to provide that minimum of security without which a normal life of trade and culture is impossible.

In 987, however, feudalism was still in its infancy, so when I use that word, the reader mustn't imagine a society living among the magnificent churches and castles of the later Middle Ages. Most of the churches built then were small, crude affairs. Some of the castles had grim, square stone keeps in the middle, but many of them were simple structures of mud and fieldstone surrounded by wooden stockades like those built in the American West to provide shelter from Indian attacks. As for poetry, music and art, they were conspicuous more by their absence. They were cultivated, to be sure, in a few monastic centers, but this was a highly sporadic affair that depended more on the taste and energy of a particular man or group of men than on any general level of learning.

But after the year 1000 things began to change, at first slowly and then with gathering momentum. As life became more secure, the population began to increase, new lands came under cultivation, commerce started flowing again and with it came the growth of towns. This rise of wealth coincided with two religious movements of importance. The first was the pilgrimage to Santiago de Compostela which induced people to abandon their lives of rural isolation. The second was the rise of the Benedictine order of Cluny with its affiliated monasteries throughout Europe, which, with its emphasis on reform of monastic life and learning, did much to revive culture. As a result of all this, a true renaissance took place. It was in the eleventh century that Romanesque architecture appeared and spread throughout Europe. It is from then that we have our first examples of polyphonic music (and since it is precisely the development of polyphony or part music that differentiates Western music from that of the rest of the world, one can say that it was in this century that Western music was born).[2] And, what is more important for us, it was towards the end of this century, around the time of the First Crusade, that we have with William of Aquitaine the first lyric poetry in any modern European language.

This period of the First Crusade, moreover, witnessed a series of events in which the West for the first time began to gain some ascendancy over the East. In the tenth century the Moslem world had been completely dominant. Not only had the Arabs controlled the Mediterranean and all its commerce, but their civilization, with its wealth and refinement, its science, art and literature, had arrived at a stage of development which it would take Western Europe several centuries to equal. And in Spain the Moslems had reached an extraordinary height of power, with Cordoba becoming the largest and richest city in Western Europe.

But in the latter part of the eleventh century the scales began to tip the other way. Between 1060 and 1090 the Normans wrested Sicily from the Arabs; in 1085 Toledo, the ancient Visigothic capital of Spain, was reconquered; in 1094 the Cid took Valencia; in 1095 the First Crusade was preached in Clermont-Ferrand; and finally in 1099 the Crusaders conquered Jerusalem.[3]

It was during this time that Occitania began its period of wealth and splendor. The Mediterranean was no longer, in Pirenne's phrase, "a Moslem lake," and the Pisans and Genoese had begun going busily back and forth with their ships. They set up their agents with their warehouses in all the principal ports of Occitania—Marseille, Arles, Saint-Gilles, Montpellier, Agde, and Narbonne—which thus found itself at the crossroads between the Mediterranean and Northern Europe. Inland, the other towns along the trade and pilgrimage routes also partook of this new wealth. This sudden prosperity, however, brought with it a certain amount of turbulence. In the first place, the Genoese and Pisan merchants were continually at each others' throats, fighting for commercial supremacy. In the second place, an entirely new class had arisen: the bourgeoisie in the towns, for whom a place had to be made in the feudal hierarchy. Sometimes this new position was not won without bloodshed, as when in 1167 the good burghers of Béziers rose up and butchered their viscount, only to have the viscount's son get his revenge two years later by butchering them in turn.

But predominantly this society moved peacefully into its newfound wealth and security. The main impression is of a world bubbling with activity. A continuous movement of noblemen, monks, pilgrims, merchants and itinerant artisans. A continuous expanding of towns, rebuilding of houses, castles, churches and walls. And a joyous world of employment and reward for masons, sculptors, painters, musicians—and poets.

All this effervescence took place, however, in an atmosphere of political chaos, which in its own peculiar way was not only ordered, but also managed to function quite well—or at least until more ordered and less chaotic groups such as the Church and the Northern French came down to shatter it. One of the prime reasons for this situation was that Occitanian feudal society had developed outside the sphere of influence of any overruling monarchy. For centuries the two parts of France—the North with its King and the South with its many noble families—had led almost completely separate lives. Nominally the king was still overlord of these southern noblemen, but this meant merely that his name appeared at the bottom of documents—"Written in the eighth year of the reign of King Louis"—no more. Throughout the twelfth century the power of the French Kings remained nil in Occitania; they had far too many troubles nearer home to be able to pay the slightest attention to their distant vassals.

So we must abandon our ideas of France as a single political unit, and instead consider the various regions in the South ruled by separate noble families as almost entirely independent petty kingdoms. In addition, these noble families are important for us, because it is from them that came the great patrons of the troubadours.

The most powerful feudal lords in all of France were the Dukes of Aquitaine, who were also Counts of Poitiers. Their lands covered most of southwestern France, from Poitiers itself down to the Pyrenees, and included such cities as Limoges, Périgueux and Bordeaux; to the east they were overlords of the Auvergne (although their effective power there seems never to have been very great). And it was an extraordinary family that ruled these lands, starting with the first troubadour, William IX (ruled 1086–1127), continuing through his son William X (1127–1137) to his granddaughter and heiress, the famous Eleanor of Aquitaine. Her first marriage to the monkish Louis VII of France ended in a divorce that was to prove very nearly fatal to the French monarchy. For shortly thereafter she married Henry of Anjou, whose spectacular rise to power was to change the political map of Europe. For Henry had already inherited Normandy, Maine and Anjou (1150–1151); by his marriage to Eleanor (1152) he gained control of Aquitaine and Poitou; and then finally (1154) he was crowned Henry II of England. His lands now stretched from Scotland to the Pyrenees and included all of western France. The French monarchy was only saved by the immense geographical dispersal of these lands, the ruling of which proved almost too much even for Henry II's extraordinary ability and energy. In addition, he was unable to cope with the remarkable brood of sons he had by Eleanor: Henry "the Young King" (as the troubadour Bertran de Born called him), Richard the Lionhearted, Geoffrey of Brittany and John Lackland, who at crucial moments would side with the French king in rebellion against their domineering father.

South and east of Aquitaine lay the very heart of Occitania —the Languedoc proper [4]—most of which had slowly come to be occupied by the family of the Counts of Toulouse. Their lands stretched from their capital all the way to the banks of the Rhône. But, except for Toulouse and Saint-Gilles, they never succeeded in dominating directly any of the other important cities of the south. The greatest challenge to their power came from the family of the Trencavels, who had come to be Viscounts of Albi, Carcassonne, Béziers, Agde and Nîmes. And there were two other families which, although their territories were by no means so vast, were important because they controlled two wealthy maritime cities: the Viscounts of Narbonne and the Lords of Montpellier.

Further south lay the other big challenge to their power— Aragon and Catalonia, which were united in 1137 under Raymond Berenguer IV.[5] For the interests of the Aragonese monarchs were by no means relegated to their lands south of the Pyrenees. They not only possessed the Roussillon and several enclaves in upper Languedoc, but they also considered themselves rightful overlords of the Viscounts of Carcassonne. However, the principal bone of contention between the houses of Toulouse and Aragon were the lands east of the Rhône— Provence.

Ancestors of both houses had married heiresses of Provence, and thus they both considered it theirs. After years of squabbling, they finally came to an agreement in 1125 that all the lands north of the Durance would belong to the Count of

Toulouse, and all those between the Durance and the sea to the Count of Barcelona, grandfather of Alfonso of Aragon. But this settlement seems to have done little to placate the squabble, for it continued—and sometimes with considerable vehemence—for the rest of the century.

So, to recapitulate: from 1154 on (which is roughly speaking when the golden age of troubadour poetry begins) we have four main areas in the South of France. Aquitaine and Poitiers ruled by the Kings of England, Toulouse ruled by a series of counts called Raymond, a united Aragon and Catalonia, and Provence divided between the houses of Toulouse and Aragon. Within the Languedoc we have three other families: the Trencavels of Albi-Carcassonne-Béziers-Agde-Nîmes, the Viscounts of Narbonne, and a series of Williams ruling Montpellier. To help the reader keep all this straight (for these names will come up again and again in the poetry), on the following page is a chart covering the crucial years from 1150 to 1250, giving the names of the various noblemen and their dates of rule.

So as not to make this chart too confusing for the reader, I have somewhat simplified things with respect to Aquitaine and Albi-Carcassonne-Béziers-Agde-Nîmes.[6] Also I have omitted Provence, since the situation there was far too complicated for me to want to burden the reader with it. Suffice it to say that it was ruled—or at least the southern portion of Provence belonging to Aragon (the only part that had any real importance in the world of the troubadours)—by a series of brothers and nephews of the kings of Aragon who changed so often as to give the impression of playing a game of musical chairs.[7]

As for the actual history of the period between 1154 and the turn of the century, there is singularly little to recount. More than anything it consisted of a continual series of minor squabbles: squabbles between the various feudal lords, between them and the church (since the church too had large landholdings), between them and the bourgeoisie in the cities, and between the ever-present Genoese and Pisan merchants. Behind the façade of all this bickering there were, indeed, two more important struggles going on: that between the French and English monarchies for the domination of the

FRANCE	ENGLAND	AQUITAINE	TOULOUSE	ALBI-CARCAS-SONE-BÉZIERS-AGDE-NÎMES	NARBONNE	MONTPELLIER	ARAGON CATALONIA
LOUIS VII 1137-1180	HENRY II 1154-1189	HENRY AND ELEANOR 1152-1169	RAYMOND V 1148-1194	RAYMOND TRENCAVEL 1150-1167	ERMENGARDE 1143-1192	WILLIAM VII 1149-1172	RAYMOND BERENGUER IV CAT. 1131 AR. 1137 DIED 1162
		RICHARD I (THE LIONHEARTED) AQ. 1169		ROGER II 1167-1194		WILLIAM VIII 1172-1202	ALFONSO II 1162-1196
PHILIPPE AUGUSTE 1180-1223	ENG. 1189 DIED 1199 JOHN LACKLAND 1199-1216		RAYMOND VI 1194-1222	RAYMOND ROGER 1194-1209	AIMERIC III 1194-1239	PETER II AR. & CAT. 1196; MONT. 1204 DIED 1213	
LOUIS VIII 1223-6 LOUIS IX (SAINT LOUIS) 1226-1270	HENRY III 1216-1272		RAYMOND VII 1222-1249	TRENCAVEL (RULE ONLY NOMINAL 1209-1246)	AIMERIC IV 1239-1270	JAMES I THE CONQUEROR 1213-1276	

soil of France (during our period the main area concerned were the English lands north of the Loire); and that between the houses of Toulouse and Aragon for the domination of Languedoc and Provence. In the midst of these two larger struggles, the lesser vassals played a continual game of backing whichever adversary was weakest—thus maintaining a balance of power and preventing any single ruler from getting strong enough to be able to check their own independence. The result was the kind of feudal chaos which the troubadour Bertran de Born so loved (and did so much to foment). But at the same time this chaos brought about a peculiar kind of stability. So much so, in fact, that for fifty years the situation in southern France remained almost completely unchanged, and a person alighting somewhere in Occitania in 1154 and then returning in 1204 would, politically speaking, have noticed almost no difference at all. This was to be in stark and tragic contrast with the next fifty years, for if the same person had been able to live long enough to return in 1254, he would have found the political situation almost unrecognizable.

For this strangely ordered, stable and prosperous chaos had one great flaw: it was maintained by a delicate balance which proved only too easy to disrupt, and of course once the balance was lost, the entire structure crumbled with extraordinary speed. And shortly after the turn of the century, two disruptive forces which had been incubating for years began to upset the balance.

First of all, in the struggle between France and England, the wily and ambitious Philippe Auguste had, until 1199, found himself struggling against two English monarchs who could play the game of feudal politics quite as well as he— Henry II and Richard the Lionhearted. But after that, the grasping, unpopular John Lackland was no match for the French king.[8] In 1203 Philippe Auguste invaded Normandy, and in a surprisingly short time he managed to recapture all the English lands north of the Loire River, and he even managed to take a large bite into the Poitou, south of the Loire.

But the second disruptive force was to prove much graver, much more tragic, for it was a religious question. A long time before, a doctrine which was a mixture of Christianity and

Manicheism had made its way from the Near East, across the Balkans and into Europe. And although in many places it made converts and caused the Church to take notice, nowhere did it meet with such acceptance and cause such alarm to ecclesiastical authorities as in Occitania.

This doctrine, known as the Albigensian or Catharist heresy, was Christian insofar as its basic text was the New Testament and insofar as it attempted to return to the poverty and simplicity of the early Church. However, it contained a dualist concept which made it fundamentally different from Catholicism. To the Cathars the world was divided between the forces of good and evil; all material things—the body, the flesh, and in short everything visible—were the creation of Satan, and the only true good lay in the spirit, in God, to whom the soul aspired. Their greatest penitence, therefore, was life on earth—this was their hell. If a person died unreconciled with God, his soul would enter another body, and so on in an endless chain of transmigrations, until finally a reconciliation was reached and the soul was at last liberated from the flesh. As a result of this idea that the flesh was evil, they were not only vegetarians, but also believed in complete chastity.

Not everyone, of course, was able to live up to such ideals of purity (the word Cathar comes from a Greek word meaning "pure"), and therefore their followers were divided into two groups: the perfects and the believers. The former were those who had passed through a series of rites culminating in the *consolamentum*, a kind of baptism conferred by the laying on of hands. The believers, those who felt themselves unable to live up to the perfects' standard of purity (or to undergo the dangers inherent in such a position), only took the *consolamentum* on their death beds, for without it their souls could not join God.

Now this sect had made inroads into Occitania that were truly astounding, and into all levels of society from simple country people and townfolk to the highest noblemen. To the point, for instance, where the mother, sister and daughter of the Count of Foix had all received the *consolamentum*, where Roger II of Béziers and Carcassonne had appointed as tutor for his son the notorious Cathar, Bertrand de Saissac, and where even the Count of Toulouse apparently doubted as to which was the true religion. And perhaps even more astonishing, the entire family of the Catholic Bishop of Carcassonne, Bernard Raymond of Rocafort, was also Cathar. Moreover, this sect flourished in Occitania amidst an extraordinary atmosphere of tolerance. The attitude of the Catholic majority is best summed up by the statement a knight of Toulouse made to the Inquisition: "I can easily see that the Catholic Church is right, and not these heretics. But all the same, I have lived among them, and I have relatives and friends who are of their persuasion, and I see that they live honestly."

Now all this could not help but alarm the ecclesiastical authorities. Yet until the turn of the century, their efforts to combat Catharism were more or less sporadic.[9] With the new, energetic Pope, Innocent III, however, things soon changed. By 1204, the year after Philippe Auguste had begun his campaigns against the English lands in the north, the south was beginning to feel the pressure of a small but dedicated group of papal legates. They traveled back and forth arguing, persuading and threatening, trying to get the noblemen to clamp down on the heretics. In 1206, two more figures appeared on the scene: the ex-troubadour Folquet de Marseille, who was now made Bishop of Toulouse and who was soon to become the implacable enemy of the count and a fanatic persecutor of heretics; and the Spaniard, Saint Dominic, who was to begin his life of poverty and preaching, trying to convert the heretics by example and by word. But Dominic's gentle ways were soon overridden by the mounting tension, which reached the boiling point in 1208, when some vassals of the Count of Toulouse murdered a papal legate.

The consequences of this murder were fatal. Not only was the Count unjustly blamed for it, made to do penance before the church of Saint-Gilles, stripped to the waist, with a rope around his neck and beaten with rods; but far worse than this personal abasement, a "crusade" was preached in the north against the heretic south. In the following summer (1209) the crusaders swarmed down on Occitania, sacked Béziers, massacring most of its inhabitants, and then took the fortress everyone had thought impregnable—Carcassonne—leaving its young Viscount to die in prison. But a man was needed to lead these crusades, to continue the struggle in the midst of the hostile south. And such a man was found in Simon de Montfort, a brilliant general and extraordinary leader of men (he time and time again won battles against overwhelming odds), but cruel and pitiless, fanatical and immeasurably ambitious. He established himself at Carcassonne and slowly began to take all the castles in the vicinity. His power grew till finally even the King of Aragon began to feel him a menace and allied himself with his ancient enemy, the Count of Toulouse.

This coalition of southern forces finally met those of Simon de Montfort in 1213 near the town of Muret, on the Garonne River just southwest of Toulouse. The outcome of this crucial battle could not have been more tragic for Occitania. Not only did Simon de Montfort utterly defeat a numerically superior enemy and send them fleeing for their lives across the countryside, but it was also in this battle that King Peter of Aragon met his death.

In order to understand the consequences of this battle, we must try to see it in a larger context of changes that were taking place in Europe. The year before, in 1212, the Spanish Christians had defeated the Moslems at Navas de Tolosa. This battle so broke the back of Moslem resistance that from now on the Christians were to be undisputed masters of the Peninsula, and within the next forty years Mallorca, Valencia, Cordoba and Seville were to fall into their hands. The childhood memory of these two battles, Navas de Tolosa and Muret, was to make the new king of Aragon, James the Conqueror, turn his back on Occitania, realizing that there was much more advantage in fighting the Moslems than in struggling against the Church and the increasingly powerful French monarchy.

Then in 1214, the year after Muret, was fought the battle of Bouvines in which Philippe Auguste defeated the combined forces of a German emperor and·John Lackland. Among the many consequences of this battle, the French monarchy emerged with extraordinarily enhanced prestige and power—

for a long time now she would be the arbitor of Europe—and the English monarchy came out of it sadly battered and helpless.

As a result of all this, Occitania lost the only two allies of any consequence it might have had—Aragon and England. It was now alone against the combined forces of the northern French and the Church, and of the two the more dangerous enemy was the latter. So much so that one sixteenth-century historian said: "There was no power on earth capable of dispossessing the Count of Toulouse of his domains, if the Church had not become involved." But he was dispossessed, and in 1215 Simon de Montfort took possession of Toulouse.

The rest of the story is a sad tale of rebellions and submissions which I will only give in outline. First the whole South went up in arms, and in 1218 Simon de Montfort was killed [10]; by 1224 the Occitanian noblemen had recovered all their lands, and the last of the detested Montfort clan had abandoned the South forever. But their restored hopes were soon dashed to the ground when the Church preached another crusade and persuaded the new King of France, Louis VIII, to lead it in person. Before this fresh onslaught the exhausted and isolated South soon crumbled. The last Viscount of Béziers and Carcassonne fled to Spain, and his lands were taken over by the crown. In 1229 Raymond VII of Toulouse was forced to sign the Treaty of Meaux, by which he gave up two-thirds of his patrimony to the French King and agreed to the marriage of his daughter and heiress, Jeanne, to Louis IX's brother, Alphonse. Now too the Holy Inquisition came into being and began its somewhat more systematic persecution of the heretics.

Later there were two more pitifully uncoordinated attempts at rebellion: one in 1240 by the exiled Viscount of Béziers and Carcassonne, and another in 1242 by Raymond VII of Toulouse. Both were quickly subdued. Then in 1244 came the siege and capture of the last Catharist stronghold, Montségur, a mountaintop castle just southeast of Foix.

During all these struggles, Provence had remained pretty much in the background. Then suddenly in 1245 the Count died, and there ensued a frenzied diplomatic scramble between the Count of Toulouse and the King of Aragon; but it was to be the last of their centuries-old squabbles over Provence. For in the midst of it, another brother of Louis IX, Charles, settled the whole dispute by marrying the heiress of Provence and taking it for himself. Then in 1249 Raimond VII died and Toulouse was inherited by his daughter and son-in-law. So for the first time, areas which had enjoyed centuries of independence were now ruled either by the French royal family—Toulouse by Alphonse and Provence by Charles—or more directly by royal agents, as in the extensive domains of the viscounts of Béziers and Carcassonne. Moreover, the Inquisition was slowly spreading its fingers throughout the south and bit by bit sapping its strength.

It was therefore but a small step to 1271, when Alphonse and Jeanne died without an heir and Toulouse was reunited with the French crown. France was now a great nation—the most powerful in Europe—but Occitania, whose past had been so glorious, was dead. It would from now on sink into the humdrum existence of provincial life within a country directed almost entirely from the north.

The Troubadours

Surely the greatest glory of Occitanian civilization—that which made it known throughout Europe—was the troubadours. They started writing their lyrics around the time of the First Crusade (1095) and continued even through the period of catastrophe and decadence until about 1295.

But what preceded them? Where did William of Aquitaine get the idea of writing in the particular forms and styles he chose? What gave rise to the notion of courtly love? This question—which is basically that of the origins of all our Western lyric poetry—is one that scholars have been trying to solve for years. Yet our knowledge of vernacular European literature before 1095 is so scanty, that trying to answer this question is almost impossible. Some maintain that it rose out of the popular poetry of the time, others that it had its roots in the Latin culture of the Church, and yet others that it came up from the Arabs in Spain. The first of these theses is the most difficult to deal with, because we know so incredibly little about the popular poetry of the eleventh century. The second thesis has in its favor the fact that all education then was in the hands of the Church, and that a man like William of Aquitaine must necessarily have come in contact with Latin religious poetry as well as with scraps of classical poetry. The third thesis has in its favor the immense superiority of Arab culture in the days preceding William of Aquitaine. For even in the eleventh century, although Moslem Spain began to decline politically, its culture in poetry, music, art and science continued unabated. To give the reader some idea of the difference between the Christian and Moslem culture of that time, it is enough to say that shortly before mid-century the largest library in northern Spain contained about 200 volumes, whereas that of the petty Moorish king of Almería, for instance, contained some 400,000 manuscripts. One might think that the linguistic or cultural barrier was too great for Arab literature to influence that of the Christians, but this objection vanishes when we remember details like that of the King of Aragon (whose widowed mother William of Aquitaine married) who at the bottom of Latin documents would sign himself in Arabic script: "Rex Pedro ben Xancho."

Which of these three theories is correct, nobody knows; perhaps all of them played their part. But until some solution is found, William of Aquitaine's poetry will always seem like some mysterious new creation, rising out of the void. And the fact that much of his poetry is humorous and even scatalogical somehow only compounds the mystery. Undoubtedly there were other men of his time writing poetry too; yet the only one whose name we even know is Eble II of Ventadorn, the father of Bernart de Ventadorn's patron—and none of his poems have been preserved.[11] So for all practical purposes, William of Aquitaine stands alone in the first generation of troubadours.

With the second generation—those poets who wrote in the 1130's and 1140's—we get three poets from widely different backgrounds: Cercamon, a Gascon jongleur; Marcabru, a foundling and also a Gascon; and Jaufre Rudel, a nobleman who wrote strange semimystical poetry.

With the third generation—those whose activity began principally after Henry II's coronation in 1154—begins the golden age of Provençal poetry. Now we start with Bernart de Ventadorn, Peire d'Alvernhe, Raimbaut d'Orange and continue through the classic poets (the ones that make up most of this anthology) till the period of decadence that begins with Muret in 1213. It was now that Occitania entered that period of chaotic stability I have described above, and this too was the epoch of the great patrons—Raymond V of Toulouse, Ermengarde of Narbonne, William VIII of Montpellier, Alfonso II of Aragon, Richard the Lionhearted and Barral, Viscount of Marseille.[12]

During this golden epoch what was the life of the troubadours like? As I have said before, they came from all classes—there were the poor foundlings like Marcabru and the servant family of Bernart de Ventadorn, and there were also monarchs like King Alfonso of Aragon, who tried his hand at composing verse (and was not without talent). But most of the poets came from what we would now call the middle classes: either from the lowest order of nobility, the simple knights (such as Arnaut Daniel), or from the bourgeoisie (such as Peire Vidal); some had even begun their careers in the Church (like Arnaut de Maruelh). Some came from families that were poor (Giraut de Bornelh), and some inherited considerable wealth (Folquet de Marseille).

Except for noblemen like Bertran de Born, whose life was spent trying to keep others at war, and Raimbaut d'Orange, whose time was divided among patronage, writing poetry and dodging his creditors, most of the troubadours probably wandered from court to court during the warmer months and during the wintertime stayed home studying, teaching or composing. Some seem to have been attached to courts in a more permanent way; but even this implied a wandering existence, since their patrons were often on the move from one castle and town to another. And those troubadours who could afford to do so traveled with one or more jongleurs who sang or recited their verses for them.

From what scraps of information we can gather here and there, we learn that patronage sometimes consisted of money payment, but often took the form of gifts of clothes, horses or land. As for the patrons, a situation developed much like that of Renaissance Italy. Not all of them were equally enlightened men, equally capable of appreciating fine poetry; however, to a certain extent, patronage was an obligation of their high station. Also it must have been what we would now call a status-symbol; just as a Renaissance nobleman ran a serious risk of being considered a nobody if he didn't hire one of the leading artists of the time, so the Occitanian nobility felt obliged to enhance the splendor of their courts by having troubadours in their service.

This relationship was frankly enough admitted so that if a nobleman showed signs of losing interest in the whole matter he was in serious danger of being called a skinflint by some poet. Now many troubadours were well enough known throughout Europe so that such an epithet was not to be taken lightly. And like most medieval men, the patrons had a strong enough feeling for the contrast between the transitoriness of political power and the permanence of art not to want to go down in history as a man whose court was a measly, unlettered, backwoods affair.

On the other side of the coin, patronage was expected to be rewarded by praises of the nobleman in the envoys of the troubadour's poems, or by the dedication of a poem to the nobleman's wife. Since the latter case involved love poetry, a certain amount of ink has been spilled by scholars on the subject of tsk-tsk what a scandalously adulterous life these people must have led. But for the most part the contents of these love poems seem to have been a matter of literary convention; and surely the troubadours had as little actual intention of diving into bed with their patrons' wives as Renaissance poets had of purchasing panpipes, taking up the life of shepherds and searching for nymphs to whom they could discourse in a delicate, Virgilian Latin.[13]

After the Battle of Muret in 1213, however, the whole world of patronage began to fall apart. The noblemen were now fighting for their very lives and were no longer concerned with enhancing the splendor of their courts. And of the great poets who had made up the golden age, some were now dead, others had entered monasteries and yet others had fled abroad.

The only court in southern France in which some patronage was still to be found was that of Provence under Ramon Berenguer IV (not to be confused with the man of the same name and number who ruled Catalonia and Aragon a century before) and his successor Charles of Anjou. The principal patrons were now to be found outside Occitania. In Spain there was James the Conqueror of Aragon-Catalonia (1213–1276), and in united Castille and Leon first Fernando III (died 1252) and then Alfonso the Wise (1252–1284).

But the greatest opportunity lay in northern Italy. Even before 1200 some poets seem to have gone there to seek their fortunes, and slightly later they started coming in droves. Then there grew up a generation of poets who were Italian—who were born and brought up there, but who took to writing in Provençal—and soon the courts of northern Italy, from Genoa to the Adriatic, were swarming with troubadours, both foreign and native born.

In the eighty-odd years from the Battle of Muret to the final eclipse of Provençal poetry, there were many poets but few really great ones. The old molds seem to have worn thin, and the best poets were those who struck out in different directions. In Occitania itself there was Peire Cardenal, inveighing violently against the Church and the northern French, somehow eluding the clutches of the Inquisition and living to be nearly a hundred years old. In Catalonia there was the versatile juggler with words, Cerverí, and in Italy there was Sordello, made so famous by Dante (and in English-speaking countries by Robert Browning). Finally there was Guiraut Riquier, called "the last of the Troubadours" not so much because he was in fact the last in date (though pretty nearly so), but rather because, with his yearning for bygone times, his endless search for understanding patronage and his rather pathetic attempts to maintain the dignity of his status as a troubadour, he represents the last gasp of this poetry in a world which had by then completely changed.

Before troubadour poetry died, however, it had already spread its influence throughout Western Europe. In northern France the trouvères were, with certain important exceptions, almost a carbon copy of their southern counterparts; in Galicia and Portugal a school of poetry arose which owed a great deal to the troubadours; in Germany the Minnesingers were open enough about this influence even to translate some Provençal poems into medieval German; but it was in Italy that this influence bore its greatest fruit.

In discussing the relationship between Provençal and Italian poetry, we must remember that when the former died out around 1295, Dante was already thirty years old. In other words, troubadour poetry was still a living thing when he was growing up. And indeed he openly acknowledged his debt to it in his *De Vulgari Eloquentia,* a debt which he was handsomely to repay by dedicating large sections of the Divine Comedy to such poets as Bertran de Born, Arnaut Daniel, Folquet de Marseille and Sordello. And it is probably thanks to Dante's extraordinary fame that the troubadours continued to be read and studied in Italy (Petrarch, for instance, was very familiar with them) far into the Renaissance.

England too received its share of influence, either directly through Provençal poetry (we must remember that one of its queens, Eleanor, was Duchess of Aquitaine, and that her son Richard the Lionhearted was one of the great troubadour patrons), or indirectly through the northern French trouvères (since the ruling classes in England were at that time almost entirely French speaking). Many of the lovely English thirteenth-century lyrics are based on Continental models, as to both form and content.

In short, there was no lyric poetry in Western Europe that remained unaffected in one way or another by the troubadours.

The Language

An adequate discussion of Provençal would involve giving a grammar, which would be out of place here. But there are a few facts about Provençal that the reader should know in order to understand the literature properly.

Firstly, it is one of a group of languages derived from Latin, called the Romance languages. It therefore has much in common with its neighbors, Spanish, French and Italian. But one thing must be made clear: even though it is spoken within the boundaries of present-day France, it is in no way a dialect of French. The two are similar, naturally, but no more so than, for instance, Portuguese and Spanish.

Another possible source of confusion is its name. A far more accurate name would be "Occitan," corresponding to the region we have called "Occitania," but that of "Provençal" has behind it such a force of tradition and usage that it would seem unwise to change it. Yet the reader must realize that the language was spoken (and the literature written) in an area far greater than the mere region of Provence.

In fact, if the reader will look at the endpaper map and follow the line starting from Bordeaux, curving up above the Auvergne, back down below Lyon and Grenoble, he will have, roughly speaking, the northern border of the Provençal language. To the south it extends to the Pyrenees and to the east to the Alps. In other words, it occupies about a third of present-day France.

Within this area we must make two exceptions. First of all, in the southwest corner of France (between the Garonne river, the Pyrenees and the sea) the people speak a dialect called Gascon. And secondly, in the southernmost province of France (the Roussillon), the language is the same as that spoken all down the east coast of Spain, through Barcelona and Valencia to Alicante as well as in the Balearic Islands, namely Catalan. Gascon was different enough so that troubadours such as Cercamon and Marcabru must have had to make a considerable effort to write in correct Provençal; whereas Catalan was so similar that it would have been quite easy for poets such as Guilhem de Cabestanh and Cerverí to make the change.

But now in using a phrase such as "correct Provençal" we come to one of the most peculiar aspects of this language. And that is that all the troubadours used a common literary language, or koine, which was completely unusual in the twelfth and thirteenth centuries. In northern France, for instance, every medieval poet wrote in the dialect of his period and region, and these dialects could differ wildly from one another at a distance of 200 miles or a time interval of 200 years. But not so with the troubadours: Guiraut Riquier wrote in the 1270s in a language that was almost identical with that used by William of Aquitaine in 1100; and Sordello, who was born and brought up near Mantua and Padua, used a language that differs scarcely at all from that of Jaufre Rudel, who was Lord of Blaye near Bordeaux.

But languages suffer the same fate as the people who speak them, and with the decline of troubadour culture and the slow centralization of France around Paris, Provençal slowly began to be either replaced or infiltrated by French. It fell tragically from a position of immense prestige throughout Western Europe to its present situation of a language spoken principally by humble villagers and country people. In the past hundred years—with Mistral and others—there has been considerable effort to revive it, but so far this effort has met with only partial success.

The Poetry

As I have said before, there is an immense variety in troubadour poetry, in tone, style and technique. Perhaps the best way to approach this variety is by starting with a brief list of the various types of poetry that were written.

Canso or *chanso* (accented on the last syllable)—the love song. In form it had to have a rhyme and/or metrical scheme different from all other poems that had preceded it; in content it was concerned with the many twists and turns of courtly love. Its form was therefore continually varied and its content conventional and stereotyped; this distinction is important for what we will say later concerning the aesthetics of this poetry. Among the earlier troubadours this type of poem seems to have been called a *vers* (see the biographies of Marcabru and Peire d'Alvernhe).

Sirventes (again accented on the last syllable). In form it had to copy the rhyme and metrical scheme of some pre-existing *canso;* in content it could take up any topic but courtly love—war, politics, morality, satire, humor, invective. It was therefore the exact opposite of the *canso;* its form was conventional and its content varied.

Between these two forms, *canso* and *sirventes,* one can account for the vast majority of troubadour verse. The remaining forms have a more peripheral interest. The ones worth mentioning are:

Tenso (again accented on the last syllable). A dialogue or debate between two poets, each taking alternate stanzas (examples on pages 98 and 104).

Partimen. A variety of *tenso* in which poet 1 (in stanza 1) selects a topic for debate, then poet 2 (in stanza 2) chooses which side he wants to defend, and the argument is off. Finally at the end they choose a judge to arbitrate their differences (see p. 208).

Planh. A lament on the death of some person (see pp. 147, 210).

Pastorela. A form in which the poet recounts his meeting with a shepherdess (hence the name) and how he tried to seduce her by praising her beauty and intimating what an honor it would be to sleep with a fine upper-class fellow like him. But shepherdesses, being apparently a quick-witted lot, didn't always fall for these tactics (see pp. 53, 123, 224, and 227).

Alba. A complaint of two lovers who have been warned by the watchman that dawn is approaching and that they must now separate. Each stanza ends with a refrain, and this refrain ends with the word *alba* (dawn) (see p. 126).

Dance songs. There are a variety of forms that fit under this heading, but their importance is so slight in Provençal literature that I won't clutter the reader's mind with their names. (For an example see p. 214.)

This list, however, must be taken with a grain of salt, for like all attempts to pigeonhole art, these categories don't always hold. Many poems in troubadour literature are unclassifiable—they seem to belong to no fixed type, or they shift from one type to another in midstream. Nevertheless, used with a little circumspection, these categories are handy tools with which to grasp some of the fundamental concepts of troubadour poetry.

First let us take up the *sirventes.* As I said above, its form was conventional and its content free. It was therefore the *sirventes* that brought to Provençal literature its rich variety of subject matter, from the high moral courage of Peire Cardenal to the backroom humor of the Monk of Montaudan, from Bertran de Born's love of war and chaos to Marcabru's intense misanthropy. It was with the *sirventes* that the troubadours could show their anger, stir up trouble (it was often used as an instrument of propaganda) or make their audiences laugh.

However with the *canso*, it was the content that was conventional. It was only concerned with courtly love—the poet complains of his lady's harshness, pleads for mercy, rejoices in expectation of the pleasure he will receive, etc. And to express himself, he uses many of the conventional terms of courtly love: *joi* (joy, pleasure, and more specifically that found in love), *joven* (youth, or the qualities of youth—qualities essential to courtly love), *pretz* (worth, merit, distinction), and, on the other side of the ledger, *gilos* (the jealous husband—the villain of the piece).

The whole mechanism of courtly love hinged on four considerations. Firstly, it thrived on the tension created by unrequited love (an emotion entirely new in Western society); secondly any hopes of its being requited were based not so much on the aspirant's charm or good looks, but rather on his ability to make himself worthy of his lady; thirdly, it was an essentially adulterous relationship—the poet never sang of his own wife or of an unmarried girl (such relationships lacked the necessary tension to set the whole mechanism in motion);[14] and lastly, it was a secretive business in which the poet referred to the lady, if at all, only by means of a *senhal*, or pseudonym.[15] In addition, the poet employed much of the terminology of feudalism, claiming to be his lady's vassal or serf, etc.

One point, however, must be made clear. Courtly, unrequited love was to the troubadours by no means synonymous with Platonic love (although it was to become more and more so as the troubadour movement wore on and began to suffer from a certain hardening of the arteries). In fact, the earlier poets are often quite explicit about what sort of "favor" it is they seek.

> unless I have her next to me,
> naked, to kiss and embrace
> within a curtained room.[16]

Now that we have some idea of the *canso* and *sirventes,* we must emphasize some points which have caused a distressing amount of confusion in troubadour scholarship. In the first place, of these two forms, that which was by far the most important and on which (with few exceptions) a poet's reputation stood or fell, was the *canso.* And the *canso* was a type of verse that was predominantly abstract and formal. By abstract I mean that the poet was not trying to express himself, deliver a message or lay bare his soul in the way of romantic poets. This is, of course, another way of saying that the content of the poem was not of prime importance, but I also mean to imply that the reader was not expected to look around behind the poem to try to find the poet. The difference between this and modern abstract art lay in the fact that the artist, instead of having to create his own frame of reference, worked in one previously agreed upon between him and his audience (in this case, one of aristocratic amateurs), and this is what I mean by formal. Perhaps the best analogy is a piece of instrumental music by Haydn or Mozart. Here too is an art that is abstract and formal, and what could be more simple and even banal than the frame of simple scales and harmonies in which these two composers operate? The listener's delight is in the imagination and musicality with which the frame of reference is manipulated, in the sense of movement and coherence the composer has succeeded in imposing on these materials common to the whole contemporary world of music, and indeed, in the somewhat paradoxical sense of freedom the composer seems to find within this straitjacket, or even in the tension created between this outer restraint and his inner (musical) need for liberty of movement.

Another point which has caused confusion in troubadour criticism is the question of the poet's "sincerity" with reference to the content of his poems. It should, however, be quite clear from what I have said above that such a question is meaningless in any art that is abstract and formal. To take another analogy from music, it is like asking if Mozart was "sincere" when he wrote *Così fan tutte* or *Figaro.* Of course he was, but not about the subject matter. He was sincere about his art, and the subject was a frame on which to construct an opera.[17]

I have been belaboring points which might seem obvious to many readers, because the battles that were fought and won so long ago in English and Spanish literature for John Donne and Luis de Góngora, for instance, have only just recently begun to be fought over Provençal literature. There are still critics who complain of the banal contents of the troubadour love lyric and who grumble over such-and-such a poet's lack of sincerity.[18]

In considering these problems, therefore, it is best to remember what Mallarmé told an aspiring young colleague who complained that he could get no ideas for writing poems: "Poetry is not made up of ideas, but of words." This dictum applies perfectly to the Provençal *canso*. Everything lay in the words, with their complex patterns of meaning, association, imagery, sound and rhythm. The result was an extraordinary variety of techniques,[19] from the dazzling virtuosity of an Arnaut Daniel and the intricately woven fabric of conceits of a Folquet de Marseille, to the ease and charm of Bernart de Ventadorn and the classical restraint and moderation of a Giraut de Bornelh. The beauty of their verse lay in its form; its magic lay in the very materials out of which their art was constructed. And they were able to bring this beauty and magic to a degree of perfection rarely surpassed since their time.

The Music

As I said at the beginning of this introduction, the troubadour was also a musician, and for the most part his poetry was sung, not recited. I say "for the most part" because we don't really know to what degree this was true. Perhaps some indication can be gained from the fact that of the 2542 troubadour poems preserved, only some 276 have been preserved with their music (in other words, somewhat less than 1 in 9); whereas with their northern French counterparts, the trouvères, the figure is roughly 1400 in 4000 (or slightly more than 1 in 3). These figures could be deceptive; perhaps they merely reflect the tastes of later generations of men who copied the manuscripts that have been preserved. Nevertheless, one does get the feeling that, though probably all troubadour poetry was sung rather than recited, the music had considerably less relative importance than it did in northern France.

When we try to delve into what the music was actually like, however, we run into difficulties that are close to insurmountable. To state the problem briefly, the music as preserved in the manuscripts is written as a single-line melody over the first stanza of the text. We can tell the pitch of the notes and which notes belong to which words of the text; but then our troubles begin.

First of all there is the question of rhythm. Twelfth-century musicians had no accurate way of notating rhythms as we have nowadays; they put the notes down and more or less hoped the performer would have either the musical knowledge or the intuition to know what the rhythm should be like. Now since our musical intuition today is very different from that of someone in the twelfth century, we can't rely on that; and our knowledge is limited to a few dry treatises on church music, with an occasional cryptic remark on how "other" music was performed. But these remarks are so sibylline as to set scholars to tearing out their hair.

Until recently, however, they thought they had found the solution. Using the poem's accentuation as a basis, they made it fit into one of a number of rhythmic molds (called "modes"). But the fit was never that snug and there was always an inordinate amount of squeezing and stuffing to try and get around passages that sounded embarrassingly awkward. And then no two scholars could ever agree on just *how* the music should fit the mold, and they thus produced a bewildering array of different transcriptions.[20]

In recent years, however, scholars have become increasingly disenchanted with this system of transcription, some even stating the extreme unlikeliness that this "modal" method can be used at all for twelfth-century secular music. As a result the whole question is now very much up in the air, so much so that I have abandoned any thought of transcribing the music "modally" in this anthology. I have included only a very few melodies in the notes, and even these I have left pretty much as they are in the manuscripts—that is, with no rhythmic indications (except for vertical lines between notes, which indicate rests).

Another problem is that of accompaniment. From contemporary miniatures and sculpture we know that this music was always accompanied by one or two instruments; but the manuscripts give nothing but the melody, leaving us totally in the dark as to what this accompaniment was like. From other sources we can surmise that it was either an embroidered version of the melody itself, or consisted of a fairly simple countermelody; we only know that this accompaniment was *not* chordal as it would be today in a similar situation.

Since music exists only as sound, and since there are so many question marks concerning the actual sound of troubadour music, the whole matter ends up being singularly frustrating. Musicologists have made valiant and often brilliant attempts at surmounting these obstacles, but so far, at least, the materials at their disposal have been too meager and too vague.

The Biographies

In many of the Provençal manuscripts the poems of a particular troubadour are preceded by a short prose biography of the man. These *vidas* ("lives"), as they were called, were composed mostly in the thirteenth century, and some even date from the beginning of the fourteenth. Moreover, all the fifty or so extant biographies are anonymous, except for two written by the thirteenth-century troubadour Uc de Saint-Circ (see p. 83) and one by Miquel de la Tor (see p. 192).

But even though these biographies were written within fifty or a hundred years after the deaths of the poets they describe, their statements must sometimes be taken with a large grain of salt. As one scholar put it, they are a bit like a modern historical novel—a mixture of fact and fiction. We must remember that they were written more to entertain an audience interested in literature than to clarify history for posterity.

The *vidas* are most reliable when they deal with the background and family of the poet. They are least reliable concerning the poet's love life (this aspect of the biographies is usually a fiction embroidered on statements gleaned from the poems themselves). On political events they are sometimes quite trustworthy, but they occasionally get horribly confused over genealogies of noble families. In general they tend to be more accurate and informative on the later poets (who are nearer in time to the actual writing of the biographies) than on the earlier troubadours.

But the aspect of these biographies which has caused the most ink to be spilled is that of the legends they might contain. The best examples in this anthology are the lives of Jaufre Rudel (with the story of the far-away princess), Peire Vidal (with the various tales of his madness), and Guilhem de Cabestanh (with the story of the eaten heart). Yet in spite of everything that has been written about them, a large air of mystery still surrounds these legends, and nobody really knows how much of them is true, or why, if they are myths, they should have become attached to those particular poets.

In addition to the biographies, individual poems are sometimes preceded by a short prose introduction called a *razo* (just as, for instance, the various Books of Milton's *Paradise Lost* are preceded by an "argument"). Everything I have said above about the *vidas* also applies to these *razos*: they were written at the same time, presumably by the same people and for much the same purpose.

But after being such a killjoy about what one can or cannot trust in these biographies and *razos*, I must now do an about-face and say that they make absolutely marvelous reading. They are fascinating not only because of what information we can glean from them (the many details that give us invaluable glimpses into the life of the time), but also because of their purely literary qualities. The stories are beautifully told, and they are couched in a simple, stately prose style with its own strange, somewhat halting rhythm in which almost every sentence starts with an "and." Although perhaps legendary, the biographies of Jaufre Rudel and Guilhem de Cabestanh, for instance, are absolutely unforgettable and have brought these troubadours far more fame than any of their poems.

Unforgettable too are some of the *razos* to poems of Bertran de Born.

In short, these *vidas* and *razos* not only give a certain special flavor of their own to troubadour poetry, but they have somehow become an integral part of it—so much so that even in an age like ours, where somewhat fictitious biographies and phantastical prose commentaries on poems are considered critical nonsense, no one would think of omitting them when presenting the troubadours.

This Anthology

I must end the introduction with a word as to how this anthology is put together. With each poet I have begun with the medieval biography, followed by a brief introduction on the man and his poetry. Then comes a selection of his verse. (The numbers in the text refer to the notes at the back of the book.)

For the sake of readers who want to delve further into the whole matter of troubadour verse, or who are simply curious as to where I got my information, I have preceded these notes with a general bibliography, and I have also preceded the notes on each poet with a short individual bibliography. This scholarly apparatus has been reduced to an absolute minimum. The notes are limited to those that will help, inform or interest the reader, and the bibliographies contain merely the works essential to orienting the reader amid the veritable jungle of literature that has grown up around the troubadours (a jungle so vast that it would take the better part of a lifetime to explore it all).

As to choice of poets and poems, I have had to make a compromise between what I like, what is important to understanding the troubadour movement as a whole, what translates well, and what poems achieved great popularity in the Middle Ages or in modern times. As a result I have included most of the early poets and then concentrated heavily on the classic poets of the golden age. As for the troubadours of the period of decadence, I have chosen only the great satirist, Peire

Cardenal; one Italian poet, Sordello; one Catalan poet, Cerverí; and the so-called "last of the troubadours," Guiraut Riquier.

My choice of poets and poems was also guided by one other consideration. Since this anthology is intended primarily for readers who have had no previous contact with Provençal poetry, I wanted to focus it strongly on the principal figures. More diffuse or "representative" anthologies can sometimes be discouraging for the beginner—he is asked to swallow forty or fifty poets represented by one or two poems each, with the result that each figure becomes blurred in his mind and he gets no essential grasp of the style and quality of each poet. In order to focus an anthology, however, one occasionally has to leave out even major figures—and of this I must plead guilty. Among the poets of the golden age I would have liked to include Raimbaut de Vaqueiras, Aimeric de Peguilhan, Raimon de Miraval, Gaucelm Faidit, and, among the later poets, Uc de Saint-Circ, Bertran d'Alamanon and Guilhem Montanhagol—these and many others. Yet I think that in the end so many names would have merely distracted the reader and blown this anthology up to such a size and scope as to make it cumbersome and forbidding.

For my aim is quite frankly one of propaganda: to persuade literate people that the troubadours have too long been overlooked and neglected beyond the small world of scholarship, and that even within this small world they have too often been misunderstood. Before it was so cruelly extinguished, Provençal literature burned with a light of singular brightness, one that was to play a great part in dispersing the shadows cast over the rest of Europe. A literature with such a destiny is great, not for any reasons of dry pedantry, but because it could breathe an extraordinary vitality into a new world of art. And now that our own values have changed and moved away from the rather narrow aesthetic views of the nineteenth century, we are freer to see why these troubadours have a right to claim our attention, and why their greatness was not some odd aesthetic error of medieval men, but something completely genuine and compelling.

William of Aquitaine

The Count of Poitiers was one of the most courtly men in the world and also one of the greatest deceivers of women; and he was a good knight-at-arms and generous in his gallantry; and he could write good poetry and sing well. And for a long time he wandered about the world seducing women.[1]

Surprisingly enough, this seems to be a fairly accurate description of William VII of Poitiers and IX of Aquitaine, the most powerful feudal lord in the France of his day and the man who has the distinction of being the first lyric poet in any modern European language (or at any rate the first whose works have been preserved). Another contemporary source describes him as an "enemy of all chastity and virtue," and he said of himself:

> I am called the "infallible master"
> for there is no woman who, after a night
> with me, will not want me back the next day;
> and, I may say, I am so knowledgeable
> on this subject
> that I could easily earn my living thereby
> in any marketplace.

His relations with the Church were, as one might expect, never of the best. Once, after being excommunicated, he waved his sword threateningly in front of the Bishop of Poitiers, shouting, "Give me absolution or I'll kill you!" "Go ahead, kill me," answered the prelate, offering his bare neck. "No," William replied, "I don't like you well enough to send you straight to Paradise." So he merely exiled the Bishop. On

* Notes accompanying this section begin on p. 241.

another occasion, when the Bishop of Angoulême reproached him for his adulterous relations with a certain viscountess, William replied, "I will only repudiate her when your hair needs a comb." But the good bishop was bald.

An unreliable but entertaining chronicler, William of Malmesbury, relates that our poet wanted to build a nunnery of whores at Niort, in which the most beautiful of the inmates was to be chosen abbess. The same chronicler also states that he used to go into battle with a portrait of his latest mistress on his shield, explaining that he wanted to have beside him in battle the same woman who had been beside him in bed.

After all this, the facts of his political career are a distinct letdown. He was born in 1071, and at the age of fifteen he inherited domains even larger than those of the King of France (they included almost all of southwestern France). But as a statesman or general he resembled more than anything an erratic, willful child, continually embarking on half-baked projects and then abandoning them as soon as they started turning sour. He traveled to Spain several times (to fight the Moors), twice tried to capture Toulouse without success, and embarked on a belated edition of the First Crusade (in 1101, after the Holy Sepulcher had already been won) in which he was lucky to escape with his life, for the rest of his army was cut to ribbons in Anatolia.

After more than forty years of rule—and misrule—he died in Poitiers in 1127 and was buried there in the "New Church." His lands passed to his son (William X), then to his granddaughter, Eleanor of Aquitaine, and finally to the English crown (for this lineage which made such a mark in history, see pp. 5–6).

As a poet—with the sole exception of Poem 4 below—William of Aquitaine is distinctly mediocre. But he commands our attention and interest because he is the first of the troubadours, and also—it must be admitted—because of his dirty mind. This latter quality needs no comment, except to say that it produced some very amusing poetry; but as for his innovating role, there is a good deal that is puzzling. His serious poetry already contains most of the essential elements of the troubadour lyric. Many critics believe that he did have predecessors (whose works have not been preserved simply because none of them had the worldly rank of William of Aquitaine), for they find it strange that an art form should have been born already developed and formalized in a way that was to change little during the next two centuries. But if he was not an innovator, then we come up against the whole problem of the origins of troubadour poetry (for which see p. 14). Or in other words, did he get his materials from popular lyrics (which a character like him would have known well), from Latin poetry (we know that he was educated by the clergy in Poitiers who would undoubtedly have taught him much of it), or from the Spanish Arabs (his family had intermarried with the Aragonese monarchs—for an Arabizing trait of which see p. 15—and, as I said above, he himself traveled several times to Spain)? Or, as Ezra Pound put this last thesis:

> And Poictiers, you know, Guillaume Poictiers,
>   had brought the song up out of Spain
> With the singers and viels.[2]

1

I   My friends, I'll write a poem for this occasion
which will contain more folly than good sense,
and I'll sprinkle it with large portions of love, joy and youth.

II   And you may be sure that he's a dolt who does not
understand it or learn it willingly by heart;
for, to a person who likes love, parting is not easy.

III   I have two splendid horses for my saddle,
valiant and well accustomed to feats of arms;
but I can't keep both, for they detest each other.

IV   If I could break them in to suit my taste,
I'd never exchange them for any others,
for I'd then be better mounted than any man alive.

V   One was the fastest of a highland breed,
    but lately she's become so skittish, wild
  and savage that you can't get near her with a currycomb.

VI   The other was raised down there below Cofolen,[3]
    and I swear I've never seen a steed so lovely;
  I wouldn't part with her for all the gold and silver in
    the world.

VII   When she was still a colt at pasture, I gave her
    to her master, but I reserved such rights
  that for every year he has her I'll have her a hundred.

VIII   Gentlemen, please advise me in my dilemma.
    Never was a choice more painful;
  I can't decide which to take, N'Agnes or N'Arsen.[4]

IX   At Gimel the castle and domain are mine,
    and I am proud of owning Niol,[5]
  for both have solemnly sworn to me their oath of fealty.

2

I   I'll write a poem as I doze,
    walk and stand in the sun.
    There are women of evil intent—
     I'll tell you which:
    those who turn a knight's love
     to scorn.

II   If a woman commits the mortal sin
    of not loving a faithful knight
    or errs to the point of loving
     a monk or priest,
    it is only right she should be burned
     with a live coal.

III   In Auvergne, beyond Limoges,
    I once was walking quietly by myself

when I met the wives of En Garin
    and En Bernart,
who gave me modest greeting
    by Saint Leonard.

IV   One of them said in her quaint speech,
"Sir Pilgrim, may God be with you.
You seem to me quite well-bred,
    I must admit,
for nowadays the world is overrun
    with lunatics."

V   Now you shall hear my answer:
I said neither "boo" nor "bah,"
nor spoke of this or that;
    my only words were,
"Barbariol, babariol,
    babarian."

VI   And then N'Agnes said to N'Ermessen,
"We've found what we've been looking for,
by God; let's take him home with us.
    He's mute, all right,
and he'll never tell a soul
    about the things we do."

VII   One of them took me beneath her coat
and brought me to her room, beside
the stove. It was pleasant there,
    the fire good,
and I warmed myself contentedly
    before the coals.

VIII   Then they gave me capons to eat—
more than two, I can assure you—
and there wasn't any cook or kitchen boy,
    but just us three.
The bread was white, the pepper plentiful,
    and the wine first-rate.

IX   "Sister, maybe this man's fooling us
and just pretending to be dumb.
Go at once and get our big brown cat;
    that critter
will make him talk if this
    is just a trick."

X   N'Agnes went to get the cursed animal;
it was huge, with great long whiskers,
and when I saw him there between us,
    I got so scared
that I almost lost my courage
    and my nerve.

XI   When the food and wine was finished,
I got undressed at their command.
From behind they brought that nasty
    snarling cat
and dragged him across my back
    from stem to stern.

XII   Then suddenly they yanked his tail
and he dug in his claws.
I got more than a hundred wounds
    that day;
but I would have sooner died
    than moved an inch.

XIII   "Sister," N'Agnes said to N'Ermessen,
"He's mute, that much is clear."—
"Well then, let's prepare a bath
    and have our fun."
Eight days or more I stayed there
    in that cauldron.

XIV   You know how many times I screwed them?
One hundred and eighty-eight to be precise; [6]
so much so that I almost broke my girth
    and harness,

and I cannot tell you how much trouble
    this has given me.

XV   No, I cannot tell you how much trouble
    this has given me.[7]

3

I   I'll write a poem of pure nothing,
    not about me or other people,
    nor about love or youth
      nor anything else—
    one I thought up while I slept
      on horseback.

II   I don't know when I was born;
    I am neither happy nor angry,
    ill-tempered or friendly, nor can I
      be otherwise,
    for thus was I bewitched one night
      on a high hill.

III   I don't know when I sleep
    or wake, unless I'm told.
    My heart is nearly rent asunder
      from mortal grief,
    and yet I swear by Saint Martial
      that I'm indifferent.

IV   I'm sick and tremble at the thought of death,
    yet I know nothing of my illness save what I hear.
    I'll find a doctor to my liking,
      but I don't know who;
    he'll be good if he can cure me, and bad
      if he cannot.

V   I have a mistress, yet I don't know who she is,
    nor have I ever seen her, I give my word;

she's never either pleased or angered me,
    and thus my nonchalance,
for never has a Norman or a Frenchman
    been in my house.

VI   I've never seen her, yet I love her very much,
she's never done me either right or wrong,
and I do very well not seeing her,
    for I do not care
since I know one who's lovelier and sweeter,
    and much more worthy.[8]

VII   Now I've written this poem (about what
I don't know), and I'll send it to him
who through another will send it
    on towards Anjou,
so that he will open his little box
    and send the key to me.

4

I   With the sweetness of the new season
when forest leaves grow and the birds
sing, each in his own way
and in a new key, it is then
that men draw near
to what they most desire.

II   From where all grace and beauty lies
there comes no messenger or letter,
and thus my heart neither laughs
nor sleeps, and I dare do nothing
until I know how this will end,
and if she will do my bidding.

III   Our love is like
the hawthorn branch
which, at night, trembles

       beneath rain and ice
       until day comes and the sun spreads
       through the boughs and green leaves.

IV   I still remember one morning
       when our war ended
       and she made me a gift
       of her love and ring.
       May God grant that I live long enough
       to have my hands beneath her cloak.

V   I care little for whatever evil talk
       could part me from my Bon Vezi,[9]
       for I know well how words
       can spread from mouth to mouth.
       Let others vainly boast of love;
       but we two hold the bread and knife.[10]

5

I   Since I feel a need to sing,
       I shall write a poem of sorrow;
       never again will I be love's slave
       in Poitou or in Limousin.

II   I shall now go into exile
       and leave my son in fear
       and danger, in a state of war
       with neighbors who will do him harm.[11]

III   It is hard for me to abandon
       my dominion over Poitou!
       I leave Folcon of Anjou in charge
       of these lands and of his relative.[12]

IV   But if Folcon of Anjou does not help him,
       nor the king from whom I hold my fief,

then felon Gascons and Angevins
will surely do him in.

V   And if he's not wise and valiant
after I have left you all,
they'll soon bring him low
when they see him young and weak.

VI   I ask mercy of my friends;
may they forgive whatever wrongs
I may have done; and I pray to Jesus
both in Romance and in Latin.

VII   I once believed in joy and prowess,
but now we've parted company,
and soon I shall go to Him
with Whom all sinners find peace.

VIII   I have often been jovial and gay
but Our Lord wishes it no more;
and now my end is so near
that my burden is no longer bearable.

IX   I have abandoned chivalry and pride,
and everything I once loved;
I accept the will of God
and pray I might be with Him.

X   I pray too that at my death
all my friends will honor me,
for I've known joy and gaiety
in my domains and far away.

XI   But now I must abandon joy and gaiety,
as well as vair and miniver and marten.[13]

Cercamon

Cercamon was a jongleur from Gascony, and he wrote poems and pastorelas *in the old style. And he wandered all over the world, wherever he could go, and that was why he was called Cercamon.*[1]

That's all the medieval biography tells us—which isn't much. To make matters worse, none of his *pastorelas* have been preserved, and we're therefore hard put to know what's meant by "in the old style."

But Marcabru's biography (see p. 44) tells us that Cercamon was his teacher. Also William X of Aquitaine (son of the preceding poet) seems to have been his patron, for Cercamon wrote a *planh* mourning his death in 1137. This fact, coupled with a probable allusion in another poem to the preaching of the Second Crusade, places his activity in the 1130s and 40s.

Cercamon is interesting mainly because he was Marcabru's teacher and because of his early date; in a sense he was the first professional poet among the troubadours. But in spite of the one poem presented here—the only one in which the occasional charm and simplicity of his verse is sustained through to the end [2]—and in spite of other nice lines here and there, his verse is distinctly mediocre, and he suffered the fate of being far surpassed by his pupil. He seems, however, to have been blissfully unaware of this state of affairs, for he takes the trouble to state in an envoy:

> My poem is simple, and I have refined it,
> ridding it of all vile, false
> or misplaced words, and it is so constructed
> as to employ only polished language,

* Notes accompanying this section begin on p. 243.

and it will be improved by being
well sung and well presented.

These last two lines being, one can only suppose, a bit of justifiable wishful thinking.

1

I   Now that the air is fresher
and the world turned green,
I shall sing once more
of the one I love and desire,
but we are so far apart
that I cannot go and witness
how my words might please her.

II   And nothing can console me
but death, for evil tongues
(may God curse them)
have made us part.
And alas, I so desired her
that now I moan and cry
half mad with grief.

III   I sing of her, yet her beauty
is greater than I can tell,
with her fresh color, lovely eyes,
and white skin, untanned
and untainted by rouge.
She is so pure and noble
that no one can speak ill of her.

IV   But above all, one must praise,
it seems to me, her truthfulness,
her manners and her gracious speech,
for she never would betray a friend;
and I was mad to believe
what I heard tell of her
and thus cause her to be angry.

V   I never intended to complain;
and even now, if she so desires,
she could bring me happiness
by granting what I seek.
I cannot go on like this much longer,
for since she's been so far away
I've scarcely slept or eaten.

VI   Love is sweet to look upon
but bitter upon parting;
one day it makes you weep
and another skip and dance,
for now I know that the more
one enters love's service,
the more fickle it becomes.

VII   Messenger, go with Godspeed
and bring this to my lady,
for I cannot stay here much longer
and live, or be cured elsewhere,
unless I have her next to me,
naked, to kiss and embrace
within a curtained room.

Marcabru

Marcabru was a foundling abandoned on the doorstep of a rich man, and thus no one ever knew from whom or from where he came. And Audric del Vilar [1] brought him up. Later on he spent so much time with a troubadour named Cercamon that he himself began to write verse. Before this, he had been called Panperdut,[2] but from then on he was known as Marcabru. In those days there was no such thing as a canso, *for any poem set to music was called a* vers. *And he was famous throughout the world; people listened to him, and they feared him because of his tongue. And he said such evil things that finally he was killed by some chatelains of Guyenne of whom he had spoken ill.*

Another biographer adds:

He was one of the first troubadours within memory . . . and he spoke ill of women and of love.

What facts about Marcabru we can glean from his poems are few. He indeed seems to have been Gascon, as the biography states, and he apparently enjoyed the patronage of William X of Aquitaine (the son of the troubadour) [3] and to a lesser extent that of Alphonse-Jourdain of Toulouse. In addition his wandering jongleur's existence seems to have carried him far afield, not only to northern France, but also to Spain, where he spent considerable time and perhaps helped fight against the Moors. His datable poems fall between 1129 and 1150.

As a poet Marcabru is primarily a moralist, castigating everything and everybody around him, from the general de-

---

cadence of the world to cuckolded husbands, prostitutes and stingy patrons. And he does so with such unrelenting energy and in such harsh terms that his moralizing gathers a terrific obsessive momentum and force. He is a sort of Old Testament prophet, or a Diogenes with a lantern searching for an honest man.

His language, which has the same virulent strength as his ideas, is a mixture of many things. There is not only the more refined troubadour speech, wielded with a prolific and very personal verbal imagination, but also a crude popular speech, spattered with peasant proverbs.[4] And he could mold it all into a rough, harsh poetic rhythm that is very effective.

> Dirai vos senes duptansa
> d'aquest vers la comensansa;
> li mot fan de ver semblansa;
> —Escoutatz!—
> Qui ves Proeza balansa
> Semblansa fai de malvatz.[5]

Yet this "powerful, strange, concise and obscure mind," as Berry put it, also had his moments of tenderness, such as the charming romance (Poem 4) which is certainly one of the minor gems of Provençal literature. But such moments are few in his verse. Even in such a courtly form as the *pastorela* (Poem 5) he introduces his own brand of realism and mordant wit.

And finally, Marcabru had an enormous influence on the troubadours that came after him. Not so much as a moralist (except perhaps for Peire Cardenal),[6] but more as a poet, as a manipulator of words, rhymes and rhythms. He was the first to attempt more involved metrical schemes and more difficult rhymes—or in other words, he was first to try his hand at the style later called *trobar clus*. It was this bold, conscious craft which made him the pathfinder for such later poets as Peire d'Alvernhe, Raimbaut d'Orange, Giraut de Bornelh and Arnaut Daniel.

1

I   I'll tell you in my own language
what I see and have seen:
this world will not last long,
according to the Scriptures,
for sons wrong fathers
and fathers, sons.

II   Youth has been led astray
and now declines,
and Liberality, his brother,
slips off stealthily,
for never did deceitful Sir Constance
take pleasure in Joy and Youth.

III   The rich man often gives bread
and wine to bad neighbors,
and if they are of evil lineage,
he'll suffer evil consequences—
if the peasant from whom comes
this proverb does not lie.

IV   The miller in his mill declares:
"He who ties well, unties well";
and the farmer at his plow says:
"Good orchards bear good fruit,
and wicked mothers, wicked children,
and bad horses, nags."

V   Nowadays two colts are often born
vigorous and handsome, but their
blond manes soon turn gray
and make them look like asses.
Joy and Youth have become deceitful,
thus making room for Evil.

VI   You goatlike husbands
      have so prepared the bed
      as to make the cunt a thief
      (and some complain of sons
      not even engendered by them).
      You must be out of your minds!

VII   But it's no use my reproving them;
      they'll always come back for more.
      And since I, Marcabru, see that they
      won't leave this way of life, I'll merely say
      that in this cunt game the husbands
      get fleeced instead of shaven.

VIII Yes, in this cunt game, the husbands
      get fleeced instead of shaven.

                    2

I   I'll tell you plainly
      how this poem begins:
      the words seem true.
            —Listen!—
      He who wavers before prowess
      shows every sign of evil.

II   Youth is broken and shattered,
      and Love is such that it taxes
      all those beneath its sway.
            —Listen!—
      Each one pays his share,
      with no special dispensations.

III   Love is like a spark, smoldering
      beneath soot, which suddenly flares up
      and sets wood and straw ablaze.
            —Listen!—
      He whom the fire devours
      knows not where to flee.

IV   I'll tell you of Love's wiles:
it looks here, winks there,
kisses this way, frowns that way.
    —Listen!—
But it will be a paragon of virtue
before I come to terms with it.

V   Love once was virtuous and straight,
but now it's twisted and jagged,
and when it cannot bite
    —Listen!—
it licks with a tongue
rougher than any cat's.

VI   Never will Love be true again,
for it takes the honey, leaves the wax,
and peels the pear for itself alone.
    —Listen!—
It would sing sweeter than a lyre
if only its tail were cut off.[7]

VII   Anyone allied with false Love
has made a pact with the devil
and needs no other punishment.
    —Listen!—
He'll feel no more pain than a man
who gouges out his own flesh!

VIII   Love is of evil lineage
and without a sword has killed thousands;
God created no better sophist
    —Listen!—
for turning fools to wise men
once it gets its hands on them.

IX   Love was perhaps once dear,[8]
but now it has turned vile
(and virginity's a thing past)
    —Listen!—

since it's become so grasping.
From now on beware.

X   Love is like a mare
who wants stallions to be
in continual pursuit
     —Listen!—
and ride mile after mile,
not caring if their stomach's empty.

XI   Don't you think I know
when Love's cross-eyed or blind?
His words are sweet and polished
     —Listen!—
and his bite is gentler than a fly's,
But the cure is far more painful.

XII   Men who follow women's wisdom
will surely come to ill,
as the Scripture tells us.
     —Listen!—
Misfortune will bear down on you,
all of you, if you don't beware.

XIII   Marcabru, son of Marcabruna,
was born beneath such a star
that he knows Love's ways;
     —Listen!—
for he's never loved a woman,
nor been loved by any.[9]

3

I   *Pax in nomine Domini!*
Marcabru made the verse and the music.[10]
    Listen to his words!
Now, through His clemency,
our Heavenly Lord has given us

a nearby cleansing place,[11]
unequaled except by that
beyond the sea toward Jehoshaphat.
To this one I exhort you.

II   We should cleanse ourselves
every morning and every evening,
    as our reason tells us.
Everyone, while he is still
sound in mind and body,
can go to this cleansing place
which is for our soul's cure:
for without it we might lodge
in Hell instead of Heaven.

III   But Avarice and Lack-of-Faith
make Youth part from his companion.[12]
    Ah! how sad it is
to see most men flying to where
their only recompense is Hell!
If we don't hasten to this cleansing place
before our mouth and eyes are closed,
then all of us, however proud we are,
will meet our adversary when we die.[13]

IV   For the Lord, who knows all
that is, was and ever shall be,
    has promised us
honor in the Emperor's name.[14]
How resplendent will be those
who go to this cleansing place!
More so than the morning star,
if we avenge God of the wrongs
done Him here, and there toward Damascus.

V   There are many of the lineage
of Cain, the first of all
    traitrous men,
not one of whom honors God.

But we will know who loves Him,
for our virtuous cleansing place
will make us one with Jesus,
thus leaving behind villains
who believe in fate and omens.

VI   Libertines, bottle-drainers,
food-crammers, coal-blazers,
    liers-down-on-the-job
will remain imbedded in their quagmire.
God wants the brave and humble
proven in His cleansing place;
the others who stay at home
will meet a powerful adversary:
these I turn away in scorn.

VII   The Marquis here in Spain, and those
over there by Solomon's temple,[15]
    bear the brunt
and burden of pagan pride,
and thus is Youth denigrated
while, through this cleansing place,
the infamy falls on the great leaders
who are decrepit and sated with prowess,
and who love neither gaiety nor joy.

VIII   The French are degenerate
if they deny the cause of God
    which I've commended.
Antioch there, Guyenne and Poitou here
all weep for Prowess and Valor.
Lord God, at Your cleansing place
bring peace to the Count's soul,[16]
and here, may the Lord who rose
from His grave guard Poitiers and Niort.

4

I   By the orchard spring, where the grass
grows green near the bank,
beneath the shade of a fruit tree,
surrounded by white flowers,
amid the singing of the new season,
I found there all alone
one who did not want my solace.

II   She was a maiden, fair of body,
daughter of a castle's lord;
and when I thought the birds,
the verdure and the gentle
springtime would bring her joy
and that she would hear me out,
she suddenly became transformed.

III   There by the fountain, tears flowed from her eyes
and sighs came from deep within her breast.
"Jesus," she said, "King of the world,
it is You who bring me sorrow—
Your suffering has caused my grief,
for the world's finest men all leave
for Your service, according to Your wish.

IV   With You goes my friend,
so handsome, gentle, valiant and noble;
and I am left with nothing but distress,
endless desire and tears.
Ah! Curses on King Louis [17]
with those pleas and commands of his
which have brought my heart such sorrow!"

V   When I heard her grieving so
by the clear stream, I drew near
and said, "Fair lady, such tears

blemish your face and skin;
you have no reason to despair,
for He who filled the woods with leaves,
can yet bring you great joy."

VI   "My lord," she said, "I know
that forever in the world to come
God will show me mercy
as with other sinners;
but He has taken my only cause
for joy, of which so little's left
since he embarked for far-off lands."

5

I   The other day, beside a hedge,
I came upon a humble shepherdess,
a person full of joy and wit,
daughter of a peasant girl.
She wore a cape, skirt and cloak,
a shirt of rough cloth,
shoes and woolen stockings.

II   I went to her across the plain.
"Young girl," I said, "lovely creature,
I'm sorry the cold so pierces you."
"Sir," replied the peasant girl,
"thanks to God and my good nurse,
I care little if I'm disheveled by the wind,
for I have both health and happiness."

III   "Young girl," I said, "sweet thing,
I turned from my path
to keep you company,
for a young peasant girl
like you shouldn't be pasturing
large flocks all by yourself
in such a lonely place."

IV   "Sir," she said, "whatever I may be,
I know folly from good sense.
And as for your company,
my lord," said the peasant girl,
"keep it for the proper time,
because with many girls
it might be just pretense."

V   "Young girl of gentle birth,
your father must have been a knight
to engender in your mother
such a courtly peasant girl.
The more I look at you, the lovelier
you seem and the greater is my joy.
But if only you were a bit more human!"

VI   "Sir, my entire lineage and family
have done nothing but go back and forth
between the pruning hook and the plow.
But Sir," said the peasant girl,
"there are those playing at knighthood
who should be doing the same thing
six days out of every week."

VII   "Young girl," I said, "a gentle fairy
blessed you, when you were born,
with a beauty unequaled by that
of any other peasant girl,
and it would be increased yet more
if only once you'd let me
lie on top, with you beneath."

VIII   "Sir, you've praised me so
that everyone will be quite envious.
And since you've so exalted me,
my Lord," replied the peasant girl,
"your recompense will be
to leave! Don't just stand there
gaping in the noonday sun!"

IX   "Young girl, a wild and felon heart
can be tamed with time.
In these few moments I've learned
that with a young peasant girl
like you one can enjoy pleasant
company and heartfelt friendship,
if neither deceives the other."

X   "Sir, a man beset with folly
swears, promises and guarantees;
but though you might do me homage,
my Lord," said the peasant girl,
"I will not for a meager entrance fee
exchange my virgin state
for that of whoredom!"

XI   "Young girl, every creature
reverts to its own nature.
We should form a couple,
you and I, my peasant girl,
out of sight beside the pasture,
and thus carry on our sweet
business in greater safety."

XII   "Yes, Sir. But each kind seeks
its own: madmen seek madness,
courtly men courtly adventures,
and peasant men peasant girls.
Old people say that to lose
all idea of proportion
shows a lack of common sense."

XIII   "Lovely creature, I've never come
across a face saucier than yours,
nor a more deceitful heart."

XIV   "Sir, the owl says that while one man
stands open-mouthed and credulous,
the other reaps his rewards."

6 (a)

I   Starling, take flight
        tomorrow at break of day
        and go to the land of one
        whom I thought loved me.
            Find her,
            and see her,
            and then tell her
            why you've come;
            and also
            ask her
        why she has been so false.

II   Is she under a spell by which
        she cannot love me or be loved?
        How great would be
        my fortune if only once
            she would let me
            make love
            to her.
            One month
            is worth three
            to whoever
        is in her company.

III   Ah! How compelling are
        her false, glib words; in this
        no other woman is her equal!
        Only fools would believe them!
            Be careful
            of her
            loaded dice,
            for many
            have been deceived
            (you may be sure)
        and tossed out in the street.

IV   It would seem that she is slier
than an old oft-hunted fox;
a while ago she kept me waiting
all night long till dawn.
> Her desires
> are changeable
> and fickle.
> Children
> sing songs
> castigating
the felony of such women.

V   A gentle fairy bewitched the man
to whom she gives her love.
There has been no woman like her
since the days of the prophet Elias.
> Fly straight
> to her
> and tell her
> that I will die
> unless I know
> whether she
sleeps dressed or in the nude.

VI   She was born with her beauty
and needs no paints or perfumes;
she's pursued by a thousand men
and loved by a thousand lords.
> Marcabru says
> that her door
> is never closed;
> but he who is
> stupid enough
> to ask for more
will find himself out in the cold.

VII   Instead of the desired true love,
she offers a many-colored flower
so enchanting that lesser fools

easily commit great follies.
    I will pardon
    the welcome
    she gave the Abbot
    of Saint Privat,[18]
    and if she
    calls me mad
I will only love her more.

VIII   I pardon too
    the wrongs
    she's done me,
    and I'll give in
    if she will only
    lie beneath me
with our two bodies intertwined.

6 (b)

I   The starling did not tarry
upon receiving his commission,
but straightaway flew off,
without a stop for food.
    He left,
    flew away,
    and finally
    found her
    dwelling place,
    and then
at once began to sing.

II   On a flowering branch
the faithful bird chirped and cried
with a voice so clear that she
understood him instantly.
    She opened
    her door
    and drew near.

"I am the bird,"
he said. "In whose
name do you sing?
What love brought you here?"

III The starling answered, "Beyond Lerida
you've had so many tournaments
with knights that it would be
impossible to justify your conduct.
 Thousands may boast
 of your favors,
 but through
 his hospitality
 only one [19]
 can take
the credit for your downfall."

IV "Starling, he took me by surprise;
but since he did not arouse my love,
nor did I promise myself to him,
I am still mistress of my destiny.
 I still love
 your master;
 and as for
 that other
 fool, I'll
 get rid
of him without a second thought.

V "True and faithful love I feel
for only one man, and I'll accept
his invitation to Love's game.
Starling, tell him as best you can
 that he's
 as cold
 as ice,
 and I'll have time
 to desire
 the abbot

if he does not give me pleasure quickly.

VI   "With an open sky above, your master
will receive unmatched joy from me
who once lay beneath him
and felt the pleasure of his sweet kiss.
    Go and tell him
    that here
    tomorrow
    under a pine
    with me
    beneath him
we'll end our lovers' quarrel."

VII   With his mission well fulfilled,
the starling let the breeze guide him
to his master, to whom he cried:
"A precious love is yours, for
    to a thousand
    courtiers she's
    given nothing
    but greetings
    and banquets;
    and in no way
been false or treacherous.

VIII   "If tomorrow
    you go
    to the place
    I'll show you,
    the struggle
    in the garden
may well vanquish and conquer you."

Jaufre Rudel

Jaufre Rudel de Blaia was of gentle birth, and was Prince of Blaia.[1] *And he fell in love with the Countess of Tripoli without ever having seen her, simply because of the good things he had heard the pilgrims returning from Antioch tell of her, and for her he wrote many fine poems, rich in melody and poor in words. But wishing to see her, he took the Cross and went to sea. In the boat he became ill, and when he arrived in Tripoli, he was taken to an inn, for he was near death. The Countess was told about this and she came to him, to his bedside, and took him in her arms. He realized it was the Countess, and all at once recovered his sense of sight and smell, and praised God for having sustained his life until he had seen her. And then he died in her arms. And she had him buried with great ceremony in the house of the Knights Templars. And then, on that same day, she took the veil for the grief she felt at his death.*[2]

Or as Petrarch put it:

> Giaufrè Rudel, ch'usò la vela e'l remo
> a cercar la sua morte . . .
> (Jaufre Rudel, who used sail and oar
> to seek his death . . .)

The only contemporary reference to him is by Marcabru, who sent a poem to:

> Jaufre Rudel, oltra mar (literally, "overseas")

which tells us that he must have gone on the second crusade of 1147. That he was Prince of Blaye (a town on the right bank of the Gironde, between Bordeaux and the sea, and famous in

* Notes accompanying this section begin on p. 248.

French epic legend as the site of the tomb of Roland) seems certain, as many of the other lords of Blaye carried this name and title; but he himself is mentioned in no document and we know nothing else about him.

Moreover, we don't even know if the biography is reliable—it could be, or then again it might well be the invention of a gifted jongleur.[3] But in any case, it scarcely matters, for the biography is in itself a minor gem, and it seems almost fitting with a poet like Jaufre Rudel that "facts" as such should be ungraspable.

For his verse is strange; there is no other troubadour like him. He takes platonic, unrequited love to its logical conclusion—where love itself becomes the aim, the thing desired, because fulfillment would destroy it or lessen its intensity. Moreover, he sings of his "distant love" in a language that is simple and direct (with *paubres motz*—"poor words"—as his biographer put it),[4] yet full of veiled, obscure allusions. He moves in a world close to that of mystics, where the sensual and the divine become fused. So close is this fusion, in fact, that some critics have taken his "distant love" as being an allegory for the Virgin Mary or the Holy Land.[5] But it is a mistake to try to interpret his verse in any one sense, to try to find a key which will unlock some specific meaning. Rudel's poetry is narrow and single-minded, and at the same time all-embracing. Or to put it another way, when the object of love becomes unimportant and the intensity of emotion is transferred to pure desire, then that object can become vague and shifting, and the poet can easily move back and forth between the earthly and the divine, or exist in a realm partway between the two.

And then when we try to find a cause for this tormented joy, we come across the most tantalizing allusion of all. In Stanza VI of the last poem given here, is he referring to some humiliation like that suffered by Abelard? We shall probably never know, but it is tempting to answer in the affirmative, for this would do much to explain the haunting melancholy of his verse.

1

I   When in May the days are long, I like
    to hear birds' sweet song from far away,
    and then, when I have gone,
    I can recall a love from far away.
    I go forth cheerlessly, with bowed head,
    so that songs or hawthorne flowers
    move me less than winter ice.

II I have faith that the Lord will grant
    I see this love from far away;
    but for every good, it brings
    two evils, since it lies so far away.
    Oh, that I might be a pilgrim there
    so that her fair eyes
    could behold my staff and cloak.

III How joyful it will be to plead
    for lodging with her far away;
    and if it please her, I shall stay
    near her, though now I'm far away.
    Then we shall talk of pleasant things—
    with the far-away lover near—
    and delight in joyful words.

IV Sad and joyful I shall leave her,
    if I see my love from far away;
    but I do not know when this will be,
    for we live in lands so far away.
    So many paths and roads lead there
    that I see nothing clearly;
    but let God's will be done.

V   I shall take no more joy in love
    if I have none from far away,
    for I know none fairer or nobler

anywhere, near or far away.
I hold it in such esteem
that, for her, I'd be proclaimed
a captive among the Saracens.

VI   God, who made all things that come and go
and fashioned this love from far away,
give me power—for desire I have—
to see this love from far away
with my own eyes, and in such
a dwelling that room and garden
will seem a royal palace.

VII   They speak the truth who call me greedy,
desiring love from far away,
for no other joy so delights me
as that in love from far away,
but what I most want I cannot have,
for my godfather cast a spell
causing me to love and remain unloved.

VIII   What I most want I cannot have;
curses upon that godfather who cast
a spell causing me to remain unloved.

2

I   When rivulet from spring flows clear
as always in this season,
and the wild rose blooms,
and the nightingale on the bough
repeats, trills, polishes
and mellows his sweet song,
I too must sing mine.

II   My love in distant lands,
for you my heart grieves;
and my only cure

is in hearing you call,
tempting me to sweet love
in an orchard or behind curtains
with you whom I so desire.

III   But since this I cannot do,
it is not strange that love
consumes me; for it was not
God's will to fashion a more gentle
Christian, Saracen or Jewess;
and he who wins some small part
of her love surely feeds on manna.

IV   My heart never stops desiring
her whom I most love;
and I will have been Love's fool
if lust take her from me.
For that pain which only joy can cure
is sharper than any thorn;
so let no one pity me.

V   I shall send this poem in no formal
parchment letter, but sung
in simple romance by Filhol,
to Hugh the Swarthy,[6] for it cheers me
that the Poitevins and Bretons
along with those from Berry and Guyenne
rejoice because of him.

3

I   How fair to me is summer, with its flowers
and birds singing beneath the blossoms,
but I find wintertime yet sweeter
for, to me, it is a time of greater joy;
and there where one finds pleasure
it is only right and proper
to feel more content and gay.

II   For now I am joyful, joyfully
received, and restored in spirit,
and never again shall I go forth
desiring others' conquests,
for now I am certain
that he who waits is wise,
and that impatience is a folly.

III   For a long time I grieved
and despaired of my estate,
and never did I sleep so soundly
that I did not wake in fear.
But now I see, think and feel
that this torment is past,
never to return again.

IV   I am now held in high esteem
by those whose words I heeded,
for my joy has again returned;
and I thank God and those
whose wishes are now fulfilled.
And, whatever I might say,
I shall stay here in this pasture.

V   But in my new estate
I pay no heed to evil tongues,
for never was I so far from love
that I am now not safe and sound.
Perhaps wiser men are wrong,
but I know that in true love
there is no treachery.

VI   Better to have been lying dressed
(of this I can assure you)
than naked beneath the covers
that night I was assailed.
My heart will always grieve,
and the way they went off laughing
still makes me sigh and shudder.

VII   But one thing still troubles me
and brings my heart anguish:
everything the brother denies me
I hear the sister granting.
And no man, no normal man
at least, has such wisdom
not to show some preference.

VIII   In the month of April, and at Easter,
when birds start their sweet cries,
then let my song be heard
and learned by those who sing.
And let it be known, too,
that I am now rich and blessed,
for I am rid of my mad burden.

Peire d'Alvernhe

Peire d'Alvernhe was from the bishopric of Clairmon.[1] *He was intelligent and well-read, and he was the son of a burgher. As a person he was handsome and of pleasant disposition. And he wrote good poetry and sang well, and he was the first good troubadour to go beyond the mountains.*[2] *And he composed the finest melodies ever written, and he also wrote the verse which says:*

> *Near the time of brief days and long nights.*[3]

He wrote no cansos, *for in those days no songs were called* cansos *but* vers; *and En Giraut de Bornelh wrote the first* canso *ever written.*[4] *He was well received and greatly honored by all the great barons of his day and by all the great ladies, and he was considered the finest troubadour in the world until the appearance of Giraut de Bornelh. In his songs he praised himself considerably and condemned other troubadours, as when he said:*

> *Peire d'Alvernhe's voice*
> *is such that he sings high and low*
> *and his melodies are sweet and pleasant;*
> *for he is master of them all,*
> *but it's a pity his meaning isn't clearer,*
> *for almost no one understands him.*[5]

He lived a long time among worthy people, according to what I was told by the Dauphin of Auvergne, who was born in that epoch; and then he did penitence and died.[6]

We also know that, like Peire Rogier, he left the Church to become a jongleur, and that he was a client of Sancho III of

* Notes accompanying this section begin on p. 250.

Castille, Raymond Berenguer IV of Barcelona and Raymond V of Toulouse. It seems reasonable to assume that his poetic career began around 1145 or 1150 [7] and that he died around 1180.

But much more important than these somewhat meager external facts about his life is his role as a poet, and this the biographer fully realized. With him we come to the first of the great troubadours; with him and Bernart de Ventadorn begins the golden age of Provençal verse. In addition, Peire d'Alvernhe was enormously important as an innovator. He himself seems to have been quite aware of this:

> Concerning the old-style poetry and the new,
> I want to speak my mind to men of knowledge
> so that future generations may understand
> that, before me, no perfect poem was written.

And later in the same poem:

> I say that I was the first
> to use perfect diction.[8]

It is precisely in this "perfect diction" that Peire d'Alvernhe's greatness lies. In his best poems there is a flawless joining of sound, rhythm, meaning and association; and with this a nobility and purity of style that few other troubadours achieved. It was in this technical mastery, coupled with a kind of artistic self-consciousness that lay his innovating role and the influence he knew only too well he would have on future generations.[9]

But for two reasons his poetry isn't easy. First, he was a disciple of Marcabru and his *trobar clus*, or hermetic poetry. Of this too he seemed quite aware, for in the lines quoted above in the biography he even jokes about it. But his hermeticism is very different from the gnarled violence of the earlier Marcabru or the dazzling virtuosity of the later Arnaut Daniel; with Peire d'Alvernhe it is more the result of poetic purification, for in his verse everything is restraint, serenity, and calm. But behind this lies the enormous force of a kind of immovable poetic necessity that becomes more compelling the more we read him.

The second difficulty is that his verse is highly objective; its content is what Jeanroy considered the "banalities" of the Middle Ages, but what other critics have understood as being the medieval belief in universal, fundamental truths rather than those which are particular and individual. To put it another way, this poetry is impersonal; and therefore its interest lies not in the content itself, but in how it is expressed, in the diction. This is perhaps poetry at its purest (if such a term can be used); and even though it is precisely in this purity and objectivity that lies his contribution as an innovator, it is also these same qualities which, until recently, have prevented his being appreciated by so many modern scholars still clinging to their romantic image of the poet's function.[10]

But it is also this quality which makes his verse almost literally untranslatable. I am only too aware of this in the pages that follow, and can do little but ask the reader's indulgence.

1 (a)

I
    "Nightingale, fly
    to where my lady dwells
    and tell her of my estate
    that she may tell you hers;
        thus will I know
        how she fares.
    But she must not forget me
        and somehow
        persuade you
    to stay there with her,

II
    instead of returning
    and telling me how she is,
    for I have no friend or brother
    of whom I so wish to know."
        And then
        the gay bird
    went straight to her dwelling,
        flying boldly,

fearlessly,
until he spied her banner.

III When the gentle bird saw
her beauty appear before him,
he began sweetly to sing
that song reserved for evening,
 but then
 he stopped
and prepared himself
 to tell her -
 calmly
that to which she deigned to listen.

IV "He who loves you faithfully
wished me to come and place
myself at your command
and please you with my singing.
 And I shall know
 what to tell him
when I see a countersign of love
 from you.
 If I know
why he waits hopefully,

V and if I bring him cause for cheer,
then this should give you great joy,
for no man born of woman
could so wish you well.
 I shall leave
 and go now,
joyfully, wherever I may wander . . .
 But no,
 not until
I have told you what is on my mind.

VI Thus will I plead my case:
he who places hope in love
must not lose precious time

and forfeit opportunity;
   for candid youth
   is soon lost
just as blossoms fall from trees,
   and far better
   to act now
before all choice is lost."

1 (b)

I
   The bird flew straight
   to his destination, and she,
   through him, sent me a message
   in accordance with mine to her:
      "Let me say
      that your words
   have pleased me very much;
      and now listen
      so that you
   can tell him what is on my mind.

II
   It was very cruel of my friend
   to leave me thus,
   for no other kind of joy
   has ever moved me so.
      Our parting
      was too hasty,
   but were I sure of him,
      I would
      be kinder;
   hence my bitterness.

III
   For I love him so that when
   I fall asleep, I can safely
   dream of sharing with him
   joy, gaiety, sport and laughter;
      and no one
      can ever know

the secret solace in imagining
   him lying
   in my arms
until his image vanishes.

IV   From the moment I first saw him,
      and yet before, he pleased me;
      and I have no desire
      to conquer one of nobler birth.
          I decided
          wisely,
      for neither wind or ice now
          torment me,
          nor summer,
      nor heat nor bitter cold.

V   In one sense true love
      is like the purest gold,
      which is of greater value
      to those who hold it in esteem.
          And thus does
          friendship
      grow daily stronger;
          and stronger
          through love
      is he to whom joy is promised.

VI   Gentle bird, go to his abode
      when morning comes
      and tell him plainly
      of my obedience."
          Quickly
          he returned
      with his role well learnt,
          and told me
          eloquently
      of my good fortune.

2

I   I'll sing, for I see I must write
        the new song groaning within my jaw;
        but singing has tormented me—
        how to sing so that it resembles
        no one else's song?
        For no singing is ever worthwhile
        which resembles that of others.[11]

II   I love to see the lark hurl himself
        into the air, against the falling sunbeams,
        and rise until he alights
        on leaves trembling in the wind,[12]
        and the gentle season—may its birth
        be joyful—pry open birds' beaks
        and let their song ring forth.

III   Who then has love, or desires it,
        and this love grows, blossoms, and is born,
        and who shows it humility and faith,
        will soon have conquered it;
        for meekness, pleasant mien
        and gentle speech quickly triumph,
        just as other means are powerless.

IV   But as for me, alas! I serve it thus
        and in return get only care;
        yet this alone brings me more joy
        than all the wealth of Pisa,
        and if it please her that I kneel down
        and throw myself at her feet,
        and utter a word of love! . . .

V   My love, you must tell me how
        things stand with us, I beg of you,
        for I can only grow lean
        not knowing my own destiny;

and though you may set your heart
against me—I never will towards you
until the soul has left my body.

VI   I only hope that she—I am immune—
pays no heed to jealous, evil tongues,
for then, though they might anger her,
little harm can come to me.
Let these jealous flatterers
hold me far or near,
provided that she side with me,

VII   and provided that I purify myself
and not be tempted by another,
for love seeks quarrels elsewhere
only when its own destruction's near;
and if I did not love her so,
I could write no poems or melodies—
nor would I, did she not exist.

VIII   Peire d'Alvernhe will worship her
both through prayer and service
until he receives his recompense.

3

I   Near the time of brief days and long nights,
when the clear air grows darker,
I want my thoughts to grow and branch forth
with new joy to bear me fruit and blossom,
for I see the oaks being cleared of leaves
and the nightingale, thrush, jay and woodpecker
withdraw from discomfort and from cold.

II   In contrast, the vision of far-off
distant love pleases me, for what matters
sleeping or waking to a man without
the one to whom he is devoted;

love wants joy and banishes despair,
and who, in moments of distress, rejoices,
must be seeking love's companionship.

III   I see, believe, and know it to be true
that love makes men grow lean and fat,
both through treachery and pleasure,
through tears and laughter;
its command brings poverty or riches,
but I still prefer my small part of it
to being crowned king of Wales or Scotland.

IV   I don't know what I should do or say,
but I am patient, for through my lady
all joy revives and valor is reborn,
so much that before her I tremble
and dare not speak (thus my distress)
for fear of losing good and gaining evil;
when I take heart, I think: why not give up?

V   Oh, if only my desires had been
divined by her noble heart
when my lady took from me
that which I most begged of her!
But I am ignorant of how to praise or flatter,
and thus my heart's feelings remain unspoken;
if this is unknown to her, I'll die gray-haired.

VI   So sweet and pleasant is the sight of her,
through the joy it brings my heart
and, above all, through the hope
it gives me that I may be the richer;
for never was I so vile or miserable
that seeing her did not at once
raises me from poverty to wealth.

VII   This is a happiness, joy, and pleasure
that many seek, and its merit
raises men to great power,

and its joy to high dominions;
discretion and beauty shelter
this love's service, which spreads and grows,
full of sweetness—green, and white as snow.[13]

VIII And so I tell myself: never leave that place
where she conquered and then crowned you,
even if King Louis were to give you France.

IX Let that villain Audric know,[14] through this poem,
that he of Auvergne says: a man without love's
service is no better than a wretched ear of corn.

4

I I'll sing of those troubadours
who sing in a myriad of styles,
and the worst of whom thinks he speaks well;
but they should take up singing elsewhere,
for a hundred yokels have got in their midst,
not one of whom knows a note of music.

II For this Peire Rogier [15] deserves reproach—
he'll be criticized first of all,
for he sings openly of love;
but he'd do better with a psalter
in some church, or holding a candelabrum
with one huge burning candle in it.

III And the second, Giraut de Bornelh,[16]
who's like an oyster dried out in the sun
with his pitiful, meager singing like that
of some old woman watercarrier;
for if he saw himself in a mirror,
he'd know how much he wasn't worth.

IV And as for the third, Bernart de Ventadorn,[17]
who's even a palm shorter than Bornelh,

his father was a humble serf,
handy with a laburnum bow,
and his mother tended an oven
and gathered brushwood.

V   And the fourth, the Limousin from Brive,[18]
a jongleur who does more begging
than anyone from here to Benevento;
when this poor fellow sings,
he seems so much like some sick pilgrim
that I can't help feeling pity.

.   .   .

X   And the ninth is En Raimbaut,[19]
who's much too proud of his own verse;
but I look down my nose at him,
for he knows neither joy nor warmth;
that's why, to me, he's no better
than those flutists who go begging alms.

.   .   .

XIV   Peire d'Alvernhe's voice
is like a frog singing in a well,[20]
yet he compliments himself in front
of everyone, for he's master of them all;
but it's a pity his meaning isn't clearer,
for almost no one understands him.

XV   This poem was made for bagpipe players
at Puivert,[21] in sport and laughter.

5

I   O Lord, living light, righteous
and truthful towards laity and clergy,
and called Christ the Savior
both in Latin and in Hebrew,

and born and after death seen saved,
arisen; thus sowing sadness among
those to whom later You gave joy.

II   O Lord, my King, I failed faithlessly,
and great evil has come therefrom
in thought and wild words
and foul infernal folly
surrounded by strange intent
and dark, demoniac desires;
I kneel before You sinful and repentent.

III   For all that which I once did
(although I lack firm, frank heart
to speak out as I must)
I lament and pray to You,
for whom Job showed such faith,
that You remember not my several sins,
but sustain me through Your grace.

IV   I cannot claim myself so wise
that I could conquer that reign
where men never feel thirst,
hunger, cold nor disquiet, unless
Your virtue, for which I cry out,
give me strength to despise
this world's departing joy

V   which makes me fail toward You,
causing my body to tremble,
and if You keep my sins
until my final spasm,
not canceling them before,
O Lord, what good is it to plead
if then they are not conquered

VI   by Your mercy, You who rescued
Shadrach from the burning flames,
together with Meshach and Abednego,

and Daniel from the lion's den,
and Jonah from the whale's belly,
and the three Wise Men from Herod,
and Susannah from the false witnesses;

VII   and You, Lord God, who on a few fish
and five loaves of bread fed so many,
and raised up Lazarus
already four days dead,
and You, who through Your word
saved the Centurion's servant [22]
and took taint of torment from the world,

VIII   and who made wine from water
at Archetriclinus' feast,[23]
and marvels too myriad
for mortal man to know
or foolishly to fathom,
and for whom Luke's portrait spoke,[24]
O rich royal ruler;

IX   and You who made earth and firmament
and everything that is or ever was
with a single sign, together with the sun,
and who confounded Pharaoh
and gave the children of Israel
milk and honeycomb, manna and honey,
and killed the serpents with the serpent; [25]

X   You gave Your people peace
when it pleased You to send
Moses hunting in the desert; [26]
and You untied Saint Peter's hands
and feet, when an angel had awoken him,
and You also gave him knowledge
of Your own piercing pain; [27]

XI   and their people sought You out
as far as Mount Oreb,

killing within Bethlehem
when Joseph fled with you
into Egypt—this we know;
and then You returned,
King Jesus, and dwelled

XII   among Your family in Nazareth;
O Father, in three people one,
with the Son and Holy Ghost,
this heavenly trinity I adore;
O Lord, Who are peak, branch, root,
God and guide of all that is,
may it please You to protect me

XIII   and grant that I willingly
do good works, so that when
You stand on a cloud and judge
on that great day, sweet Savior,
I receive not Your enmity, and that I,
mighty, merciful King of Kings,
may joyously join the blessed.

XIV   O Lord, forsake me not, for
without You I have no sustenance;
and now, believing in Your name, I cross myself:
In nomine patris et filii et spiritus sancti. Amen.

Bernart de Ventadorn

Bernart de Ventadorn was from the Limousin, from the castle of Ventadorn.[1] He was of a poor family, the son of a servant who was a baker and heated the oven to bake the castle's bread.[2] And he grew up to be handsome and intelligent, and learned how to sing well and write good poetry, and he became courteous and knowledgable. And his lord, the Viscount of Ventadorn,[3] took a great liking to him, to his poetry and to his singing, and he honored him greatly.

And the Viscount of Ventadorn had a wife[4] who was young, noble and gay. And she took a liking to En Bernart and his songs, and she fell in love with him, and he with her; he thus wrote his songs and verses for her, about the love he felt for her and about her merit. Their love lasted a long time before the Viscount or anyone else took notice of it. But when the Viscount did notice it, he parted company with En Bernart, and had his wife locked up and guarded.[5] And he had her take leave of En Bernart and made him depart and go far from his lands.

And he left and went to the Duchess of Normandy,[6] who was young and of great merit, and who understood worth and honor and words of praise. And she was very pleased by En Bernart's songs, and she received him and gave him a warm welcome. He remained at her court for a long time, and fell in love with her and she with him, and he wrote many fine songs for her. And while he was with her, King Henry of England[7] married her and took her from Normandy and brought her to England. En Bernart stayed behind, sad and mournful, and went to the good Count Raymond of Toulouse,[8] and there he remained until the count died. And En Bernart, because of the grief he felt, entered the order of Dalon,[9] and there he ended his days.

* Notes accompanying this section begin on p. 256.

And I, N'Uc de Saint Circ, wrote this according to what was told me by the Viscount N'Eble de Ventadorn, who was the son of the Viscountess that En Bernart loved.[10] *And he wrote the songs you shall hear, those written below.*

Apart from this biography, which is unfortunately not too reliable as a historical document (see the notes), we know almost nothing about Bernart de Ventadorn. From scraps of information in his poetry and some other isolated facts, we can gather that he must have started writing between 1145 and 1150, that he was in England around 1154 (contrary to what the biography says), that he was in Puivert in 1170 (see Peire d'Alvernhe's satire on p. 77), and that he did in fact enjoy the patronage of Raymond V of Toulouse. We don't know when he died, but scholars assume that his poetic career ended around 1180.

But our interest in Bernart de Ventadorn is as a literary figure. He is certainly one of the greatest of the troubadours, and as a love poet he has rarely been surpassed in any age or language.

His role among the troubadours, however, is somewhat special, and this singularity of his is so intimately bound up with his greatness that it is difficult to separate the two. Perhaps the best way to approach this problem is to compare him with his contemporary Peire d'Alvernhe, whose production is so much more typical of the troubadours.

Both poets were aware of their own greatness, but each boasted of it in different and very precise terms. As we have already seen, Peire d'Alvernhe said:

> I was the first
> to use perfect diction.

whereas Bernart de Ventadorn wrote:

> Singing is worthless unless
> it arises from within the heart . . .
> and thus my song excells;
> and for joy in love I use
> mouth, eyes, heart and mind.[11]

and also in the first stanza of our Poem 7:

> It is no wonder that I sing
> better than any other singer
> for my heart impels me more towards love
> and I am better made for its command.

Notice how Peire d'Alvernhe proclaims himself the crafts-man, the man for whom the art is an end in itself; whereas Bernart de Ventadorn is the romantic (to use a much over-taxed word), the man for whom art is an expression of intense personal emotion.[12]

But this emotion of his is many-sided: it is sensitive, tender, occasionally highly sensual—

> May she have the courage
> to have me come one night
> there where she undresses
> and make me a necklace of her arms.[13]

It is also often suffused with a strange mixture of joy and grief, emotions that frequently exist side by side in his poems. This is in a sense a natural result of the paradox of love, which feeds on desire rather than on fulfillment, but the reader will see how beautifully and sometimes abruptly he can shift from one to the other. All of these elements give his poetry its highly characteristic note of melancholy.

But more than anything, one is struck by the pitch of inten-sity his emotion can reach. At times it approaches a mystic point, where the whole being becomes suffused with love and the conscious self vanishes in a delirious forgetfulness:

> When I see the lark joyously move
> his wings against a ray of sunlight
> and forget himself and fall,
> his heart pierced with rapture . . .[14]

This quality of emotion in his verse brings him closer to Jaufre Rudel than to any other troubadour, but by making yet another comparison we can begin to appreciate Bernart de Ventadorn's genius. The earlier poet's emotions were perhaps even more intense and complex, but they did not find totally adequate expression; his poetry fell somewhat short of the feeling behind it. But with Bernart de Ventadorn there is an invisible welding of emotion and expression, of content and form. The versification, which is sometimes quite intricate, appears natural and inevitable, and the words themselves, which seem so effortlessly chosen (and all this I'm sure is an illusion), develop a music which often holds the reader spellbound. Try, for instance, reading out loud the original of the opening stanza of our Poem I:

> Lo tems vai e ven e vire
> per jorns, per mes e per ans,
> et eu, las! no·n sai que dire,
> c'ades es us mos talans.
> Ades es us e no·s muda,
> c'una·n volh e·n ai volguda,
> don anc non aic jauzimen.

and see how, through careful repetition and insistence on certain sounds and words, there is a steady build-up through to the end, and then a sudden break, with the full force of his melancholy stated in that one flat, bleak last line.

But his verse is full of passages like this, and I leave the reader with the meager pickings of eight of the many poems one could include in an anthology.

1

I   Time comes and goes and turns,
      through days, through months and through years,
      but I, alas! am left speechless,
      with my desire always the same.
      Always the same and unchanging,
      for she whom I wanted and still want,
      has never brought me joy.

II   Her endless laughter
      pains and wounds me.
      She made me play a game
      in which I got the worst twice over,

for love upheld by one side only
is surely lost
until the two somehow agree.

III   It is only right
that I should blame myself,
for no man born of woman
ever served so much in vain;
and if she does not punish me,
my folly will only grow, since
"fools are fearless until beaten."

IV   I shall never sing again
nor belong to the school of Eble,[15]
for my singing is of no avail,
nor are my trills or melodies;
nor does anything I say or do
seem to be of any use to me,
nor do I see my state improving.

V   Though I may seem joyful,
my heart is filled with grief.
Who ever saw a man do penitence
for a sin not yet committed?
The more I beg, the crueler
she becomes, and unless she changes,
we'll be forced to part.

VI   It is best that she should
bend me to her every wish,
for then, if she does me wrong
or puts me off, she'll have compassion.
Because the Scripture says
one day of happiness
is well worth a hundred.[16]

VII   As long as I, safe and sound,
may live, I'll never leave her,
for after the grain has fallen,

the chaff swings aimlessly in the wind;[17]
and if she takes her time,
it's not for me to blame her—
but if only she could mend her ways!

VIII O love which I so covet,
well-formed body, thin and smooth,
fresh skin and high color
which God fashioned with His hands,
I have always wanted you,
for nothing else so pleases me,
no other love so tempts me.

IX O wise, gentle lady, may He
who fashioned you so beautifully,
grant me that joy which I await.

2

I My heart is so full of joy
that all seems changed:
winter's cold transformed to flowers
white, red, and yellow,
for with the wind and with the rain
my joy increases,
and thus my merit mounts and rises
and my song improves.
Such love lies in my heart,
such joy and sweetness,
that ice seems as flowers
and the snow verdure.

II I can go unclothed,
naked in my shirt
for I am protected by true love
against the cold wind.
But it is madness to be insolent
or indiscreet,

and thus have I been cautious
    since I begged for love
from one of such great beauty
    and from whom I await such honor
that I would not exchange her wealth
    for that of Pisa.[18]

III   She keeps her friendship from me,
    but I yet have hope,
for I've at least obtained
    some outward signs;
and with my wish thus fulfilled
    my joy is such
that on the day I see her
    I'll feel no grief.
    My heart's near love
    and my soul runs towards it,
but my body's elsewhere, here,
    far from her, in France.

IV   But for all the hope I have,
    it does me little good,
since I am tossed about
    like a ship on waves;
to flee the melancholy overwhelming me,
    there's nowhere I can hide.
All night I writhe and turn
    upon my bed:
    I endure more pains of love
    than Tristan, the lover
who suffered such endless grief
    for blonde Isolde.[19]

V   Oh God, why am I not a starling
    who flies through the air,
so that in the depth of night
    I may come to her?
Worthy, joyful lady,[20]
    your lover is dying!

I fear my heart will melt
 if it continues thus.
Lady, for your love
I join hands and worship you.
Gentle body with fresh skin,
 what grief you bring me!

VI   There is nothing in this world which
    so troubles me that when
I hear her mentioned, my heart
   does not turn towards her
and my face become all radiant,
   so much that, in spite
of what I say, you will think me
   on the verge of laughter.
  But my love for her is such
  that often it makes me weep,
for I prefer the bitter
  taste of sighs.

VII   Messenger, go quickly
   and tell my sweet lady
of the pain and grief I bear,
   and the martyrdom.

3

I   Since you ask me, my lords,
to sing, I shall sing,
but when I sing, I weep
the moment I begin.
You'll never hear a singer
sing well amid ill fortune;
but is my fortune thus with love?
No, it has never been so good!
Why then do I feel such sorrow?

II   I know that God does me
            great favor and great honor,
            for I adore the loveliest of women,
            and she me (as far as I can tell),
            but I am here, far away,
            not knowing how she is.
            Thus I die of grief,
            unable to see her
            as often as I would wish.

III   But I feel such pleasure
            when I think of her
            that I am deaf
            to shouts or screams.
            Her beauty draws my heart
            so sweetly from my breast
            that many say I'm here,
            and believe this to be true,
            though they don't see me with their eyes.[21]

IV   Love, which way should I turn?
            Will I be cured through you?
            I'll surely die
            of longing and desire
            if that beauty does not call me
            near her, there where she lies,
            to let me caress and kiss her
            and press against me
            her white, soft, smooth body.

V   I don't cease loving
            because of harm or grief;
            and when God shows me favor,
            I don't refuse it or despise it;
            and when no favor comes,
            I can bear ill fortune,
            for sometimes only
            distance can alter
            its fateful course.

VI   Gentle lady, have mercy
on your true lover
who, in good faith, swears
he's never so loved anyone.
With joined hands and bowed head
I give and commend myself to you;
and if some day you find
occasion—smile on me;
that is my greatest wish.

VII   My God grant
My Squire [22] and me to wander
throughout the world;

VIII   and let him take along
whatever he most wants,
and I My Aziman.[23]

4

I   When I see the lark joyously move
his wings against a ray of sunlight
and forget himself and fall,
his heart pierced with rapture,
oh! I feel such envy
of those whom I see joyful
that I marvel how desire
does not instantly melt my heart.[24]

II   Alas, I thought I knew so much
about love, and yet I know so little!
For I cannot keep from loving her
whose favor I shall never have.
She took away my heart, my life,
herself and all the world;
and taking this, left me nothing
but desire and a yearning soul.

III   I was no longer master of myself,
        nor was I mine from the moment
        I first saw my image in her eyes,
        in that mirror so dear to me.
        O mirror, since I saw myself in you,
        sighs from deep within have killed me,
        and I have perished, as once did perish
        fair Narcissus in the fount.[25]

IV   I despair of women; never again
        shall I have faith in them;
        and those whom I once upheld
        I shall now forsake. Since none
        will help me against the one
        who confounds and destroys me,
        I mistrust and fear them all
        (for I know they are all alike).

V   In this my lady truly
        is a woman; thus my complaint.
        She doesn't want what should be wanted,
        and desires what is forbidden.
        I've fallen into disgrace and acted
        like the fool crossing the bridge; [26]
        and I don't know why this is, unless
        perhaps I've reached too high.

VI   Yes, pity's truly lost
        (and I never knew it),
        for if she who should have most
        has none, where should I seek?
        Who, looking at her, would think
        that this poor, love-sick man
        whose life is meaningless without her,
        would be allowed to die, unaided?

VII   Since nothing serves me with my lady,
        not prayers, pity, or the rights I have,
        and since my love displeases her,
        I'll never speak of it again

but rather part from her and leave.
She's killed me, and through death I answer her:
I shall go now—since she doesn't stop me—
forlornly, into exile, I know not where.

VIII Tristan, you'll have nothing more from me,[27]
for I am going, forlornly, I know not where.
I shall renounce and give up singing,
and hide myself from joy and love.

5

I When flowers bloom near green foliage
and the sky turns serene and clear
and in the forest birds' sweet songs
soften and revive my heart
(each bird with a different melody),
I, whose heart is full of joy,
should also sing, for all my days are joy
and song—I think of nothing else.

II She whom in all the world I most want
and most love, in heart and faith,
joyfully and willingly hears my words,
heeds and retains my prayers;
and if loving well could cause death
I would surely die, for in my heart
I bear her a love so sincere and true
that my most loyal friends seem false.

III When I undress at night
I know well that I won't sleep.
I rob myself of sleep and lose it
all for you, my ever-present lady;
for "where lies a man's treasure
there also must lie his heart."
If I don't see you, my lady, you who mean most to me,
then no sight is worth the beauty of my thoughts.[28]

IV   When I think how I used to love
one who was false and merciless,
such anger comes over me
that I almost abandon joy.
My lady for whom I sing and live,
wound my heart with your mouth
through a sweet kiss of heartfelt love
to bring back joy and banish mortal grief.

V   There are some whose pride increases
with good fortune or great joy;
but I am of a different sort,
more open—when God favors me.
I was once at the brink of love, but now
from that brink I've reached the heart.
Have mercy, my lady; I am unequaled, unsurpassed.
I lack nothing, provided God save you for me.

VI   My lady, if I don't see you with my eyes,
know well that my heart sees you;
and may your grief be less than mine, for I know
that because of me you're treated harshly.
But if some jealous person strikes your body,
take care that he not strike your heart.
Return in kind whatever pain he causes you
and never, within you, let evil conquer good.

VII   May God keep my Bel Vezer from grief and evil,
whether I am far away or by her side.

VIII   If God preserves my lady and my Bel Vezer,[29]
my wishes are fulfilled—I ask for nothing more.

6

I   With joy I start and begin my poem,
and with joy it continues and ends,
and if it ends successfully,
then I'll consider the beginning good.

From this good beginning
I get joy and happiness;
and thus should I welcome its good ending,
for at their end all good things are praised.

II   Joy so seizes and conquers me
that I marvel how I can bear it,
and I will not tell or hint
for whom I am so gay and joyful;
    but then true love is never
    free from fear and doubt.
For men are afraid to fail in love,
and thus do I lack courage to speak out.

III   My better judgment helps me in one way:
no one ever inquired about my joy
that I did not willingly tell a lie,
for I do not think it is good sense,
    but mere childishness and folly,
    for him whose love is blessed
to wish that he might open up his heart
to those who cannot help or serve him.

IV   There is no curse, fault,
or baseness, it seems to me,
greater than that of one who spies,
desiring knowledge of another's love.
    You scoundrels! Of what use
    is my grief or care to you?
Each man to his own, yet you confound me,
and I fail to see what joy this brings you.

V   It is only right for a woman to show courage
among base people and evil neighbors;
and if a strong heart does not protect her,
she'll find nobility or courage difficult.
    Thus I pray (so my lovely lady,
    in whom I trust, may remember it)
that words may not make her change heart,
for all my enemies are dying of envy.

VI   I did not think her lovely smiling mouth
        could kiss me so treacherously,
        for one sweet kiss killed me—
        unless she now cure me with another;
            so it was
            with Peleus' lance,
        from whose attack there was no cure
        unless it wounded once again.[30]

VII   Fair lady, your gentle body
        and lovely eyes have so conquered me,
        as have your sweet look, your clear skin,
        and the beauty of your manner,
            that when I judge you
            I can find no equal.
        Either you are the loveliest of women, or the eyes
        with which I gaze on you no longer see you clearly.

VIII   Bel Vezer,[31] in my eyes
            your merit only grows,
        for you know so well the acts and words of joy
        that no man could refrain from loving you.[32]

7

I   It is no wonder that I sing
            better than any other singer,
            for my heart impels me more towards love,
            and I am better made for its command.
            I've given it my heart and body,
            wisdom and sense, strength and power;
            this bridle so leads me towards love
            that I'm attracted by nothing else.

II   He is dead who in his heart
            hasn't some sweet taste of love;
            and life without meaning is useless

except to annoy one's fellow men.
May God not so despise me
that He let me live another day or month
if I am guilty of such annoyance,
or have no more care for love.

III   I say guilelessly that there is no one
finer or more beautiful than the one I love.
And this love is such that my heart sighs
and my eyes cry; and thus my pain.
But what can I do if Love has seized me
and if that prison in which it's put me
can be opened by no other key but mercy,
and I find no mercy there?

IV   This love so gently wounds
my heart with its sweet taste
that a hundred times a day I die
of grief and am reborn another hundred.
But this evil is a pleasant one,
for I prefer it to the good of others;
and since my evil seems so good to me,
how much better will be pleasure after pain.

V   Oh God! if only one could know
false from true lovers;
if only flatterers and traitors
had horns upon their heads.
I would give—if I could—
all the gold and silver in the world
only to have my lady know
how faithfully I love her.

VI   When I see her, my eyes, face,
and color bear me witness,
for out of fear I tremble
Like a leaf against the wind.
Love has seized me with such strength
that I have less judgment than a child;

and towards a man so subjugated
a lady should show great mercy.

VII   Good lady, I ask nothing
except to be your servant,
and I would serve you well
no matter what the recompense might be.
Lady, with a humble, gay and courtly heart
you see me now at your command.
But be not as a bear or lion; do not
kill me when I give myself to you.

VIII   To my Cortes,[33] where she is now,
I send this poem, and may it not
disquiet her that I have been away so long.

8

I   *Peire*   My friend Bernart de Ventadorn,
how can you refrain from singing
when you hear the nightingale
rejoicing night and day?
    Listen to his joy!
All night he sings beneath the flowers;
he understands love better than you.

II   *Bernart de* Peire, I prefer my sleep and peace
Ventadorn to hearing nightingales;
you'll never persuade me
to return to a state of madness.
    I am, thank God, free
of chains while you and all the other
lovers remain as mad as ever.

III   *Peire*   Bernart, it's scarcely proper or courtly
that a man be unable to deal with love;
nor will it ever cause you such pain

as not to be worth more than other
　　　pleasures,
　　for it quickly gives good for ill.
There is little pleasure without its share
of pain, and joy soon conquers grief.

IV　　*Bernart*　　Peire, if for two or three years
the world were run according to my
　　　desires,
I'll tell you how women would be treated:
they'd never be asked for anything,
　　but made to suffer,
and they would honor us, and ask
of us, rather than we of them.

V　　*Peire*　　Bernart, women shouldn't ask—
it isn't right; but rather, men
should ask of them and cry for mercy.
And it strikes me as madness,
　　like sowing in sand,
to blame them or their worth—
it only shows bad breeding.

VI　　*Bernart*　　Peire, my heart fills with grief
when I remember one false lady
who killed me, I know not why,
except that I loved her faithfully.
　　I have fasted long,
but I know that if I fasted even longer
I'd find her no better disposed towards me.

VII　　*Peire*　　Bernart, you're mad
thus to alienate love from which
men gain worth and valor.

VIII　　*Bernart*　　Peire, love is senseless,
for those traitresses have absconded
with all joy and worth and valor.

Raimbaut d'Orange

Raimbaut d'Orange was lord of Orange and Courthézon [1]
*and of a great many other castles. And he was clever and well
educated, and a good knight-at-arms and gracious in his conversation. He had a great liking for honorable ladies and honorable gallantry. He wrote good* vers *and* chansos; *but he preferred to write in difficult, subtle rhymes.*

*And for a long time he loved a woman of Provence whose
name was Maria de Vertfuoil, and he called her "Jongleur" in
his songs.* [2] *For a long time he loved her and she him. And for
her he wrote many fine songs and did many other good deeds.*

*And then he fell in love with the good Countess of Urgell,
who was from Lombardy, daughter of the Marquis of Busca.* [3]
*She was honored and esteemed over all the other noble ladies
of Urgell, and Raimbaut, without having seen her but simply
because of the good things he heard tell of her, fell in love
with her and she with him. And he then wrote his songs for
her, and he sent them to her by means of a jongleur called
Nightingale, as he states in one song:*

> *My Nightingale, though
> you are full of grief,
> rejoice through my love
> in a little song you shall take
> for me without delay
> as a present for the worthy
> countess who lives in Urgell.* [4]

*For a long time he courted this countess, without ever hav-
ing the opportunity of going to see her. But I heard her say,
after she had become a nun, that if he had come she would
have granted him his pleasure and permitted him to touch
her bare leg with the back of his hand.* [5]

° Notes accompanying this section begin on p. 262.

While yet in love with her, Raimbaut died without male heir, and Orange was inherited by his two daughters.[6]

Aside from this biography, which is more entertaining than informative, we know a certain amount concerning Raimbaut d'Orange thanks to the fact that he was a nobleman with a minor role in local history. He was born about 1144, the youngest of four children. Through his mother he inherited Orange and Courthézon, and through his father (younger brother of the powerful lord of Montpellier, William VI) Omelas and various other castles west of the Rhône.[7]

His father died in 1156 leaving him a heritage of debts, and Raimbaut (as we can gather from his poems), not having much propensity for a life of austerity, did little to alleviate the situation. Because of the continual pawning of his lands to raise money, and mainly because of the division of inheritances among members of his family, his dominion over his various towns and castles was more titular than real.[8]

Aside from his continual preoccupations with keeping the wolf from the door, he undoubtedly took part in the local wars of the period (as an ally of his cousin William VII of Montpellier and of the Counts of Barcelona against Raymond V of Toulouse), and at the same time tried to maintain (insofar as his finances would permit it) his position as patron of other troubadours.[9]

But all this was cut short when he died at Courthézon in 1173 at the early age of twenty-nine, mourned by his friend and client, Giraut de Bornelh.[10]

As a poet, Raimbaut d'Orange gives the impression of a gifted dilettante, one who enjoyed experimenting with new verse techniques as well as entertaining his friends with light occasional verse. The experimental side of his character, however, that which produced his most obscure poems, is of considerable historical importance because it provides the connecting link between Marcabru and Arnaut Daniel. But with Raimbaut, the effort to make poetry fit the mold of extremely complex technical devices never really succeeded; it was his fate merely to break the ground which Arnaut Daniel was later to cultivate so masterfully.

As a light poet, however, he can be very entertaining. I've therefore chosen only one of his *chansos* (the one that was by far the most widely read in the Middle Ages), his famous debate with Giraut de Bornelh, and three of his humorous poems.

1

I   Since within me grows the knowledge
that I can write (and I say so frankly),
it would be wrong to hide my talent,
and I'd be blamed if I abandoned it,
for what a man boasts of with his tongue
he should always clearly keep in mind,
since there is no worse sin
than a promise unfulfilled.

II   I feel joyful now because the cold weather
is over and shelters remain unused;
the little birds—and their nature's such
that they never renounce their singing—
are cheerful each in his own tongue,
for the new season coming on,
and the trees, so long dried out,
now line their branches with green leaves.

III   And whoever was once devoted to love
should not uproot himself therefrom,
for with the awakening of the new season
each man's heart should be the richer;
and who cannot with his tongue
say fitting things, let the new joy
teach him to express himself,
for thus Merit wishes men to act.

IV   I have loved faithfully and truly
a woman who deceived and tricked me,
and because her love brought torment,
I shall always feel resentful;

and I no longer want her tongue
to bind me in its chain of words,
for another man is close to her
and has captured what I hunted.

V   Let spite and deceit remain
with them both, for a joy
has now seized and inflamed me
of which I'll believe no evil;
may someone cut out my tongue
if I give ear to slander
or renounce her love, even
if I would thus lose Orange.

VI   I cannot be untrue to her,
for never have I had such
good fortune; the Lord himself
almost erred in making her—
he could scarcely make his tongue
say, "This I wish her to become,"
for he did not want others
aspiring to such beauty.

VII   Lady, I cannot plead for long,
but you can either make me a beggar
or richer than any king—
I am entirely in your power!
You have only to let your tongue
tell me how to act, for
my heart will never change
or turn towards another.

VIII   Lady, I ask nothing with my tongue
save that I may embrace and kiss you
some place where we might be alone,
and with my arms encircling you.[11]

2

| I | Raimbaut d'Orange | I'd like to know, Giraut de Bornelh, why you're always criticizing trobar clus, and what your reasons are.[12] |

        Tell me now:
        if you so prize
what's common to every man, then
all things must have equal value.

| II | Giraut de Bornelh | Senh'en Linhaure, I can't complain [13] if each man writes according to his taste, but my own sense of judgment tells me |

        that a poem's better
        loved and prized
if easy and understandable to all;
but please don't misunderstand me.

| III | Raimbaut | Giraut, I don't want my poetry put in such confusion that it be praised by the good, the small and the great. |

        And it will never
        be praised by fools,
for they don't comprehend (or care about)
that which has most worth and value.

| IV | Giraut | Linhaure, if on this account I lie awake and turn my pleasure into care, I'd seem afraid of popularity. |

        But why write
        if you don't want
everyone at once to understand you?
For singing has no other value.

| V | Raimbaut | Giraut, it's enough to bring forth, improve and recite my verse; beyond that, I don't care if it's not spread abroad. |

        For nothing vile
        is ever worthy;

just as men prefer gold to salt,
so it is with any song.

VI	*Giraut*	Linhaure, a true lover usually

speaks the truth in an argument.
And thus I'll admit it worries me
    when some horse-voiced
    jongleur, who's not
been properly paid, recites badly
and thus spoils my lofty songs.[14]

VII	*Raimbaut*	Giraut, by the heavens, the sun

and the spreading light,
I don't know what we're talking about,
    nor where I was born,
    and my confusion
comes from dwelling on such great joy
that I can think of nothing else.

VIII	*Giraut*	Linhaure, she whom I court

shows me the red of her shield,[15]
making me wish for God's help.
    What mad
    wild thoughts
have brought me such disloyal doubts?
Did she not raise me to a noble rank?

IX	*Raimbaut*	Giraut, it pains me, by Saint Martial,

that you must leave by Christmas time.

X	*Giraut*	Linhaure, I am going now

to a rich, powerful royal court.[16]

3

I   Listen now! But I do not know,
gentlemen, what it is I'm starting.
It's not a *vers, estribot* or *sirventes*,[17]
nor can I find a name for it,

nor do I know how it should be written
and have it turn out in such a way
that no one ever saw its equal made by man or woman
in this century or in the one that's past.

II   Although you think me mad,
        I cannot refrain
        from stating how I feel;
        and let no one blame me.
        Everything seems worthless
        compared to what I now behold.
And let me tell you why. If I'd begun it and then not
finished it, you'd consider me a fool; for a bird in the
hand is worth two in the bush.

III   I beg my friend not to fear
        that he might displease me.
        If he does not wish to help me now,
        let him do so after a long delay;
        no one can deceive me so easily
        as she who has conquered me.
I say all this because of a lady who makes me languish
with fine words and keeps putting me off—I don't know
why. Do you think any good can come of this, gentlemen?

IV   A good four months have passed
        (they're like a thousand years to me)
        since she gave in and promised
        she would grant me what I most sought.
        Lady, since you hold my heart,
        relieve my bitterness with sweetness.
God help me! *In nomine patris et filii et spiritus sancti!* What will happen to us, my lady?

V   Because of you I'm gay and full of grief:
        sad and joyful, you make me want to write
        my poems; and I have left three women
        who, except for you, have no peer.

My courtly singing is so good
that people call me "Jongleur."
Lady, you can do whatever you want with me, just like
N'Ayma who stuck the sword in where it most pleased
her.[18]

VI Now I've finished my *Don't-know-what-it-is*,
 for this is what I think I'll call it;
 and since I've never heard of such a thing,
 I certainly should name it thus.
 And to enjoy it, you must recite it,
 after learning it by heart.
And if anyone asks who wrote it, tell him it was the one
who knows how to do all kinds of deeds well when he
wants to.[19]

4

I I know well how to speak of love
 and give advice to other lovers;
 but about myself (which matters most)
 I'm lost as to what to say,
 for neither kindness and praise,
 nor evil, hostile words are any use to me;
 but now towards love I'm
 true and good, frank and loyal.

II So I'll teach the rules of love
 to those others who chase after women;
 and if they follow my instructions,
 they'll make as many conquests
 as they could ever wish!
 Let disbelievers be hung and burned,
 for glory will crown those
 who use the key I give them.

III If you wish to conquer ladies
 and have them do you honor,

then if they answer you with vile
mean words, start to menace them;
and if then their reply is even worse,
plant your fist across their nose;
and if they get wild, get even wilder.
From great harm will come great peace.

IV   And there's more I want to teach you
so you can conquer the finest ladies.
Do everything with foul words,
ugly singing and much boasting;
and treat the worst of them
respectfully and praise their faults.
And make sure your houses
aren't like ships or churches.[20]

V   If you do that, you'll be all right.
But I'll behave quite differently,
since I'm not interested in love.
I wouldn't want to take the trouble
even if they were all my sisters!
That's why I'll be faithful,
humble, frank, and loyal,
gentle, amorous, true and open.

VI   But don't follow my example,
for what I do will be sheer madness.
Don't be caught playing the fool,
but cherish what I've taught you
if you don't want to suffer grief
and pain and endless tears.
For I'd also treat them badly
if I sought their hospitality.

VII   Hence my sense of pride, for I
(to my great dishonor) feel no love
and don't know what it is.
But I do love My Ring [21]—thus my radiance—
for it was on my finger . . . but I've gone

too far! Stop, tongue! Too much talk
is worse than a mortal sin;
I'd better keep my heart enclosed.

VIII But my fine Jongleur [22] will know
her worth and how dear she is to me
and that she'll never do me any harm.

IX And now that it is finished, she'll receive
this poem in Rodez, my native town.[23]

5

I I've been silent for a long time now,
but God doesn't want me to keep
my deficiencies a secret any longer,
and this fills me with grief and horror.
So listen, knights, and see
if indeed I don't lack something.

II You may rest assured on one score:
I've lost those things which make
men gayest—and hence my shame;
and I don't dare say who did it.
But you can see I speak the truth
when I admit to such chagrin.

III The reason I so willingly confess
the cause of my endless grief
is that I want to relieve, without
delay, all husbands of any fear,
anxiety or worry which might have
made them look at me askance.

IV Though I seem likable and pleasant,
I'm really thin, nasty and cowardly
(with or without my armor),
leprous and foul smelling,

a vile, niggardly host, and the worst
soldier you have ever seen.

V   So any man is clearly a fool
to worry if I court his wife;
why should he drive me off,
since no harm
could ever come to him
from my endless wretched sighs?

VI   For even without this deficiency
(which makes me tear out my beard in rage)
I have so much else on which to preen myself
—other evil sins into which I've fallen—
that to no woman whole in body [24]
would I be worth a moment's thought.

VII   And if I'm allowed to do so, I'll sing,
for this I will never abandon.
Let every husband grow a pimple
on his snout if he gets angry
when I wish to hide my grief
behind a mask of gaiety.

VIII   I've commended myself to ladies
so that I may have some joy,
which I'm powerless to realize
in bed; so I'll grow fat
merely from desiring
and looking—I seek nothing else.

IX   I'd like the countess at Monrosier
to hear of my perfect joy.[25]

The Countess of Die

The Countess of Die,[1] wife of William of Poitiers, was both beautiful and gracious. And she fell in love with Raimbaut d'Orange and wrote many fine poems for him.

These two sentences have caused more tearing out of scholarly hair than any comparable passage in the Provençal biographies. The confusion can be summed up by saying that we know of no Countess of Die who fits the above description, that there are five characters called William of Poitiers wandering across the pages of the histories of this period,[2] and that we also know of two Raimbauts d'Orange.[3]

But this noblewoman, whose "personality has obstinately eluded the research of historians" as Jeanroy put it, and of whom only four poems have been preserved,[4] is a figure unique in the Middle Ages. This is not only because she was a woman poet—there were several others among the troubadours, although none of them as good as she—but also because of an almost startling directness in her verse. First of all there is a stylistic directness, with simple forms and unadorned language; but mainly one is struck by an emotional directness, in which she lays bare the feelings of her obviously passionate and sensual nature. So for a brief moment we get a glimpse, not of the idealized woman sung by male troubadours, but of a specific woman whose emotions can still touch us even though the intervening eight hundred years have obliterated her own figure from history.

* Notes accompanying this section begin on p. 266.

1

I   For a while now a certain knight
has caused me great distress,
and I want it known, once and for all,
how excessively I have loved him;
    yet I've been betrayed
on pretext of not giving him my love,
and ever since, in bed or dressed,[5]
    my life's been one of grief.

II   How I would like to hold him
one night in my naked arms
and see him joyfully use my body
as a pillow, for I am more
    in love with him
than Flore with Blanchefleur,[6]
and offer him my heart, my love,
    my mind, my eyes and my life.

III   My handsome friend, gracious and charming,
when will I hold you in my power?
Oh that I might lie with you
one night and kiss you lovingly!
    Know how great is my desire
to treat you as a husband;
but you must promise me to do
    whatever I may wish.

2

I   Although I do not want to, I must sing
of that which makes me bitter:
a man whom I love more than anything.
But with him all pity and courtesy is useless,
as well as my beauty, merit or intelligence;

for I have been deceived and tricked,
treated as if I were contemptible.

II   My only comfort lies in knowing, my friend,
that I have never been unfaithful,
but love you more than Seguin loved Valence,[7]
and I am glad that I surpass you in love,
my friend, because of your great valor;
but why with me are you so haughty
and yet so open with other people?

III   I am amazed how haughty your heart has become,
my friend, towards me, and it makes me grieve;
no other love should draw you from me
no matter what is said or granted.
But remember how our love began;
God could not wish
to blame me for our separation.

IV   The valor dwelling in your heart
disturbs me, as does your great merit,
for there exists no woman whom,
desiring love, you cannot attract;
but you, my friend, have sense enough
to recognize the one who is most faithful
and to remember the promises we made.

V   Remember, too, my merit and nobility,
my beauty and, even more, my loyal heart;
thus to you in your dwelling place
I send this song as messenger.
And I want to know, my handsome, charming friend,
why you're so cruel and harsh with me,
whether through ill will or haughtiness.

VI   But you must also tell him, messenger,
that haughtiness can wreak great damage.

Giraut de Bornelh

Giraut de Bornelh was from the region of Excideuil in the Limousin, from a powerful castle belonging to the Viscount of Limoges.[1] He was of low birth, but he was wise in matters of letters and had great natural intelligence. And he was the best troubadour of any of those who came before or after him. For this reason he was called Master of the Troubadours, and is still considered as such by those who understand subtle, well-placed words concerning love and reason. He was greatly honored by men of valor and understanding, and also by ladies who understood [2] the masterful words of his songs.

His life was such that he spent all winter in school learning [3] letters, and all summer going from court to court, taking with him two jongleurs who sang his songs. But he never wanted to marry, and everything he earned he gave to poor relatives and to the church in the town where he was born, which church was—and still is—called Saint Gervais.

And here are written a great number of his songs.

Aside from what we can glean from this biography, our information about Giraut de Bornelh's life is scanty. His poetic career seems to have extended from about 1165 to 1200 (or perhaps 1211). He traveled widely in the South of France and Spain, and he included among his many patrons the kings of Aragon and Castille and Richard the Lionhearted. We also know that he accompanied his lord, Ademar of Limoges, on the Third Crusade.

In addition, his literary reputation has suffered strange vicissitudes. As the biography plainly states, he was regarded by his contemporaries as the greatest of the troubadours. But after that his reputation began to decline. Dante was the first to dethrone him—in favor of Arnaut Daniel. But in spite of

* Notes accompanying this section begin on p. 267.

his saying in the *Divine Comedy* (Purgatory, XXVI, 120), "let fools pretend that he of Limoges is better (than Arnaut Daniel)," Dante still seemed to hold him in considerable esteem, for he quotes four of his poems in the *De Vulgari Eloquentia*.

With time Giraut de Bornelh's image became more and more worn and besmudged, until the inimitable Jeanroy could say, "This so-called 'Master of the Troubadours' seems to us like an infatuated pedant, pompously spinning out his banalities . . . He reminds one of a tenor as pleased with himself as he is displeased with a public whom he cannot forgive for not going into ecstacies over his vocal flourishes." [4]

But since then, fortunately, the pendulum has begun to swing the other way. Riquer, for instance (in his *Lírica de los Trovadores*), passes a very fair and sound judgment on Giraut de Bornelh.

The difficulty in appraising his poetry stems, I think, from the fact that of all the great troubadours he has the fewest distinguishing characteristics by which he can be pigeon-holed. He hasn't the tenderness of Bernart de Ventadorn, the brilliance of Arnaut Daniel nor the virility of Bertran de Born. He is a poet without idiosyncracies. Each of these other poets became famous for cultivating a particular form or style, whereas Giraut de Bornelh worked in a variety of forms and styles. Moreover, his poetry never relies on isolated, quotable passages—there are no "moments" in his verse as there are in Bernart de Ventadorn; nor does his greatness rely on any one or two poems (the beautiful and justifiably famous *alba*—Poem 6 below—is not at all characteristic), but rather on the whole body of his verse.

Giraut de Bornelh could therefore be called the most classic of the troubadours. He is not an innovator, but rather a figure who, when the troubadour movement was at its height, summed up most of its many facets. As a technician, he is a master, with complete control of diction and form, and with a craftsmanship of endless resourcefulness. But there is something more to his verse, a quality which is rather difficult to define. It has a density (which might best be described as a kind of poetic saturation), an immutable, hard, almost rock-like quality. As a result his verse is not pretty or particularly attractive; it is not easy and almost completely lacks any instantaneous appeal (except perhaps for the *alba* mentioned above). Dipping into a few passages here and there will be singularly unrewarding. Giraut de Bornelh requires greater effort and appeals to a deeper poetic sense on the reader's part. But the more one reads his poetry, the more compelling and impressive it becomes, and one begins to understand why his contemporaries considered him the Master of the Troubadours.

1

I   "Ah, I'm dying!" *"Why, my friend?"*
        "I've been betrayed!"
        "And how, pray tell?"
"Because I put my faith in one
who seemed to welcome me."
"Is that why your heart is broken?"
        "Precisely."
"And is your heart there with her?"
        "Indeed it is."
"So this is why you're near death."
"Yes, more than you'll ever know."
"But why did you let this happen?"

II   "Because I'm too timid and sincere."
        "You've asked for nothing?"
        "Good Heavens, no!"
*"But then why worry when you
have no idea how she feels?"*
"Because I live in constant fear."
        "Of what?"
"Her love, and the anxiety it brings.".
        *"But that's absurd;
do you expect her to make the offer?"*
"No, but I can't get up my nerve."
"Then you'll just continue suffering."

III   "But what should I do, my lord?"
       "The proper courtly thing."
      "And what is that?"
"Go at once before her
and plead for her love."
"She might think it impertinent."
     "So what!"
"But she might answer me with insults."
   "Just be patient,
for patience can conquer anything."
"What if her husband catches me?"
"There's no danger if you both are careful."

IV   "Both?" *"Yes."* "If only that could be!"
      "It will." "What?" *"Believe me."*
      "I hope you're right!"
"If you conquer your fears and talk
to her, your joy will be unbounded."
"The mortal grief I've felt, my lord,
      is such
that it must now be shared with her."
   "May your judgment
and courage stand you in good stead."
"Yes, and all my hopes too."
"Make sure to express yourself well."

V   "I'll never be able to do that."
      "Why not, pray tell?"
      "Because of her presence."
"Won't you even be able to talk to her?
Are you that far gone?"
"Yes, when I'm before her, I . . ."
    "Tremble?"
"So much that my mind goes blank."
   "That's what happens
to anyone who's hopelessly in love."
"I know, but I'll try to get up courage."
"But you must delay no longer."

VI   "Love has led me
to the point that I am now like those
who live badly since they die of desire.
I therefore can't feel sorry for myself."

VII   *"Go to your pleasure;
go, my friend, while it's still a secret.
And be sure you do not lose your nerve,
for happiness can vanish in a moment."*

2

I   When the cold with its ice and snow
departs and the warm weather returns
bringing on spring verdure,
and when I hear the birds trill,
    I so love
the sweet time at the end of March
that I feel more agile than a leopard,
livelier than a deer or chamois.
And if she to whom I've given myself
    would honor me
to the point of suffering
me to be her faithful lover,
I'd be the richest man on earth.

II   Her body is so gay and lithe,
with such charming hues, that never
from a rose or other plant
did a fresher flower bloom;
    nor would Bordeaux
have a more gallant lord than I
if she would deign to receive me
and allow me to be her serf.
And let them call me a Bézierite [5]
    if any man
hears me divulging secrets

which she privately has told me,
thus angering her lovely heart.

III   Good lady, the ring you gave me
has rendered great service
in lessening my sorrows,
and the sight of it makes me happier
    than a starling;
moreover, for you I feel such courage
that I am sure neither lance nor dart
nor steel nor iron could harm me.
And yet, through excessive love
    I feel as lost
as a ship driven from its course,
lashed by wind and waves—
thus do my thoughts afflict me.

IV   My lady, as when a castle
is besieged by powerful lords,
when towers are crumbled by catapults,
battering rams and siege engines,
    and from all sides
the battle rages with such ferocity
that no wiles or tricks can help,
and so great are the shouts and cries
of the anguished men inside
    that it would seem
they could only plead for mercy,
so do I for mercy humbly beg,
my good, noble and valiant lady.

V   Lady, just as a lamb is helpless
against a bear, so shall I be
if your valor does not help me,
for I feel more fragile than a reed,
    and my life
shall be four times shorter
if you delay in repairing
the wrongs you've done me.

And you, True Love, be kind
   (for you should keep
true lovers from committing follies)
and guide me, leading me towards
the lady who has conquered me.

VI   Jongleur, take this new song
and bear it with all speed to that
lovely lady, source of all wealth,
and tell her that I am hers even more
    than her own cloak.

3

I   Now you will hear a perfect song, for I
am a perfect lover, daunted by nothing!
   Listen! Was a greater folly
   ever uttered in a song?
   Surely harm will come
   from comparing myself with her
   to whom I'm bound in servitude.
   O earth, how can you endure me?

II   Ah, foolish talk has so often taken joy
from my grasp that my hair's turned gray,
   and my heart, which knows
   that happiness is all too rare,
   wanted me to sing gay songs,
   for until its eyes were opened
   it had justice quite reversed,
   so much was it lost in love.

III   But what say you? If knowledge is rare
and the heart light, what good is excess love?
   None, for she is so highborn
   and rich—we'll not discuss the rest—
   that my praises are no use,
   however enticing they may be;
   and thus I raise my songs
   like a fool deprived of reason.

IV   No alarm seemed serious to me
        until my idle talk took joy away,
            and now I say that Love
            has tricked me with appearances
            and made me lose what cannot
            be regained with gentle speech,
                and through my mouth, which is to blame,
                I'm like a captive held in chains.

V   Why can't I, now that prayers might help,
        beg for mercy? I can, and since my love
            is so determined and does not
            seek another, then let my poems
            ask for mercy—sing them who may—
            from the one I once could vilify.
                —You mad fool, do you think you'll
                find what you are looking for?

VI   *And even if you were burned alive, could you*
        *repay her favors?—*There was only one kiss!
            —Ridiculous! Can a man with
            determination not slowly better
            *his state?—*That's childishness!
            —And if she gave more than was due,
                you who are worse than a Bézierite,[6]
                what gratitude have you shown?

VII   —Such gratitude that my eyes look out to sea [7]
        and my heart feels gentle, frank and true
            towards her who is clothed in joy,
            who is far from vileness and deceit
            and far from me. My ceaseless thoughts
            have turned me thin and sickly,
                tossed me to and fro, and made me
                sadder than a poor lay monk.[8]

VIII   Do you think I'm troubled or harmed by thirst
        or by hunger? No, my sweet thoughts
            and a few crumbs of bread
            can sustain me all year long!

  —You fool! Who on earth
  would believe such nonsense?
  —Anyone; they need only ask
  my Linhaure, there beyond Lers.[9]

IX Joios,[10] only a hopeless fool
  is sad when things go well.

4

I I'll write a song both good and bad,
  but for what reason I don't know,
  nor for whom, nor how, nor why,
  nor can I even say what I have in mind;
  and though I don't know how, I'll write it,
  and whoever wants to, will be free to sing it.

II I'm sick, though my health was never better,
  and I mistake wicked men for good
  and make gifts when I have nothing left
  and wish evil on those who wish me well;
  without being in love, I'm such a true friend
  that I lose those who curry my favor.

III I go with whoever does not call me
  and beg from those who cannot give.
  I feel splendid when I'm with Jaufré,[11]
  for then I do what suits me best,
  rising when I should lie down
  and singing when I should cry.

IV Folly encircles and surrounds me,
  and thus do I know more than Cato,[12]
  and unless restrained by some madder person,
  I attach the bit to the tail,
  for my earliest teaching was such
  that now my folly knows no bounds.

V For a while my love was without
  deceit and yet treacherous;

I proudly pleaded mercy for others
as if for me, and thus without
wanting to, I'll meet my end begging
for things I will not give myself.

VI   There's a lady whom I hope does not speak
to me, or pardon me if she does me wrong.
If she wanted to lie with me,
I'd almost swear upon my faith
that I'd make her beg and plead;
yet one mustn't be too disdainful!

VII   If she's kind to me, as a reward
I will find an opportunity
to end my service towards her.
— ¹³

who think evil makes them prosper
and vileness raises their esteem.

VIII   I won't know of what this song is made
or how, unless someone tells me;
for within me there is such mad knowledge
that I know nothing concerning myself.
She who does not want me as her friend
has caused me to lose my mind.

IX   Although I think I speak discreetly,
I must be carefully watched.

X   I'd regain my sanity at once
if only she would deign to love me.

5

I   The other day, on the first of August,
I arrived in Provence, beyond Alest; ¹⁴
I was riding with sad demeanor,
    full of anguish. But then
I heard a shepherdess
singing near a hedge,

and so sweet a sound
echoed through the valley
that I turned in surprise
and saw her picking ferns.

II   When she had stretched her skirt tight
to avoid sharp branches, and before
I could ask, "Where are you from?"
        she held my stirrup
        and said, "What path
        has brought you here?
        You seem sad; but please
        don't think me too inquisitive.
        Since you're alone, I have the right
        to ask such questions."

III   "Young girl, since you asked so sweetly,
I'll tell you (though it's not easy)
why fortune makes me sorrowful.
        I need to find a woman
        who'll be true and faithful,
        for the one I've just left
        was false and treacherous,
        and led me far astray;
        she would have been my guide
        had she not been so changeable."

IV   "Noble Sir, alliances with highborn
ladies can only bring grief, no matter
how much a man has seen or heard;
        for a noblewoman wants
        her good deeds recompensed
        and her treachery forgotten.
        Beware if you are not
        prepared to do such things,
        for they're a fickle lot,
        always changing course."

V   "Young girl, may God bring her
the suffering she's brought me

and make her lose sleep and appetite.
    But you with your swarthy skin,
    don't think that I prefer you!
    Yet since you've been so sweet,
    I'll tell you frankly
    how grateful I am
    that you didn't flee
    when you first saw me."

VI   "Sir, I must be very careful,
    since I've not yet given my 'yes.' [15]
    My body's small and my mind chaste
        (even though I seem obliging),
        and I think I'll be well married
        in accordance with my poverty;
        but since you ask so little,
        I'll be frivolous, and if
        you give your solemn word,
        my love will be entirely yours."

VII   "Young girl, that would doubtless
    cure me, but my love has grown
    such deep roots there beyond Lobera [16]
    that the evil, although now dormant,
    could yet do me even greater harm."

VIII   "Sir, you have little courage
    if you're afraid the evil you now
    flee will seek you out; but since
    you're so attractive, let us
    lie together in the shade."

IX   "Young girl, N'Escaronha [17]
    is my guide; she was my true love
    and gentle, courtly companion;
    through her my troubles vanish."

X   "Sir, you make a big mistake
    to talk about possessing someone

else, even though it's only
vanity that makes you do so!"

6

I   Glorious King, true light and clarity,
Lord God all powerful, if it please Thee,
help my companion faithfully, for I
have not seen him since night came on,
    and soon it will be dawn.

II   Fair companion, do you sleep or wake?
Sleep no more, but get up gently,
for in the East the morning star rises,
bringing day—I can see it clearly—
    and soon it will be dawn.

III   Fair companion, I call to you in song:
sleep no more, for the birds sing too,
seeking daylight through the woods,
and I fear some jealous fool might come,
    for soon it will be dawn.

IV   Fair companion, come to the window
and look at the stars in the heavens!
You shall see I'm a faithful messenger;
you must, or harm will come to you,
    for soon it will be dawn.

V   Fair companion, I have not slept
since I left you, but remained on my knees
praying God, the son of Saint Mary,
to bring back your loyal companionship;
    now soon it will be dawn.

VI   Fair companion, outside on the stairs
you begged me not to be drowsy
but to watch all night till day came,
and now my song and presence displease you,
    yet soon it will be dawn!

VII   Fair sweet companion, so rich is my delight
       that I wish dawn and day would never come,
       for the gentlest lady ever born of mother
       I now hold in my arms; what then care I
          for jealous fools or dawn!

7

Razo

Giraut de Bornelh loved a woman from Gascony whose name
was N'Alamanda d'Estancs,[18] and who had granted him pleasure in love. But it came to pass that she felt her worth had
been diminished because of what he had wanted from her. So
she let him go and withdrew her love in favor of another man,
and because of this she was very much blamed, for he was
excitable and malevolent. Giraut de Bornelh was therefore sad
and sorrowful for a long time on account of the harm that was
his and the blame that was hers, for it was not right that she
should take the other man as her lover.

He therefore composed this song, complaining of her treachery and saying he no longer cared for joy, gaiety or pleasure.

I   I will not entirely abandon
       singing, joy, or laughter, no matter
       how little desire I may have.
          But because I no longer
          take pleasure in hope
       or solace, I do not want to waste
          my golden words on myself
          alone, but rather clench
          my lovely songs between
          my teeth, since I do not
          dare recite them; for I
          see scarcely anyone
             taking pleasure
          in joy, or feeling
       envy at my happiness and gaiety.

II   But I have received more injury—
       far more than I can ever tell—
       from my evil, treacherous lady,

and it was surely madness
to have believed in her,
for now with her I am defenseless.
    Since I behaved so badly,
    I'll be patient;
    good and happiness
    will slowly return.
    For lovers know nothing
    of love (they are only
        quick to anger),
    but Love's law demands
that one forgive the other's wrongs.

III   It is quite true that she deprived me
           of her love—I cannot hide this fact;
           but since grass is cut by force,
               what good is truth to me?
               It would be far better
           if my heart's attentions would turn
               somewhere else;
               for irresistible power
               makes my rights useless.
               But then the little
               wisdom I may have
               leads me to think
                   I'll be destroyed
               if I'm untrue to her;
           for she alone can drown or save me.

IV   But if I had some true friend
           who took pleasure in my well-being,
           one sincere, frank and faultless,
               who was discreet
               and not inquisitive,
           he could help restore my joy with her.
               Is this so unattainable?
               My suspicious heart,
               my mind and fear, all
               fight with one another;
               but then no robber

ever plunders alone
   a well-guarded house
without his heart, mind and fear
making his anxiety almost unbearable.[19]

V   Now she can delight in the thought
         of holding my life in her hands!
         For I've had no gaiety or happiness
            since a cunning fool
            led me into error,
         got my confidence and fed me lies,
            after which the dandy
            helped me no more
            than those thoughts of her
            which fire my soul.
         And nobody
            envies a lover
               his high charge,
            even were he an emperor,
         for Love wants no man's dominion.

VI   A man must be submissive, patient,
         and admit to his being conquered
         (unless he's evil in other ways),
            for acts of daring
            are never recompensed
         but only cause annihilation.
            Humility alone attracts
            people of discernment.
            —*But won't you learn
            that pride is useless,
            and that suffering
            (without boasting)
               can bring you
            to kiss and caress her?*
         —But that's what I've been saying!

VII   Never has worth (which crumbles through
         vileness or through welcoming vile fools)
         not endeavored for a place of decency.

Thus the evil
ill-bred rich
should not strive for such great power.
    —*With justice they would strive
    in vain!*—You think so?
    —*Yes!*—Do you consent
    to scoundrels taking
    advantage of whatever
    chance they might have
        with a lady
    of charm and gentle birth?
No, a man not in earnest renounces love.

8

Razo

After Gui, the Viscount of Limoges,[20] had had Giraut de Bornelh's house robbed of all his books and clothes, and when Giraut saw that worth had fled and solace had gone to sleep and gallantry was dead and prowess come to nought and courtliness lost and wisdom turned into vulgarity, and that both lovers and the beloved had become full of deceit, he wanted to recover solace, joy and worth, and he therefore made this song which says:

I   I thought I might try
        to reawaken solace
        which has slept too long,
        to receive and recover worth
        which has been banished,
        but now I've given up; for I
        have failed, and found that such
        an undertaking is interminable:
    the greater my desire and will become,
    the more the obstacles and harm increase.

II   I find it hard to bear;
        I say this to you who know
        how people once loved
        well-being and abundance.

But who has not seen
torture racks
or villeins forced
into knightly service?
It is ugly, painful and unseemly when
men lose God and fall into disgrace.

III   You've seen tournaments announced
and attended by men handsomely
fitted out, and then afterwards
you've discussed the various blows;
but now only those who pilfer
or rob sheep are prized.
Shame on the knight who thinks
to pursue a course of love
after making off with bleating lambs,
stealing from churches or robbing pilgrims.

IV [21]   Where have they fled, the jongleurs
who once were so well received?
For those who were guides
now themselves need guidance,
and since worth has failed
(and here I blame no one),
they walk alone
who once had
companions—how many I cannot tell—
handsome, well-dressed and gay.

V   And you used to see jongleurs
with good clothes and shoes [22]
going from court to court
praising ladies; but now
no one even mentions them,
so much has their worth
vanished.—*But what brought on
this evil of slandering them?*—
Whom, the lovers or their ladies?—
Both, for deceit has stained their worth.

VI   And I myself, who used to praise
      men of valor and distinction,
      am so confused that I don't
      know what course to take.
      Indeed, from courts
      I hear, instead of
      enlightened conversation,
      cries of joy over the tale
of the Bremar goose,[23] as if it were decent
poetry of noble deeds, of time past and present.

VII   But to soften hearts
      which have become too hardened,
      should men not recall
      old forgotten deeds?
      For it is hard to abandon
      a thing already under way,
      and one needs no medicine
      for an ill already cured.
The things a man now sees make him turn
and toss; they press about him on all sides.

VIII At least I can boast
      that they never invaded
      my little house;
      they all respected it—
      brave men and cowards alike—
      and they did me only honor.
      Wherefore my distinguished
      lord must think
that I bring him little praise and glory
by praising them and bemoaning him.

IX   But I'll complain no more!—*Why?*—Don't ask.
      What a pity it would be to end my song this way.

X   Thus says the Dauphin, who knows about good songs.[24]

Arnaut de Maruelh

Arnaut de Maruelh was from the bishopric of Périgueux, from a castle called Maruelh;[1] he was of a poor family and became a clerk. But since he could not live by his letters, he went out into the world. And he could write good poetry, and he was a man of intelligence. The heavens and fortune brought him to the court of the Countess of Burlatz, who was daughter of the good Count Raymond and wife of the Viscount of Béziers, called Taillefer.[2]

This Arnaut was handsome, and he sang well, and read romances. And the Countess did much for him and honored him greatly. And he fell in love with her and dedicated his songs to her, but he did not dare tell her nor anyone else that it was he who had written them, but instead he pretended somebody else had done so.

But finally love forced him to write a song which begins:

La franca captenensa

and in this song he told her of the love he felt for her. And the Countess, instead of shunning him, listened to his entreaties, welcomed them and was grateful for them. She gave him many presents, did him great honor, and gave him courage to sing of her; and he became an honored courtier. He thus dedicated many fine songs to the Countess, and these songs show that she treated him sometimes very well and sometimes very badly.

A *razo* goes on to say that King Alfonso of Aragon, who was also in love with the Countess, found out about all this, and being a jealous man, had Arnaut kicked out of Béziers, after which he went to the court of William VIII of Montpellier.

* Notes accompanying this section begin on p. 272.

We know little else about him, except that his poetry was probably written between 1171 and 1190, and that he seems to have traveled to Italy.[3] We also know that a troubadour called Pistoleta started out as his jongleur, and that the Monk of Montaudan, in his satyric gallery of troubadours (see p. 186), pictures him as begging his lady for mercy and shedding floods of tears with each new song.

As a poet he seems to have enjoyed considerable fame in his own lifetime; he was, in fact, among the dozen or so most widely read of all the troubadours. The quality of his verse was best summed up by Ezra Pound in *The Spirit of Romance:* "For the simplicity of adequate speech Arnaut of Marvoil is to be numbered among the best of the courtly 'makers.' " But this simplicity is not banal or vacuous; it is rather the result of a technique honed down to the point where all signs of effort vanish, where the words, sounds and rhythms flow past with a mellifluous ease, resulting in a poetry of extraordinarily gentle and delicate beauty.

But it also makes his poetry like a rare flower, which when tampered with ever so slightly, wilts and dies. And since translation is nothing if not tampering, I have decided to give only one poem—the one that seems to have been best known—and to include the original of the first stanza in the notes so the reader can get some idea of the charm of his verse.

1

I   You and Love have such sway over me, my lady,
       that I dare not love you, nor can I refrain therefrom:
       the one makes me flee, the other holds me back,
       one brings me courage, the other fear,
       and I don't dare plead for you to give me pleasure;
       but like a man mortally wounded,
       who knows he must die yet clings to life,
       I desperately implore you for mercy.

II   Good Lady, where lineage and nobility
       are greatest and merit highest,

there too should one find more humility,
for worth has no place with pride
unless it be sweetly veiled in clemency.
And since I cannot refrain from loving you,
I pray that your sense of mercy and humility
will let me find in you some pity.

III   I am not unnerved by your high merit,
for I shall never cease exalting it;
since I first saw you, all my powers
have been used in praising this worth of yours
and making it known far and wide.
And should you deign to show me gratitude,
I would ask nothing else of your friendship,
for such recompense would be enough.

IV   All the wrongs and ceaseless complaints
of which you could accuse me
come from your having been more charming
than any other creature I have ever seen.
No, my lady, I am guilty of no other sin
than having recognized and chosen you
as finer and more beautiful than any other.
That is the only wrong I have committed.

V   Your lovely eyes, your fresh complexion,
and the sweet charming way you act with me
have made my desire and my need so great
that I love you more as my despair increases,
and it is madness that I cannot leave you.
But when I consider for whom I languish,
I think of the honor and forget the madness,
I flee my judgment and follow my desire.

VI   Precious Jewel, you need no greater eulogy,
and may he who mentions the Marquis of Montferrat
praise him no more, for he has done so enough already.[4]

Bertran de Born

Bertran de Born was a chatelain from the bishopric of Périgord, lord of a castle called Autafort.[1] He was always at war with his neighbors, the Count of Périgord, the Viscount of Limoges, his own brother Constantin, and Richard when he was Count of Poitiers.[2] He was a good knight, a good warrior, a good courtier of women, a good troubadour, knowledgeable and clever of speech; and he was a man who knew how to make the best of any situation. Whenever he so wished, he could dominate King Henry and his sons, but he always wanted them to be at war with one another—father, son and brother. And he always wanted the kings of France and England to be at war with each other. And if there was a peace or truce, he would try by means of his sirventes to undo it and prove how each had been dishonored by this peace. And he reaped great rewards and suffered much harm from the troubles he stirred up.

There is another version of this Provençal biography which is quite different; but the only portions of it worth transcribing contain the marvelous judgment of King Alfonso of Aragon, who "gave Giraut de Bornelh's *chansons* in marriage to Bertran de Born's *sirventes*," and the statement that "after living for a long time in this world, he [Bertran de Born] entered the order of Cîteaux."

From various documents of the time, scholars have been able to deduce that he must have been born around 1140, had two brothers (Itier and Constantin), was twice married and had at least five children. His datable poems fall between 1181 and 1197, and at this latter date he had already entered

* Notes accompanying this section begin on p. 274.

the monastery of Dalon (of the Cistercian order, as the biographer said),[3] the same monastery to which Bernart de Ventadorn retired at the end of his life (see p. 82). As for the date of his death, we only know that it took place some time before 1215.

As a poet Bertran de Born is an extraordinary and completely original figure. He could, like the other troubadours, write love poetry, and some of it is excellent (see the first two poems below), but it was as a war poet, as a maker of *sirventes*, that we can see him in his true light. Yet he did not write of war, like most poets, to complain of its horrors, nor did he write of it just to describe its pageantry, as for instance it is depicted in a Uccello painting or the miniatures one finds in medieval chronicles. He seems actually to have loved war and everything connected with it: not only the pageantry, but also the excitement of the sight, smell and feel of it, and even its horrors.

> we'll soon see fields strewn with bits
> of helmets, shields, swords and saddlebows,
> and bodies split open from head to foot,
> and horses wandering about aimlessly,
> and lances protruding from ribs and chests,
> and joy and tears, and grief and happiness.[4]

And yet more extraordinary is the fact that he can make the modern reader, for whom war no longer holds much charm, feel his excitement. This is probably due to the amazing sense of immediacy in his verse; he is like Villon in that he can drag the reader back through centuries and make him momentarily see the world through the poet's eyes, to the point where he can even interest us in his own personal petty squabbles (see Poem 4, for instance, which is about his own troubles with his brother Constantin). Part of the effect is achieved through the use of vivid, everyday speech—one can almost hear him talking:

> Guilhem de Gordo, that's a crazy
> clapper you've put inside your bell.[5]

Yet that is only part of it. The rest is an indefinable poetic magic.

But in discussing his love of war, one thing must be made clear. He loved it not only for its own sake, but also because it was the only means by which minor noblemen such as he could maintain their position and independence. They wanted and needed a state of mild but continual feudal anarchy, which was achieved by making sure the more powerful lords were always at war with each other. Bertran de Born was quite frank about this:

> I want great barons always
> to be angry with one another.[6]

Pattison summed up the situation very well: "when the vassal dared, he joined the enemies of his own overlord"—as did Bertran by joining Henry the Young King against Henry II— "or if two suzerains were involved, the more remote and consequently less exacting"—as with Bertran's desire (in Poem 8) to see King Richard return and help him against his immediate local overlords, who were undoubtedly leaning on him a bit too heavily. The one thought which terrified minor noblemen such as he was that of long periods of peace, with a royal administration becoming more and more stable, entrenched and centralized, sending out its agents to stick their noses into every detail of local life.

But unfortunately this need for feudal anarchy and consequent love of war not only made him try to embroil the English crown with Philippe Auguste of France and Raymond V of Toulouse, but also induced him to fan the fires of warfare between Henry II and his sons, Henry the Young King, Richard the Lionhearted and Geoffrey of Brittany. This is why Dante put him in Hell among those who created divisions and broke up the unity of mankind.[7]

> I saw, and still seem to see,
> a headless trunk walking as were
> other members of that sad troop,
> and in its hand, swinging like a lantern,
> it held its severed head, which
> looked at us and cried, "Woe is me!"
> Of itself and for itself it made a lamp,
> and they were two in one, one in two;
> how this could be, only God knows.

When it was just below the bridge,
it raised its arm, and with it the head,
so that I could better hear its words,
which were: "Now you see my grievous punishment,
you who, breathing, go gazing on the dead;
see if any other is greater than mine.
And so you may bring forth news of me,
know that I am Bertran de Born
who gave evil counsel to the Young King
and put rebellion between father and son:
Ahithophel did no worse for Absalom and David
with his wicked goadings.
Because I parted those so joined,
I carry my brain, alas! parted
from its roots within this trunk.
Thus do I receive my retribution.

1

Razo

Bertran de Born and Count Geoffrey of Brittany called each
other *Rassa,* and this count was a brother of the Young King
and of Richard, Count of Poitiers.[8] Both Richard and Geoffrey
were in love with Maeut de Montanhac,[9] as were also Alfonso
of Aragon and Raymond, Count of Toulouse. But she turned
them all away for Bertran de Born whom she had taken as her
lover and counselor. And he, in order to make them cease
courting her, wanted to tell Count Geoffrey who it was he
loved, and praise her in such a way as to make it appear he
had seen her in the nude and possessed her. He wanted people to know that his lady was Maeut, the one who had turned
away Poitou—that is to say, Richard who was Count of
Poitiers—and Geoffrey who was Count of Brittany, and King
Alfonso who was lord of Saragossa, and Count Raymond who
was lord of Toulouse. . . .[10] And for these reasons, he wrote
the *sirventes* which says:

I   Rassa, she who is without deceit
         so soars and rises in worth
         as to put all others to shame
         and be out of harm's reach;
         the mere sight of her beauty
         makes great men beg for mercy.
         And those of deepest understanding
         are constant in their praise of her

and hold her in high esteem,
for, by wanting only one suitor,
she preserves her honor unstained.

II   Rassa, my lady's delicate and fair,
charming, gay and young;
her hair is blond with a ruby tint,
her body as white as hawthorne,
with soft arms and firm breasts
and a rabbit's suppleness in her back.
Those who wish to know
who it is I love
can easily recognize my lady
by her delicate, fresh complexion,
her merit and her worthiness.

III   Rassa, with great men she's haughty
yet sensible in her girlish way,
for she does not want Poitiers,
Toulouse, Brittany or Saragossa,[11]
but rather so seeks merit
as to choose poor knights.
And since she's made me her suitor,
I pray she holds this love dear
and prefers a worthy vavasor [12]
to a count or deceitful duke
who will only bring her dishonor.

IV   Rassa, great men who give nothing,
nor welcome or converse with people,
and who accuse unjustly and do not
pardon those who beg for mercy,
these annoy me, as well as anyone
who does not recompense good service.
And great men who like hunting
annoy me too, as well as those who use
buzzards and act as if they're goshawks [13]
(and who among themselves
never mention love or war).

V   Rassa, I hope you prefer
great men who do not tire of war
or desist therefrom through threats
until they're done no more harm
—this is far better than hunting,
which has no merit at all—or men
like Maurin, who gained his lord Aigar's
respect by making war on him.
May the viscount defend his honor
and the count demand it of him by force,
and may he be among us for Easter.[14]

VI   Marinier, the honor's yours;
we have left a lord who's fond
of tourneys for one who is a warrior.
And I pray that this song of mine
not frighten Golfier de las Tors.[15]

VII   Papiol, take this song to the court
of my wicked Bel-Senhor.[16]

2

Razo

Bertran de Born was in love with a young gentlewoman of
great merit whose name was Maeut de Montagnac, and she
was the wife of Talairan, brother of the Count of Périgord;
she was also the daughter of the Viscount of Turenne and
sister of my lady Maria de Ventadorn and Aelis de Montfort.[17] And according to what he says in this song, she turned
him away and took leave of him, which made him very sad
and downcast. And he realized he would never win her back
nor find another so beautiful, so good, so charming and so cul-
tured. And since he could find none equal to his lady, he
thought to fashion one by borrowing traits from other lovely
and worthy ladies, taking from each one a particular quality
of beauty, expression, charm, speech, conduct, stature or figure.
And thus he went about asking each of the good ladies to
give him one of the gifts you have heard me mention, in order
that he might refashion the lady he had lost. And in the

sirventes he wrote on this subject you will hear him name all the women he asked for help and assistance in making his "borrowed" lady. And here is the *sirventes* he wrote on this theme:

I　　Lady, since you care little
　　　for me, and without cause
　　　have turned me away,
　　　　　I know not where to seek;
　　　　　　　for never
　　　will I find a joy so rich;
　　　and if there exists no other
　　　woman to my liking, one equal
　　　to you whom I have lost,
　　　I shall never love again.

II　　But since I cannot find another
　　　so lovely and worthy as you,
　　　nor with such a rich, joyous body
　　　　　so beautifully fashioned,
　　　　　　　nor so gay,
　　　nor with such rich, true merit,
　　　I shall wander about
　　　begging traits from others
　　　to make a borrowed lady,
　　　till you come back to me.

III　　Natural, fresh complexion
　　　I'll take from you, Bel Cembeli,[18]
　　　and your sweet loving look;
　　　　　but I presume too much
　　　　　　　in leaving all
　　　the rest, for you lack nothing.
　　　From my lady Aelis I ask
　　　her gay, clever speech,
　　　so that my borrowed lady
　　　will not be dumb or mute.

IV　　From the Viscountess of Chalais
　　　I must have at once
　　　her throat and both her hands.

Then I'll continue
    on my way
to Rochechouart and ask
Agnes to give me her hair,
for in this she could surpass
Isolde, Tristan's lady, whose
fair locks were known to all.

V   From Audiart, though she wish
me ill, I want the manners
with which she clothes her presence
    (for since her love
      is unchanging
and unbroken, her honor's whole).
From my Mielhs-de-Be I ask
her shapely, prized young body,
which, as far as one can see,
would be pleasant to hold naked.

VI   From Faidida I want a gift
of her lovely teeth,
her affability and the sweet replies
    with which she greets
      her guests.
Bel Miralhs must let me have
her gaiety and lovely stature;
she can be so amiable
(she's known for this)
without the least deceit.

VII   Bel Senher, I want you only
to be as jealous of this lady
as I am of you, for
    the fond love risen
      within me
gives me such great desire
that I prefer to beg your mercy
than to embrace another.
Why does my lady turn me away
knowing I love her so?

VIII　　Papiol, go tell my Aziman
in song that love knows
no gratitude and thus has fallen
from its former heights.

3

I　　The Count has urged and commanded,
through N'Aramon Luc d'Esparro,[19]
that I write such a song
as will shatter a thousand shields,
pierce and smash helmets,
hauberks, doublets and actons.[20]

II　　Since he's told me his wish,
I must attend to the matter,
for once his mind's made up,
I cannot say no;
otherwise the Gascons, to whom
I am beholden, will blame me.

III　　At Toulouse, beyond Montagut,
the count will unfurl his banner
at the Prat Comtal, beside the Peiro; [21]
and when he's set up his tent,
we'll take quarters around it and lie
on the bare ground three nights running.

IV　　And with us will have come
potentates and barons,
and all the most honored
and best-known soldiers in the world,
who will have assembled for gain,
through summons or for glory.

V　　And when we've all arrived,
the tourney in the fields will start,
and the Catalans and Aragonese

will fall thick and fast
unhorsed and wounded
by the blows we'll rain on them.

VI   And it can't be helped if bits
of lances fly up in the air,
and if cendal, ciclatoun
and samite are torn to shreds,[22]
along with ropes, tents, hooks,
stakes and pavillions.

VII   Let the king who lost Tarascon,
and the lord of Mont Albeo,
Roger, the young Bernard Oto
and Count Peire help them, along
with the Count of Foix, Bernardo,
and Sancho, brother of the conquered king.[23]

VIII   They make their preparations
while we sit here waiting.

IX   I want great barons always
to be angry with one another.

4

Razo

Bertran de Born, as I have said in other *razos*, had a brother
called Constantin de Born, who was a good knight-at-arms
but cared little for valor or for honor. He always harbored ill
feelings towards Bertran, and once he took from him the castle
of Altafort, which belonged to both of them in common. But
Bertran recovered the castle and expelled his brother. Then
Constantin went to the Viscount of Limoges asking for help
against Bertran, and the Viscount agreed to help him. And
King Richard agreed to help him too . . .[24]

I   I've made a *sirventes* without a line
missing, and it cost me nothing.

I'm the sort of man that if I have
a brother, cousin or relation, I'll share
    my last egg or farthing with him,
but if he then wants my part too,
    out he goes without a thing.

II   My wits are still safe and sound
even though Ademar and Richard [25]
have caused me endless trouble.
They've harassed me for a long time,
    but now they're in such a squabble
that if the King can't stop them,
    their children will have a bellyfull.

III   Guilhem de Gordo, that's a crazy
clapper you've put inside your bell
(and I like you, God knows),
but the two viscounts consider you
    a fool and simpleton ever since
that treaty, and they're just itching
    to have you on their side.[26]

IV   Every day I fight and struggle,
spar, scramble and defend myself
while people wreck and burn my land
and lay waste to my forests
    and mix straw with my wheat.
My enemies, both the brave ones
    and the cowards, all assail me.

V   Every day I resole and restitch the barons,
melt them down and remold them—
I thought I could bring them into shape,
but I was a fool to try
    for they're made of worse metal
than Saint Leonard's chains, and a man's
    mad to give them thought.

VI   Talairan neither trots nor gallops,
nor moves an inch from his castle,

nor throws lances or darts,
but just lives like a Lombard.[27]
   He's such a lazy oaf
that when others get up and go,
   he just yawns and stretches.

VII   At Périgueux, so near the walls
I could hit them with my mace,
I'll come armed on Baiart,[28]
and if I find some fat Poitevin
   he'll see how my sword cuts,
and on his head I'll make a mash
   of chain mail and brains.

VIII   Barons, may God keep, preserve,
   protect and help you,
and make you say to Richard
   what the peacock said to the crow.[29]

5

I   If all the grief and tears and sorrow,
and the pain, affliction and misery
known to man in this sad world were brought
together, they would seem as nothing
beside the death of the young English King
which makes Worth and Youth sorrowful
and turns the world somber, dark and shadowy,
void of all joy, full of woe and sadness.

II   Woeful, grieving and full of sorrow
one can see the courtly soldiers,
the troubadours and gracious jongleurs.
In death they've found a deadly warrior
who has taken away their young English King,
next to whom the most generous seemed mean.
There never was nor will be in the world
an equal to this loss for grief and sadness.

III   Cruel Death, bearer of endless sorrow,
       you can boast of having taken
       the finest knight that ever was,
       for nothing in the way of worth
       was lacking in the young English King.
       And it were better, had God listened to reason,
       that he should live, than many other scoundrels
       who only wound noble men with woe and sadness.

IV   If from this miserable world, full of sorrow,
       love flees, I must count it as deceitful,
       for there's nothing which does not turn to pain,
       and each today is worth less than yesterday.
       Let everyone think on the young English King,
       who was the most valiant of worthy men!
       His fine, amorous body is gone now,
       and nothing's left but grief and sadness.

V   He who took flesh, moved by our sorrow,
       in order to deliver us from evil
       and received death for our salvation,
       to Him we beg mercy, as to a kind
       just lord, that the young English King
       be pardoned (if it please Him, fount of mercy)
       and be placed among honorable companions
       where there is no pain or sadness.

6

Razo

King Henry of England held En Bertran de Born besieged
within Altafort and was attacking him with siege engines. He
bore him great ill will, for he held En Bertran responsible for
the entire war the Young King had waged on him; he had
therefore come to Altafort to dispossess En Bertran. And the
King of Aragon joined King Henry's army before Altafort.[30]
And when Bertran knew of this, he was overjoyed that the
King of Aragon had joined in the siege, for they were close
friends. And the King of Aragon sent his messengers within

the castle asking En Bertran to send him bread, wine and meat, and he sent him a goodly amount. And he told the messenger to beg King Alfonso to have the siege engines moved elsewhere, for in the place where they were attacking, the walls were all broken. Yet King Alfonso, with an eye to King Henry's great wealth, told him everything En Bertran had said. And King Henry put even more siege engines against that part of the wall he now knew to be broken, and he made the walls crumble to the ground and took the castle.

En Bertran, with all his people, was brought to King Henry's pavilion and there was received very badly. And King Henry said to him, "Bertran, Bertran, you once said you never needed more than half your wits, but now you may be sure that you will need them all." "My Lord," said En Bertran, "it is true that I said that, and I spoke the truth." And the king said, "But now it would seem you have lost your wits altogether." "My Lord," said En Bertran, "indeed I have." "And how is that?" asked the king. "My Lord," said En Bertran, "the day your son, the valiant Young King died, I lost my wits, judgment and mind." And when the king saw En Bertran's tears and heard what he said of his son, a great grief entered his heart and eyes, and he could not keep from fainting. And when he had recovered, he called out and said in tears, "En Bertran, En Bertran, it was only right that you should lose your wits for my son, for he loved you more than any other man in the world. And I, for love of him, shall set you free—your person, your belongings and your castle—and I shall grant you my love and my favor, and I shall also give you five hundred marks of silver for the injury you have received." And En Bertran fell at his feet, giving him thanks and gratitude. And then the king went off with his entire army.

And when En Bertran found out that the King of Aragon had done him such felony, he was very angry with King Alfonso. And then he also learned that he had joined King Henry as a hired mercenary, and that the King of Aragon came of a poor lineage from the Carladès. . . .[31] And for these reasons En Bertran de Born wrote the following *sirventes.*

I   Since the gentle season of flowers
        spreads forth joyful and gay,
        a desire has entered my heart
        to compose a new *sirventes,*
        so the Aragonese may know
           that their king
        (and of this they may be sure)
        came here beneath an evil star,
        dishonored—a mere hired mercenary.

II   I know that the fortune of his base
            extraction will finish like a *lai,*
            and return to its humble origins
            in Milhau and the Carladès.[32]
            When each man's reconquered what's his,
                let the king go to Tyre.[33]
            But at sea the wind will surely
            do him in, such a coward as he is,
            so feeble, weak and lazy.

III   He's losing Provence, from whence he came,
            for they prefer his brother Sancho;
            he thinks of nothing but growing fat
            and drinking in the Roussillon,
            from which Jaufré was dispossessed; [34]
                and at Vilamur
            near Toulouse, all those with whom he'd sworn
            allegiance consider him a perjurer,
            for he abandoned them through fear.[35]

IV   The king who holds Castrojeriz
            and the palace of Toledo
            I praise for the strength he's shown
            towards the son of the Barcelonés
            who is his treacherous vassal.[36]
                I'd prefer the court
            and following of the Brigand King [37]
            than that by which I was betrayed
            the day I offered it my services.

V   The good king García Ramírez,
            had he lived longer, would have
            recovered Aragon, usurped by the Monk,
            and the good King of Navarre, to whom
            it rightfully belongs, will surely
                soon regain it.[38]
            Just as gold is of more value
            than lapis lazuli, so is he of greater
            worth and merit than the false king.

VI   For the sake of the good queen [39]
to whom he's married (and since
she's reassured me) I'll desist.
But if she wishes, I'll remind her
of Berenguer de Besalú,[40] although
    royal wrongs are always
glossed over (yet how terrible
it was thus to betray and kill a man
and leave his lineage so dishonored).

VII   Like the false, treacherous king he is,
he betrayed the Empress in an ugly way
when he hauled off by the cartful
the money Manuel had sent
and robbed her of her belongings;
    then, with felon heart,
when he'd taken everything green and ripe,
he sent her back across the sea
along with the Greeks he had betrayed.[41]

7

Razo

No matter what En Bertran de Born said to King Philip in *coblas* or in *sirventes,* nor how much he reminded him of the wrongs or dishonor done him, he never wanted to wage war on King Richard.[42] But Richard set out to wage war anyhow when he saw King Philip's weakness; he robbed, plundered and burned castles, villages and towns, and killed and captured men. Thus all the barons who disliked peace were overjoyed, and En Bertran de Born more so than any other, because he wanted war more than any of them, and because he believed that King Richard (whom he called "Yes-and-No") had started the war on account of what he, Bertran, had said, as you will hear in the *sirventes* he wrote upon finding out that King Richard had gone to war.

I   I can no longer refrain from writing a song
now that Yes-and-No has brought fire and drawn blood,
for war makes the avaricious generous.
I like to see kings display pomp

and use stakes, ropes and pommels [43]
setting up tents to sleep outdoors,
and call us together in hundreds and thousands,
so that later men can sing of our heroic deeds.

II   A man without skill or taste for war
is shameful and worthless; thus I doubt
that Yes-and-No will abandon Cahors
and Cajarc—he's far too clever.
And if the King gives him the treasure
at Chinon, then he can wage war; [44]
he's so fond of trouble and expense
that he puts both friend and foe in turmoil.

III   I would have received blows on my shield
and seen my white banner dyed red,
but I'll desist, for I know too well that
Yes-and-No has loaded the dice against me.
Since I hold neither Lusignan or Rancon, [45]
I cannot fight far away without money;
only for those who show gratitude do I place
a shield around my neck and a helmet on my head.

IV   Had King Philip burned a ship
before Gisors, or staved in a dike, [46]
thus entering the forest of Rouen by force,
or besieged him through hill and dale
so only pigeons could carry his letters out,
then I'd know he wanted to be like Charlemagne,
the greatest of his forefathers, through whom
Apulia and Saxony were conquered.

V   Never did a ship at sea, with its longboat gone,
in the midst of a storm, about to strike reefs,
flying like an arrow before the wind,
rising and falling with the crashing waves,
suffer more than I because of her; [47]
and I'll tell you why—she'll neither
come to terms nor keep me by her side,
and thus my joy turns to bitterness.

VI   Go, Papiol, run quickly to Treignac [48]
      so you arrive before the feast day.

VII   Tell Rotgier and his relations that I've
      run out of rhymes in *-omba, -om* and *-esta*.[49]

8

I   Now comes the joyful season
          when our ships arrive, and when
          the gallant, brave King Richard too
          will come, more king than ever.
      We'll see gold and silver handed out,
      catapults released and fired, walls crumble,
      towers totter and crash down,
      the enemy captured and put in chains.

II   I don't like it when our barons
          make mysterious pacts together;
          but now they'll be ashamed,
          like wolves trapped and caught,
      when our King comes and surveys his reign.
      There'll be no excuse for what they've done,
      and each will say, "I've taken part in no
      conspiracies, but rather pledge myself to you."

III   I love to see the press of shields
          with their hues of red and blue,
          of ensigns and of banners
          many-colored in the wind,
      and the sight of tents and rich pavilions pitched,
      lances shattered, shields pierced, shining
      helmets split, and blows exchanged in battle
                          .   . [50]

IV   I hate the company of highwaymen
          as I hate that of greedy whores;
          I'm disgusted by the piles of money
          they earn through fraud.

These grasping mercenary captains should be hung [51]
along with the rich who sell their generosity,
just as one shouldn't lend an ear to women
who willingly lie down for cash.

V   I love the lion's custom
     of sparing his fallen prey,[52]
     yet meeting arrogance with arrogance.
     Among these barons there's no equal
     to the king; but when they see him cornered,
     each one tries his best to do him in.
     Don't think I've written this for pay, but—
     it's always wise to fight for a lord so rich.

9

I   I'll write a half-*sirventes* about both kings,
     for soon we'll see which has more knights:
     Alfonso, the valiant king of Castile,
     who I've heard is looking for mercenaries,
     or Richard who'll throw around gold and silver
     by the bushel, taking pleasure in spending
     and giving, wanting no security in return
     and seeking war as a hawk seeks quail.

II   If both kings are bold and fearless,
     we'll soon see fields strewn with bits
     of helmets, shields, swords and saddlebows,
     and bodies split open from head to foot,
     and horses wandering about aimlessly,
     and lances protruding from ribs and chests,
     and joy and tears, and grief and happiness.
     The loss will be great, but the gain yet greater.

III   We'll soon see trumpets, drums, banners,
     pennants and standards, horses both white
     and black; and the times will be good,

for usurers will be parted from their money,
and beasts of burden will not travel safely
in broad daylight, nor townsmen without fear,
nor merchants on their way from France;
only those who rob will be rich.

IV   But if the King comes, I have faith in God
      that I'll either be alive or quartered,

V   and if I'm alive, great will be my joy,
      and if I'm dead, great will be my liberation.

10

I   I love the gay season of spring
      which brings forth leaves and flowers,
      and I love, too, hearing the merriment
      of birds as they make their song
          resound through the woods;
      and I love seeing green fields
      covered with tents and pavilions;
          and great is my joy
      when the countryside is lined
      with knights and horses in armor.

II   And I love seeing scouts spread panic,
      making people flee with their belongings,
      and I love seeing them followed
      by great hosts of armed men;
          and deep in my heart
      I love seeing strong castles besieged,
      with the ramparts broken and crumbled,
          and troops at the banks
      of the moat, and a thick, strong
      palisade surrounding the battlements.

III   And I love, too, when a baron
      is the first to attack,

on horseback, armed, without fear,
thus by his valor and bravery
    giving courage to his men.
And when the battle's under way,
each of them should be ready
    to follow unflinchingly,
for no man's worth his salt till he's
given and received blow on blow.

IV   Maces, swords, many-colored helmets
and shields we'll see broken and shattered
when the struggle is at its height,
along with vassals striking left and right,
    and the horses of the dead
and wounded wandering aimlessly about.
And when he's in the thick of battle,
    each nobleman thinks only
of breaking heads and arms, for better
to be dead than alive and vanquished.

V   I tell you that I find less pleasure
in eating, drinking or sleeping
than in hearing the cry of "Charge!"
from both sides, and hearing riderless
    horses whinnying in the shade,
and hearing shouts of "Help! Help!"
and seeing the great and small
    fall beside the moat,
and seeing the dead with bits of lances
and banners protruding from their sides.

VI   Barons, better to pawn
your castles, towns and cities
rather than give up making war!

VII   Papiol, go at once
to Yes-and-No and tell him
he's been at peace too long.[53]

Arnaut Daniel

Arnaut Daniel came from the same region as Arnaut de Maruelh, from a castle called Ribairac [1] *in the bishopric of Périgord, and he was of gentle birth. He learned his letters well* [2] *and took great delight in writing poetry. And then he abandoned his letters and became a jongleur, and began writing a kind of poetry with difficult rhymes, which is why his songs are not easy to understand or to learn. And he loved a lady of noble lineage from Gascony, the wife of En Guilhem de Buovilla,* [3] *but it would seem that the lady never gave him pleasure in love, which is why he said:*

> I am Arnaut who gathers the wind
> and hunts the hare with the ox
> and swims against the incoming tide. [4]

From his poetry we can gather that his career extended from about 1180 to 1210, that he may well have been a friend of Bertran de Born (Ribérac is less than forty miles from Hautefort), and that his travels took him as far afield as Paris, where he apparently attended the coronation of Philippe Auguste in 1180. [5]

In his own land, his fame never equaled that of Giraut de Bornelh, but later Italian poets considered Arnaut Daniel the greater poet. There is the well-known scene in the *Divine Comedy* [6] in which Dante meets his predecessor, Guido Guinicelli, and says to him:

> "The ink of those sweet lines
> of yours will remain dear
> as long as the modern style endures."

But Guinicelli points to another shade and says:

* Notes accompanying this section begin on p. 283.

"He was the better craftsman of the mother tongue.[7]
In verses of love and tales of romance
he surpassed them all; let fools talk
who thinks he of Limousin was better." [8]

Dante draws nearer to the shade, who speaks in Provençal, the only such passage in the *Divine Comedy:*

"Ieu sui Arnaut, que plor e vau cantan."
(I am Arnaut, who weep and sing as I go.)

To characterize Arnaut Daniel there is no better word than Dante's: the craftsman. Few poets have ever taken craft to such heights of virtuosity, few have ever manipulated the words, sounds and rhythms of poetry with such mastery. As an example, let the reader try to read aloud the opening lines of one of his poems:

L'aur' amara
fa·ls bruoills brancutz
clarzir
qe·l dous'espeis'ab fuoills,
e·ls letz
becs
dels auzels ramencs
ten balps e mutz,
pars
e non pars.[9]

Here, within an extremely complicated rhyme and metrical scheme (each line rhyming with corresponding lines in successive stanzas in addition to the repeated *-utz* and *-ars* within the stanza, and lines that are actually short segments of longer and more standard eight-syllable lines), he has manipulated sound and association so as to engrave indelibly his words and the scene he is describing on the reader's mind. Notice, for instance, all the alliterations of soft sounds in the first four lines to make one hear the wind in the trees, and then the sudden change to harsh sounds in line 5 to describe the chattering birds. The result is an extraordinary intensity of language, with each word serving a multitude of purposes.[10]

But there is another side to Arnaut Daniel, one which is

perhaps a natural outcome of such self-conscious craft—that of humor. He wrote one poem that is undoubtedly the most hilarious and violently scabrous satire ever written on the subject of courtly love—and this at a period when it was, in theory at least, at its moment of greatest flowering.[11] The famous Sestina (Poem 2 below), amid its incredible display of technical virtuosity, is not without its flashes of humor. And then, like Mozart in Don Giovanni, he parodies his own most famous lines in another poem (see Note 26 to Poem 3).

The result of this is not to make Arnaut Daniel a "humorist"; there are, in fact, few humorous passages in his works. But they act as a kind of seasoning which brings us up short and, what is surprising in twelfth-century art, gives us glimpses of the poet standing outside his work observing it, or observing himself creating it. The effect is to set in motion our awareness of a complex and curiously shifting relationship among poet, poem and reader.

So truly we have words serving a multitude of purposes. But of course there is, in this kind of mysticism of technique and in the attempt to make poetry so many-faceted, something immensely Quixotic. Yet here again Arnaut Daniel sees himself quite clearly and, as might be expected, invites us to see him seeing himself:

> Ieu sui Arnautz q'amas l'aura,
> E chatz la lebre ab lo bou
> E nadi contra suberna.[12]

1

I
      I hear sweet calls
     and cries, lays, songs
  and trills of birds, each of them
in his own language entreating his mate,
just as do we with those we love, and since
I've set my sights upon the noblest of them all,
I must write a song finer than any other,
without a false word, with no rhyme unanswered.

II   I did not err
        or take a wrong turning when I
first entered within the castle's boundaries,
there where dwells my lady, for whom I hunger
more than ever did the nephew of Saint Guilhem.[13]
A thousand times a day I yawn and stretch
for that lovely lady who surpasses all others
just as true joy surpasses ire and anger.

III   I was well received
        and my words accepted
(for I was not stupid in my choice,
in preferring pure gold to copper)
the day I and my lady made love
and she shielded me with her blue coat,
so that talebearers with their adder tongues
would not see us and spread their evil stories.

IV   May it please
        the gracious Lord by whom
the blind Longinus' sins were absolved,[14]
that I may lie together with my lady
in that room where we made our rich covenant,
from which I await the great joy of having her,
amid kisses and laughter, disclose her fair body
that I may gaze at it beneath the lamplight.[15]

V   What are you saying,
        mouth? You could easily set
to flight those promises which would honor
the Emperor of Byzantium, the lord of Rouen,
or the king who holds both Tyre and Jerusalem.[16]
I am mad to want so much that I might then
repent, for Love could not protect me;
only the witless would make joy flee.

VI   I do not fear
        vile, sharp-tongued creatures,
even though they've caused the lord of Galicia

to err, for which we rightfully blame him;
for he took prisoner his relative, Raymond
the Count's son, while he was on a pilgrimage,
and King Fernando will not easily regain
his reputation unless he sets him free at once.[17]

VII   I would have seen him, had I not gone
to the good King of Étampes' coronation.[18]

2

I   The firm desire which enters
my heart cannot be taken from me by the beak or nail
of that talebearer whose evil words cost him his soul,
and since I dare not beat him with a branch or rod,
I shall at least, in secret, free from any spying uncle,
rejoice in love's joy, in an orchard or in a chamber.

II   But when I think of that chamber
which, to my misfortune, no man enters
and is guarded as if by brother or by uncle,
my entire body, even to my fingernail,
trembles like a child before a rod,
such fear I have of not being hers with all my soul.

III   Would that I were hers, if not in soul
at least in body, hidden within her chamber;
for it wounds my heart more than blows of rod
that I, her serf, can never therein enter.
No, I shall be with her as flesh and nail [19]
and heed no warnings of friend or uncle.

IV   Even the sister of my uncle [20]
I never loved like this with all my soul!
As near as is the finger to the nail,
if it please her, would I be to her chamber.
It can bend me to its will, that love which enters
my heart, better than a strong man with a sharp rod.

V   Since flowered the dry rod,[21]
     or from Adam came forth nephew and uncle,
     there never was a love so true as that which enters
     my heart, neither in body nor in soul.
     And wherever she may be, outside or in her chamber,
     I shall be no further than the length of my nail.

VI   As if with tooth and nail
      my heart grips her, or as the bark the rod;
      for to me she is tower, palace and chamber
      of joy, and neither brother, parent or uncle
      I love so much; and in paradise my soul
      will find redoubled joy, if lovers therein enter.

VII   Arnaut sends his song of nail and uncle
      (by leave of her who has, of his rod, the soul)
      to his Desirat, whose fame all chambers enters.[22]

3

I   To this gay, charming air
     I will put words so honed and pared
     that when they've passed beneath
     my file, they'll be true and sure;
     for love at once smooths and gilds
     my song, which proceeds from her
     whom Merit guides and sustains.

II   I continually improve and purify
     myself, for I serve the gentlest lady
     in the world (and say so openly).
     I am hers from head to toe,
     and even amid cold winds,
     the love raining within my heart
     keeps me warm in harshest winter.

III I hear and offer a thousand masses,
     light candles and lamps of oil

praying that God give me success
with her, for no defense avails me;
and when I look at her blond hair
and gay, graceful body, I love her more
than he who would give me Luserna.[23]

IV   I so want and love her, that I fear
my excess desire will take her from me,
if one can lose a thing through love.
For her heart submerges mine beneath
a flood that makes it drown; [24] and she
has done her usurer's work so well
as to possess both shop and artisan.

V   I do not want the Empire of Rome,
nor to be elected Pope, if I
cannot return to her for whom
my heart burns and cracks;
and if she does not cure my ills
with a kiss before the new year,
she'll kill me and condemn herself.

VI   Yet in spite of the ills I suffer,
I shall not desist from loving,
even though I remain in solitude,
for I can still set words to rhyme.
Love makes my lot worse than that
of a peasant—yet the lord of Montcli
did not love Audierna one whit more.[25]

VII   I am Arnaut who gathers the wind
and hunts the hare with the ox
and swims against the incoming tide.[26]

Peire Vidal

Peire Vidal was the son of a furrier from Toulouse. And he sang better than any man in the world. And he was one of the craziest men who ever lived, for he believed to be true whatever he liked or wanted. And he wrote poetry with greater facility than any man in the world, and it was he who composed the most beautiful melodies and recounted the craziest things in matters of arms and of love and in speaking ill of others. And it is true that a knight of Saint Gilles cut his tongue for letting it be known that he was his wife's lover. And N'Uc de Baux had him cared for and cured.[1]

And when he was cured, he went overseas.[2] *He returned with a Greek woman whom he had married in Cyprus. He had been given to understand that she was the niece of the Emperor of Constantinople and that through her he was rightful heir to the Empire. He therefore put all his earnings into building ships, intending to go off and conquer the Empire. And he bore imperial arms, and had himself called Emperor and his wife Empress.*

And he took a fancy to every woman he saw and begged each one for her love; and they all gave him permission to do and say whatever he wanted. He therefore thought they were all in love with him and pining away for him. And he always rode fine horses and bore splendid arms and was always followed by an imperial retinue.[3] *And he thought there was no knight in the world finer or more loved by women.*

Other stories were told by the medieval biographer of Peire Vidal. First of all there was the one of how

he courted my lady N'Alazais, who was the wife of En Barral, Lord of Marseille.[4]

* Notes accompanying this section begin on p. 288.

He was fonder of Peire Vidal than of anyone else in the world, both for his splendid poetry and for the splendid mad things he said and did; and they called each other "Rainier." And Peire Vidal was more intimate with En Barral, both in public and in private, than any other man in the world.

And En Barral knew perfectly well that Peire Vidal was courting his wife, but he took it in good humor, as did everyone else who knew about it. . . . But then one morning when Peire Vidal found out that En Barral had arisen and that the lady was alone in her room, he entered, went over to my lady Alazais' bed and found her asleep. And he knelt down before her and kissed her on the mouth. When she felt the kiss, she thought it was En Barral, her husband, and she woke up laughing. But when she opened her eyes and saw it was the madman Peire Vidal, she began to cry out and make a great commotion. Upon hearing this, her ladies-in-waiting entered and asked, "What is it?" And Peire Vidal ran away. And the lady called for En Barral and made great complaint of Peire Vidal for having kissed her. With tears in her eyes, she begged him to seek revenge at once. But En Barral, being a man of valor and justice, took it all in good humor and began to laugh and scold his wife for making such an outcry over what a madman had done. . . .

Meanwhile Peire Vidal, afraid for the folly he had committed, embarked on a ship and went to Genoa. And he stayed there till he could go overseas with King Richard.[5] . . . And he remained overseas a long time, not daring to return to Provence. And En Barral, who, as you have heard, was very fond of him, pleaded with his wife till she finally forgave the stealing of the kiss and instead granted it as a gift. And En Barral sent for Peire Vidal, letting him know that he was forgiven and restored to his wife's good graces. And with great joy he returned to Marseille, and with great joy he was received by En Barral and my lady N'Alazais . . .

Another story tells how

Peire Vidal, because of the death of the good Count Raimond of Toulouse,[6] felt great grief and sadness. And he dressed all in black, cut the tails and ears off

*all his horses, and had his head and that of all his servants
shaven, at the same time prohibiting them from cutting their
beards or nails. For a long time he went about like a man mad
with grief.*

Then, after an interlude in which the biographer tells how
King Alfonso of Aragon and all his barons tried and finally
succeeded in cheering him up, the story starts off on yet another tack.

*And he loved Loba [literally "She-Wolf"] of Pueinautier
. . . who was from the Carcassès, and for her sake Peire Vidal
took the name of Lop ["Wolf"] and bore wolf arms. And he
had shepherds hunt him through the mountains of Cabaret
with mastiffs and greyhounds as if he were a wolf.[7] And he
dressed in a wolf's skin so the shepherds and dogs would make
no mistake about his being one. And the shepherds with their
dogs hunted him down and caught him in such a way that
he was brought half dead to the house of Loba de Pueinautier.
When she saw that it was Peire Vidal, she began to feel
great joy for the madness he had committed and to laugh a
great deal, and her husband did the same. And the husband
had him taken in and put in a quiet place. And he called for
the doctor and had him treated until he was all well again.[8] . . .*

Though somewhat more banal than these stories, the facts
of Peire Vidal's career are as follows. His datable poems fall
roughly between 1180 and 1205. His principal patron was
Barral, Viscount of Marseille,[9] but he had many others and
few troubadours wandered as far afield as he. He traveled
not only to Spain and Italy, but also to Hungary, Malta and
Cyprus, and perhaps also to the Holy Land and to Constantinople (with the Fourth Crusade).

Even though the stories of thinking himself Emperor, of the
stolen kiss, of cutting off his horses' tails and ears, and of having himself hunted like a wolf are probably legends, one won-
ders how they could have sprung up about him in such relative profusion. It isn't difficult to imagine the planting of a
single seed (as in the case of Jaufre Rudel or Guilhem de
Cabestanh) and having it soon grow into a full-blown myth.
But so many? Then too there is his wanderlust, his traveling

from one end of Christendom to the other. Even in his poetry there is a kind of restlessness, a certain dislike of staying too long on one topic (see Poem 3 below, which is not at all untypical).

Modern critics tend to discount—a bit angrily at times—his madness as a pure invention of his medieval biographers. Perhaps it was, or perhaps it was a mask, a literary disguise to amuse his patrons, or perhaps the mask, Hamletlike, turned out to fit only too well. In any case, his poetry is a wild and often humorous mixture of many things. There is his absurd boasting (or *gap,* as it was called in Provençal) along with great meekness, beautiful passages of love poetry mixed with forthright requests for money (or a good horse, as in Poem 1), and personal or political diatribes intermingled with stanzas full of religious and crusading fire.

Although perhaps not one of the very greatest troubadours, Peire Vidal has been one of the most popular, both in the Middle Ages and in modern times. This is partly because his verse has a lovely charm and ease (notice the biographer's remark on this score) mixed with a marvelous quality of incisiveness and vigor, and partly also because of his versatility —few troubadours touched on such a wide gamut of emotions and styles. But then there's something else too. The boasting we mentioned above never concerns him as a poet or craftsman; it is always as a great knight or lover, or even as "Emperor," that he presents himself, and this gives to his poetry a certain air of tragicomic buffoonery, of something Quixotic in a much more personal sense than that of Arnaut Daniel. It is this aspect, I think, that has made him such an attractive figure and has brought down on him the reputation of the great madman of Provençal letters.

1

I   Sir Dragoman, if I had a worthy steed [10]
      my enemies would be in bad straits,
      for the mere mention of my name makes men

tremble like quail before a sparrow hawk
and feel their life not worth a penny,
such is my renown for bravery and ferocity.

II   When I've put on my doubly strong coat of mail
and the sword En Gui [11] gave me a while ago,
the earth trembles beneath my feet
and my enemies, however proud, instantly
clear roads to let me pass, such is the fear
caused by the mere sound of my footfall.

III   I'm the equal of Roland and Olivier for courage,
and of Berart de Mondesdier for gallantry; [12]
my prowess has brought me such fame that I
am besieged by messengers bearing gold rings,
black and white ribbons, and declarations
of love that fill my heart with joy.

IV   I not only appear to be a knight,
but I am one; I know the trade of love
and all things concerned with gallantry,
for no one can be more charming in bed
nor more terrible or powerful in battle.
Even from afar I'm loved and feared.

V   Now if I had a good war horse, the King
could be more tranquil there by Balaguer,
and sleep more calmly and untroubled;
for I'll keep peace in Provence and Montpellier
so that thieves and highwaymen won't
lay waste to the Autavès and Crau.[13]

VI   And if the King returns to the Strand at Toulouse,
and the Count comes out with his miserable lancers
who continually cry "Aspa!" and "Orsau!," [14]
I'll strike the first blow and wreak such havoc
that they'll run back inside with me
behind them, unless they close the gates.

VII   And if I get my hands on some talebearer
whose evil words spoil the happiness of others
and kill their joy, he'll know what sort
of blows I mete out, and even were he made
of steel or iron, this would protect him
scarcely more than would a peacock feather.

VIII   Na Vierna, thanks to Montpellier [15] you will now
love a knight in battle; thus will my joy
be increased through you, praise be to God.

2

I   With each breath I draw in the air
I feel coming from Provence;
I so love everything from there
that when people speak well of it,
I listen smiling, and with each
word ask for a hundred more,
so much does the hearing please me.

II   For there is no gentler dwelling than that
which lies between the Rhône and Vence,
enclosed by the sea and the Durance,[16]
nor any place where shines such joy.
For among those noble people—with
a lady who turns sorrow to laughter—
I have left my joyous heart.

III   For no one can despair when thinking
upon her, for in her joy is born.
And whoever praises
or speaks well of her
can never lie, for she
is the finest and gentlest lady
the world has ever seen.

IV If I speak or act worthily, it is
  thanks to her, for she has given me
  the science and the knowledge
  to be joyful and to sing.
  Whatever I may now do well
  comes from her lovely body,
  even to my most heartfelt thoughts.

3

I I am not dead through love or other ills,
  and yet my life is surely like a death
  when I see that the creature I most love
  and want brings me only pain and suffering.
  Death is evil, but yet worse is the thought
  that she and I will soon be old,
  and thus will be lost my youth and hers,
  mine regretfully but hers a hundredfold more.

II My good lady, you could easily kill
  your liege man, if this would give you
  pleasure, but you would be held to blame
  for having committed a mortal sin.
  I and everything I have is yours, yet
  beneath unjust lords men abandon fiefs,
  and noblemen without their men are powerless,
  As Darius, King of Persia, finally realized.[17]

III I cannot help but love with all my heart
  this lady who does not deign to see or hear me.
  What shall I do since I cannot leave,
  and since clemency and pity are of no avail?
  I shall beg eternally like some tiresome
  pilgrim, since from the cold snow is born
  a crystal which can start a blazing fire.[18]
  Those who wait patiently always win.

IV   I've never seen anyone act so strangely
as she when I've done or said something
which I think might give her pleasure.
Night and day my mind's on no one else,
yet everything I do seems to her vile and base,
and neither through pity nor through love
of God can I find clemency with her;
she wrongs me and sins against me.

V   Thus have I now become indifferent,
like the coward who, when his mortal
enemies hunt him down, forgets to flee
and dares not turn or save himself.
My only comfort lies in knowing that, like
the Jew, by harming me she harms herself;
but meanwhile, in my blind self-defense
I've lost all strength and courage.

VI   So I turn my song towards the celestial King
whom we should all honor and obey; it is only
just that we should serve Him in such a place
where we will conquer everlasting life.
For the Saracens, those treacherous Canaanites,
have captured and destroyed His kingdom,
seized His cross and sepulcher, and this
should fill our hearts with horror.[19]

VII   Count of Poitou,[20] both I to you
and God to me cry out against you
(for you have foully betrayed both):
He for His cross, and I for my money.

VIII   Count of Poitou, my lord, you and I
have received the whole world's praises:
you for doing and I for speaking well.

Folquet de Marseille

Folquet de Marseille was the son of a rich merchant from Genoa called Ser Anfos. And when his father died, Folquet inherited a large fortune. And he was a man who understood valor and merit; and he put himself in the service of worthy barons and worthy men. . . .

And he was rewarded and honored by King Richard and by Count Raymond of Toulouse and by his own lord, En Barral of Marseille.[1]

He wrote good poetry, was handsome in appearance and charming in manner. And he courted the wife of his lord, En Barral. And he pleaded for her love and wrote his songs for her. But neither through his entreaties nor through his songs was he ever able to find any mercy with her, for she would grant him none of love's favors. This is why he always complains of love in his songs.

And it came to pass that this lady died, as well as her husband En Barral, the lord who had so honored him. And good King Richard also died, and the good Count Raymond of Toulouse and King Alfonso of Aragon.[2] And then he, out of grief for his lady and the princes I have named, abandoned the world and, along with his wife and two sons, entered the Cistercian order. And he was made abbot of a rich abbey in Provence called Le Thoronet.[3] And then he was made Bishop of Toulouse, where he later died.

Even though we know more about Folquet de Marseille than about any other major troubadour, he nonetheless remains one of the most enigmatic figures in Provençal literature. During his brief poetic career (his datable poems fall between 1179 and 1195) he not only was involved with most

* Notes accompanying this section begin on p. 292.

of the principal barons of southern France and with many
other troubadours (Bertran de Born and Peire Vidal, to name
just two), but also attained a pinnacle of fame reached by few
other Provençal poets. Then suddenly, in 1195, he abandoned
this way of life and, as the biographer says, entered the Cistercian monastery of Le Thoronet along with his wife and children. In 1201 he was elected abbot, and in 1205 he was made
Bishop of Toulouse.

There he rapidly rose to another more sinister kind of fame.
He was now in a position of great power in the very center
of the turmoil over the Albigensian heresy. When Simon de
Montfort's "crusaders" began wreaking their work of destruction on southern French culture, Folquet did not hesitate to
side with them against his own people and against the son
of his former patron, Raymond of Toulouse. Moreover, he carried out his work with such vehemence that the Count of Foix
accused him of having been responsible for the death of five
hundred people, and a contemporary chronicle (in verse)
says of him:

> and when he was elected Bishop of Toulouse
> he spread such fire throughout the land that no amount
> of water will ever suffice to extinguish it;
> he snuffed out, in body and in soul, the lives
> of more than fifteen hundred people, great and small.
> Upon my faith, by his deeds, words and conduct
> he is more an Antichrist
>   than a messenger of Rome.

To what degree such assertions are reliable, we cannot tell;
in any case, few people concerned with the Albigensian crusade evoked such violent passions as Folquet de Marseille. The
southern French hated him with all the bitterness reserved for
one who betrays his own, whereas the rest of the world (including Dante later) considered him almost a saint, partly for
his work against the heretics, and partly for his friendship with
Saint Dominic and for his being instrumental in the founding
of the Dominican Order.

After more than twenty-five fanatic, turbulent years as
Bishop of Toulouse, he died on Christmas day of 1231, and in
a final twist of irony, he was buried in the Abbey of Grand-

selve alongside one of his former patrons, William VIII of Montpellier.[4]

This was the man of whom the story was told that once in Paris, when he heard a minstrel sing one of the songs he had written earlier in his career, he imposed penance on himself. Although we will probably never know why he changed his way of life so abruptly and considered his former troubadour existence so sinful, we cannot help but take it as a tragic symbol of the crumbling of southern French civilization. Here was one of its greatest exponents turning his back on it and doing his best to destroy it from within.

In any case, before his "conversion," he wrote remarkable poetry. I can think of no better way of characterizing it than to say it is *richer* than any other troubadour verse I know. He not only has a marvelous control over words, rhythms and sounds, with beautiful use of alliteration and word repetition that remind one of Bernart de Ventadorn, but he can also, like Peire d'Alvernhe, use syntactically intricate sentences in such a way as to make them seem smooth and effortless. And all this takes place within the framework of a poetry that hasn't the slightest waste motion—every word and sound is made to count, to form part of a complex and beautiful pattern. Listen, for instance, to the opening stanza of Poem 3:

> En chantan m'aven a membrar
> So qu'ieu cug chantan oblidar,
> Mas per so chant qu'oblides la dolor
> E·l mal d'amor;
> Et on plus chan, plus m'en sove,
> Que la boca en al re non ave
> Mas en: merce!
> Per qu'es vertatz e sembla be
> Qu'ins el cor port, dona, vostra faisso
> Que·m chastia qu'ieu no vir ma razo.[5]

But the one thing that distinguishes Folquet de Marseille from most of the other troubadours, is the fact that he often interweaves his verse with a splendid fabric of conceits (a good example are Stanzas II and III of this same Poem 3, where he rings a wonderful series of variations on the idea of his lady's image being locked within his heart). In this he has much in common with the English metaphysical poets, with whom he also shares the fate of having been considered ridiculously artificial by nineteenth-century critics. But there the similarity ends, for John Donne and the others have long since been rehabilitated, whereas Folquet de Marseille continues being ignored or belittled.[6] But there is no longer any reason why we shouldn't see him for what he is—one of the half a dozen or so greatest of the troubadours. His contemporaries certainly felt he was, and Dante referred to him as:

> *questa luculenta e cara gioia del nostro cielo*
> (that shining and precious jewel of our heaven).[7]

1

I   Love, have mercy! Let me not die so often,
for you could easily kill me outright,
but instead you hold me on the brink of life
and death, thus increasing my martyrdom;
but though half-dead, I'm still your servant,
and this service I prefer a thousand times
to any other facile recompense.

II   For you know, Love, that it would be a sin
to kill me, since I've not rebelled against you;
but too much service often does great harm
and—or so I've heard—makes friendship flee.
I've served you and still don't turn away,
but since you know I await some recompense,
I have now lost you and the service too.

III   But you, my lady, who have the power,
persuade Love and yourself, whom I so desire,
not for me, but merely out of pity
and because my sighs thus plead with you.
For when my eyes laugh, my heart cries,
and through fear of seeming troublesome
I fool myself and bear the grievous loss.

IV   I did not think your proud person
could bring me a desire so unending,
but through fear of redoubling my woes
I do not dare discover them to you.
Ah! if your eyes could see my martyrdom,
you might then be merciful, unless your
sweet look of pity were nothing but a lie.

V   If only I could show you the grief I feel
and yet hide it from others; but never could I
pour out my heart to you in secret, and so,
if I can't be discreet, who will do so for me,
and who will be faithful if I betray myself?
A man's secrets cannot be kept by others
who receive no benefit therefrom.

VI   Lady, I cannot tell you of my loyal heart
out of fear of seeming foolish, but I hope
your wisdom will perceive the words unspoken.

VII   But Sir Aziman says that I betray him,
and Sir Tostemps accuses me of being too sly,
because to them I will not open up my heart.[8]

2

I   I am so pleased by the amorous thought
which has lodged within my loyal heart,
that no room is left for others,
nor does any seem so sweet and pleasant.
I live sheltered from mortal pain,
and true love lightens my martyrdom
through promises of joy; but those sweet
appearances keep me waiting far too long.

II   I know that I am completely helpless.
What can I do if Love wants to kill me?

He has knowingly brought me such a desire
that can neither conquer nor be conquered.
But no, it can be conquered—gently killed
by sighs, for I receive no help from her
whom I so want, nor from elsewhere
(since I have no wish for another's love).

III   Good lady, if it please you, suffer that I
love you, since it is I who suffer therefrom,
and thus would I be unharmed by pain,
but rather we would share it equally;
yet if you wish me to turn elsewhere,
take away that beauty, sweet laugh
and charming look which drive me mad,
and only then shall I depart.

IV   Since each day you're more lovely and charming,
I curse the eyes with which I gaze on you,
for their subtle contemplation can never be
to my advantage but only cause me pain.
Yet in the end I know I'll be more helped
than wounded, my lady, for I should think
that you'd get little joy from killing me,
since the pain would be yours as well.

V   Thus, my lady, I do not love you wisely,
for I am true to you and yet betray myself;
I fear to lose you yet am not master of myself;
I try to harm you and yet only harm myself.
Thus, although I dare not tell you of my grief,
my heart's thoughts are written on my face:
I start to speak and then repent,
while shame and ardor rise to my eyes.

VI   My lady, I dare not say how much I love you,
and I don't repent my former loves,
for witnessing others' conduct has only
made my love increase a hundredfold.

VII   Go, my song, to Nîmes (whomever this might
        displease), for I'm sure you will be welcomed
        by the three ladies to whom I shall present you.[9]

3

I   In singing I sometimes remember
            what, through song, I tried to forget,
        yet I go on singing to forget my grief
                and unhappy love;
            but the more I sing, the more I recall
        that my mouth can utter no other word
                but "Mercy!"
            For it seems both true and just,
        my lady, that within my heart I bear your image
        which reproves me for my mind's vagaries.

II   And since Love so wishes to honor me
            as to let me bear you in my heart,
        I beg of you to keep it from the flames,
                since I fear for you
            much more than for myself;
        and since, lady, my heart has you within,
                if it is harmed,
            you, inside, will be harmed as well;
        do with my body what you will, but keep
        my heart as if it were your dwelling place.

III   For it will keep you and hold you so dear
            as to make the body seem a foolish thing
        by employing every bit of reason, wit and valor,
                thus leaving my body
            in error by the reason it has taken away;
        for often when men speak to me, I know not
                what they say,
            nor do I hear them when they greet me;
        I therefore should not be reproached
        if their salutations go unanswered.

IV   But the body should not blame the heart
         for whatever harm it might have done,
for it has been taken from a place of deceit
        and faithlessness
       and made to serve a more honorable lord;
thus justice always returns to its own master.
        Yet I don't think
       that she, unless mercy help me,
will allow herself to enter my heart, and,
in place of rich gifts, deign to hear my song.

V   But if you deign to hear it out,
        my lady, you cannot help but feel pity.
But I must forget her rich beauty
        and the eternal
       praises I have sung thereof,
since my praises bring me more pain
        than benefit
       and make my burning ardor grow;
for a fire, if fanned, springs to life,
but if left untouched soon dies.

VI   I can die now,
        Aziman,[10] and I'll complain of nothing,
not even if my woes multiply as if doubling
from square to square across a chessboard.

VII   Go quickly, my song,
        towards Montpellier, and beg
Don Guilhem [11] for me, if it not displease him,
that his increasing worth grant me pardon.

The Monk of Montaudon

The Monk of Montaudon was from the Auvergne, from a castle called Vic which is near Orlac.[1] He was of gentle birth and was made a monk in the abbey of Orlac. And then the abbot gave him the priorate of Montaudon,[2] and there he did a great deal for the good of the house. While he was in the monastery he wrote coblas *and* sirventes *on subjects that were popular in that region. And knights and barons brought him forth from the monastery, did him great honor and gave him whatever he wanted or requested; and he took everything back to Montaudon, to his priorate.*

He greatly increased and improved his church while he still wore the monk's habit. And he returned to Orlac, to his abbot, showing him how he had improved the priorate of Montaudon; and he begged the abbot to allow him to follow Alfonso of Aragon's advice, and the abbot consented. For the king had commanded him to eat meat, court women, sing and write poetry, and thus he did.[3] And he was made lord of Puoi Santa Maria and was chosen as the one to give the sparrow hawk.[4]

For a long time he was lord of the court of Puoi, until it came to an end. And then he went to Spain, and there all the kings and barons did him great honor. And he went to a priorate there in Spain called Villafranca, which belongs to the abbey of Orlac.[5] And the abbot gave him this priorate. And he enriched it and improved it. And there he died and was buried.

Even though the biographer seems intent on painting the good monk as a saintly character who was torn away from his devotions by royal command, his poetry (which falls roughly

* Notes accompanying this section begin on p. 295.

between 1180 and 1213) gives a somewhat different impression. His principal concern seems to have been enjoying the good life. He had, for instance, strong feelings on the subject of food—he once swore by Saint Martin that

> . . . if there's anything I hate
> it's a lot of water in a little wine

and in another poem he said how he loved

> a fat salmon at the hour of nones.

And, judging from Poem 2 below, he suffered from no angelic innocence on the subject of women. Yet in the midst of all his ribaldry, he remained a stickler for decorum.

> I cannot bear a knight who takes
> three helpings of cabbage and sauce,
> or a suitor who is always farting.

One can still imagine this red-faced Friar Tuck chortling as he pinches girls' bottoms, or sitting at table with a napkin tucked under his double chin and with knife and fork in ready position, or amusing his hosts by singing one of his delightful songs in a hoarse, croaking baritone.

1

I The other day I was in Paradise,
   which is why I'm gay and joyous,
   for God, whom all things obey—
   earth, sea, valleys and mountains—
   was most friendly towards me.
   "Monk," he said, "why have you come,
   and how are things at Montaudon
   where you have more company than here?"

II "Lord, I've been locked up
   in the cloister for a year or two
   and thus lost the barons' friendship;

they now treat me coolly
merely because I love and serve You.
En Random, lord of Paris,[6] for instance
(a man without deceit or falsehood),
regrets I stopped my traveling."

III   "Monk, I'm not happy either
seeing you locked up in a cloister,
engaged in wars, disputes,
and arguments with neighbors
over control of lands.
I prefer singing and laughter;
it makes the world a better place,
and even Montaudon benefits thereby."

IV   "Lord, I fear it might be a sin
to write *coblas* or *chansos*,
for he who knowingly tells lies
loses both Your love and You;
thus I'll leave that way of life,
and, in order not to hate myself,
return to my divine offices
and forego my trip to Spain."

V   "Monk, you're making a big
mistake not to go at once
to the king who rules Olairos [7]
and who was such a friend of yours;
I can see why his love has waned.
Ha! How many good marks of sterling
he would have lost in gifts to you,
for it's he who raised you from the mire."

VI   "Lord, I would have gone
to see him had it not been for You,
for You permitted his captivity.[8]
And as for those Saracen ships,
You care little how they roam the seas;
for once inside Acre, the Turks will be

that much more formidable; only a madman
would follow You into such a fray!"

2

I   Another time, quite by chance,
I attended a gathering in Heaven
at which the holy images complained
of the make-up women wore;
I saw them cry out to God against
those who heighten their complexion
and make their faces shine with that
which should be used on statues.

II   And God replied quite frankly,
"Monk, it's wrong that holy images
should lose what rightfully is theirs;
so, for love of Me, run earthward
and make women cease this practice.
I want no more complaints,
and if they won't stop, I myself
will wash their make-up off."

III   "Lord God," I said, "You should have
more mercy and moderation where women
are concerned, for it's only natural
that they should paint their faces.
This should not anger You, nor should
the images complain, for otherwise
they surely will receive
no more offerings from women."

IV   "Monk," said God, "that's no excuse!
It's sinful and insidious
that my own creatures should beautify
themselves without permission.
Soon those whom I make grow older
day by day will be like Me,

if through paint and make-up
they can restore their youth."

V   "Lord, you talk too proudly
and judge from too high a place,
for the use of make-up will not cease
without some sort of covenant:
either you make ladies' beauty
last until their death
or cause make-up to disappear
entirely from the earth."

VI   "Monk, it is not right that women
should beautify themselves with paint,
and it is indeed unreasonable
that you should try to justify them.
Yet even though you praise them for it,
they should not suffer things that spoil
their skin for beauty's sake, and then
are lost when they piss but once." [9]

VII   "Lord, she who paints well sells well;
that's why they take such care
to make their preparation thick and hard
so it won't leave with their first piss.
Since you will not make them beautiful,
why be angry if they take the task
upon themselves? Instead, be grateful
that they can do it without your help."

VIII   "Monk, this sort of make-up makes them
receive all kinds of blows in their nether
regions; and do you think they like
having men make them bend over?"

IX   "Lord, let them burn in Hell's fires!
For I can never fill their holes;
and when I think I've reached the shore,
I find my swimming has just begun!"

X   "Monk, we'll let them be; and since
pissing will destroy their make-up,
I'll just give them such a malady
as will keep them pissing day and night!"

XI   "Lord, whomever you make piss,
You must spare Helis de Montfort,[10]
who has never painted herself or caused
complaints from images or altars."

3

I   Since Peire d'Alvernhe has sung
of those troubadours now past,
I will sing, as best I can, of those
who have appeared more recently;
and let them not be angry
if I criticize their failings.

II   The first is from Saint-Didier,
Guilhem by name, who sings not only
willingly but most agreeably.
But what good's a man who dares not
ask for what he wants? One must
conclude that he's of little worth.[11]

III   The second, the Viscount of Saint Antoni,
has never been rewarded with love's joy.
He had bad luck, for the first
lady he loved became a heretic,
and since then he's sought no other,
and thus weeps night and day.[12]

IV   And the third is from the Carcassès—
Miraval—who pretends to be so courtly,
always giving away his castle; but he's
never there more than one month a year,

and never for the feast day. So why
should he care if another owns it? [13]

V   The fourth, an Auvergnat called Peirol,
has worn the same clothes for thirty years
and is more dried out than burning wood,
and his singing has gone quite stale,
for since he took up with whores in Clermont,
he hasn't turned out one decent poem.[14]

VI   And the fifth is Gaucelm Faidit,
who changed from lover to husband of a lady
who had quite a following, and since then
we haven't heard his trills and cries.
But his singing was never in high repute
except between Uzerche and Agen.[15]

VII   And the sixth is Guilhem Ademar—
never was there a worse jongleur.
He accepts old clothes as payment
and dedicates his songs to such a lady
as brings him a good thirty competitors;
thus I always see him poor and miserable.[16]

VIII   With Arnaut Daniel that's seven: in his
entire life he's sung nothing but a few
crazy words that no one understands.
And ever since he hunted the hare with the ox
and swam against the rising tide,
his songs have been completely worthless.[17]

                              .   .   .

X   The ninth is Arnaut de Mareuil
whom I always see downcast,
for his lady is without pity.
It is wrong of her not to welcome him,
for his eyes are always crying mercy,
and the more he sings, the more the water flows.[18]

                              .   .   .

XIII   And the twelfth will be Folquet
de Marseille, a little merchant
who made a crazy vow when he swore
he'd never write another song;
but they say he's done so many times,
and thus committed perjury.[19]

. . .

XV   Peire Vidal's the last: not only
is he lacking a member or two,
but this villein and former furrier
had better get a tongue of silver,
for ever since he was made a knight
he hasn't shown a bit of common sense.[20]

. . .

XVII   With the sixteenth that'll be enough:
he's the false Monk of Montaudon
who argues and quarrels with everyone,
and who left God for lard. What's more,
just for writing *vers* and *chansos*,
he should be strung up in the wind.[21]

XVIII   The Monk wrote and recited this *vers*
at Caussade for the first time,

XIX   and then took it quickly beyond Lobeo
as a present for En Bernart.[22]

Guilhem de Cabestanh

Guilhem de Cabestanh was a knight from the region of Roussillon, which borders on Catalonia and the Narbonnais.[1] *He was very charming and valiant, humble and courteous.*

And in that region there lived a woman called my lady Seremonda, wife of En Raimon de Castel-Roussillon.[2] *This man was very rich and noble, but also cruel and harsh, fierce and arrogant. Guilhem de Cabestanh loved the lady with a great love; he sang of it and wrote his songs for her. And she, young and noble, lovely and charming, loved him above all other creatures. This was told to Raimon de Castel-Roussillon who, in a jealous rage, made inquiries and, finding it was true, had his wife put under guard.*

And then one day Raimon de Castel-Roussillon saw Guilhem de Cabestanh passing by unescorted and killed him. He had his heart removed from his body and his head cut off. He had the heart cooked and seasoned with pepper, and gave it to his wife to eat. And when this lady had eaten it, Raimon de Castel-Roussillon asked her, "Do you know what you have eaten?" And she answered, "No, I only know that it was savory and very good." Then he told her she had eaten the heart of En Guilhem de Cabestanh; and in order that she should have no doubts, he had the head brought before her. And when the lady heard and saw this, she lost her sense of sight and hearing. Upon recovering, she said, "Sir, you have given me such a fine thing to eat, that I shall never eat again." When he heard this, he leapt at her with sword in hand, intending to strike her on the head, but she ran to a balcony and threw herself down. And so she died.[3]

Or, as Ezra Pound put it:

* Notes accompanying this section begin on p. 298.

And she went toward the window and cast her down,
    'All the while, the while, swallows crying:
Ityn!

      'It is Cabestan's heart in the dish.'
      'It is Cabestan's heart in the dish?
      'No other taste shall change this.'
And she went toward the window,
      the slim white stone bar
Making a double arch;
Firm even fingers held to the firm pale stone:
Swung for a moment,
      and the wind out of Rhodez
Caught in the full of her sleeve.
    . . . the swallows crying:
'Tis. 'Tis. Ytis! [4]

It is this story, much more than his poetry, which has spread Guilhem de Cabestanh's fame far beyond the small circle of men interested in Provençal literature.[5] But how this legend— and it indeed seems to be a legend, for exactly the same story was told of a Breton harper called Guiron, of the German minnesinger Reinmar von Brennenberg, and of the French trouvère, the Châtelain of Coucy—became attached to Guilhem de Cabestanh, nobody knows. Perhaps he did come to some violent end, and then the story was embroidered to fit the legend of the eaten heart.

But this is only a guess, for as a historical figure Guilhem de Cabestanh is almost nonexistent. A person of that name appears in a document of 1162 and in another of 1212 (the latter a list of men from the Roussillon who fought in the battle of Navas de Tolosa), but we don't know which of these —if either—refers to the poet. He dedicates several of his songs to a Raymond, whom we assume to be the lord of Castel-Roussillon. And that's where our information ends.

As a poet Guilhem de Cabestanh is a minor figure in Provençal letters. A few of his poems, nevertheless, seem to have been widely read in the Middle Ages. And he could write verse of great charm and musicality (in the poetic sense, for none of his music has been preserved). His entire output is love poetry in the classic troubadour vein; his language is always simple, and his resources are limited, but within this framework he achieves moments of considerable beauty.

1

I   The day I first saw you, my lady,
when it pleased you to let me do so,
my heart abandoned all other thoughts,
and all my desires converged on you,
for with your sweet smile and gentle look
you brought my heart such longing that I
forgot myself and all that was mine.

II   For the great beauty, sweet solace, courtly
words, and amorous pleasure you let me glimpse
so robbed me of my wits that never since,
my lady, have I recovered them, but rather
bequeath them to you, with true and thankful
heart, that they may glorify your name,
for I could find no better love than yours.

III   For I love you, my lady, so faithfully
that Love leaves me powerless to love another,
yet courting others could give me occasion
by which I might relieve my grief;
but when I think of you, to whom Joy bows,
I forget and forsake all other love
and stay with you, who are nearest to my heart.

IV   And remember, if it please you,
the covenant we made upon parting,
which brought my heart such happiness
for the hope you commanded me to have;
and though my lot has since worsened, I had
great joy and will again, if it please you,
my good lady, for I continue to wait patiently.

V   I would not care what evil might befall me
if only I were sure, my lady, that you
would give me some joy while I yet live;

but these pains make me rejoice,
if only because I know Love commands
true lovers to forgive great wrongs
and suffer pain in hope of recompense.

VI   And thus it will be, my lady, when I see
that out of mercy you will honor me
by deigning merely to call me your friend.

Peire Cardenal

Peire Cardenal was from the Velay, from the city of Le Puy Notre-Dame; [1] *and he was from an honorable, noble family, for he was the son of a knight and a lady. And when he was still a young boy, his father had him entered as a canon in the greater canonry* [2] *of Le Puy; and he learned his letters and became familiar with reading and singing.*

And then when he reached the age of manhood, he took great pleasure in the vanities of this world, for he was gay, handsome and young. And he wrote many poems on lovely themes and with lovely melodies. He wrote chansos, *but only a few; however he wrote many* sirventes, *all of which were splendid and beautiful. And in these* sirventes—or at least for *those who understood them—he propounded many fine arguments and examples, for he greatly chastised the folly of this world and greatly vilified false clergymen, as one can see in these poems of his. And he traveled to the courts of kings and noble barons, taking with him a jongleur to sing his* sirventes. *And he was greatly honored by good King James of Aragon* [3] *and by noble barons.*

And I, Master Miquel de la Tor, [4] *scribe, hereby make known that En Peire Cardenal, when he passed from this life, was close to a hundred years old. And I, the aforementioned Miquel, have copied these* sirventes *in the city of Nîmes.*

From his poems (the first of which can be dated from 1205) and from the fact that we find him named as a secretary of the Count of Toulouse in 1204, we can assume that Peire Cardenal must have been born around 1180. And since his last poems date from 1272, he must indeed have been close to a hundred when he died.

° Notes accompanying this section begin on p. 299.

Such a life span, which began when the troubadour culture was still in its prime and ended after the last hopes of the Southern French were dashed by the reuniting of Toulouse to the French Crown in 1271, involved Peire Cardenal in the whole drawn-out agony of this particular way of life. And in a world in which everything was crumbling, the finely chiseled artifacts of earlier poets seemed to find little place. From now on the best verse was to be written in anger or in sorrow. In Guiraut Riquier we feel the sorrow, the yearning for times gone by. But with Peire Cardenal everything is anger. With him the spirit of Marcabru rises again, in a different vein to be sure, but still vituperating against all the corruption seething about him.

Peire Cardenal, however, reserves his anger especially for those he considers responsible for the destruction of his society, the Northern French and the Church. He even goes so far as to hurl epithets at the Dominicans. Now because of their role as inquisitors, this was an extremely risky thing to do. As Jeanroy put it, "It is a pity we don't know where, in what circumstances or beneath what sort of protection were written the poems of this intrepid pamphleteer, as well as those of many others, no less daring, whom the Inquisition probably actively pursued and which exposed their authors to the direst of punishments." But this raises an even more tantalizing question: did Peire Cardenal write such diatribes merely out of a sense of moral outrage, or out of sympathy with the persecuted heretics, or did he go so far as to accept their beliefs? Theories have been propounded on all sides, but the truth of the matter is that this whole question is still a mystery.

In any case, "Peire Cardenal, caustic and fulminating, more eloquent than poetic" [5] stands out as the great figure of Provençal literature after the Battle of Muret. With his only weapon—that of words—he courageously tried to redress the wrongs about him. But their roots went much deeper than even he probably realized, with the result that his efforts could only prove vain and Quixotic. His ultimate tragedy was being doomed to live long enough to witness the final crumbling of whatever hopes he might have had.

1

I   Now I can boast that Love takes away
neither my sleep nor my appetite,
nor makes me feel hot and cold,
nor causes me to yawn and sigh,
    nor to wander aimlessly at night;
nor am I vanquished and tormented,
nor in a state of pain and anger,
    nor must I pay some messenger,
nor am I betrayed or deceived,
but escape with my wits intact.

II   I have no greater pleasure than not
betraying or causing betrayals;
now I don't fear traitress or traitor,
nor jealous husband with his wild rages,
    nor do I perform mad deeds,
nor am I wounded and overthrown,
nor am I captured and despoiled,
    nor do I sit waiting stupidly,
nor am I subjugated by Love,
nor is my heart taken from me,

III   nor do I die for some sweet lady,
nor languish for a lovely creature,
nor do I give praise and adoration,
nor do I beg and yearn,
    nor do homage,
nor do I give myself to her,
nor am I her feudal serf,
    nor is my heart pledged,
nor am I chained in captivity;
instead I have escaped in time.

IV   Men should, to tell the truth, praise
the victor and not the vanquished,
for the victor bears the laurel, while

the vanquished are laid in their graves.
    He who rids his heart
of treacherous desires, which cause him
to do mad unreasonable things
    and other outrageous follies,
will be more honored by such a victory
than by conquering a hundred cities.[6]

2

I

Churchmen pass for shepherds
but they're murderers.
Dressed in their robes
they seem so saintly,
but they remind me
of Isengrim,[7] who,
to enter a farmyard
guarded by dogs,
dressed in a sheepskin,
thus fooling them all,
and then gorged himself
on everything in sight.

II

Kings and emperors,
dukes, counts and viscounts,
and knights as well
used to rule the world;
but now I see
churchmen holding sway
with their thefts and treachery
and their hypocrisy,
their violence and their preaching.
Since they can't bear
not being given everything,
they procure it by any means.

III

And the mightier they are,
the less is their virtue,

and the greater their folly
the less their truthfulness,
and the greater their lying
the less their nobility,
and the greater their deception
the less is their holiness.
I say this of false
clergymen, for never
did God have such enemies
since time immemorial.

IV I consider it no honor
to be in a refectory,
for at the highest table
the worst scoundrels sit
and serve themselves first.
And it is worse to think
that they dare come at all
and that no one throws them out.
And I've never seen some poor
beggarly scoundrel sit next
to one who's rich—they'd
never commit a sin like that!

V Let caliphs or sultans
have no fear
that abbots and priors
will swoop down
and seize their lands.
It would be too much work;
they'd rather be here scheming
how to make the world theirs
and how to flush
Frederick from his lair;
but those who attacked him
had little cause for joy.[8]

VI Clergymen, whoever thought
your hearts are free of treachery

has made a grave mistake,
for a worse lot I've never seen.

3

I'll write an *estribot* [9] that will be masterful,
full of art, new words and holy thoughts.

For I believe in a God born of mother,
a holy virgin, through whom the world is saved.
He is the Father, Son and Holy Trinity,
and thus three persons in one, and I believe
that He opened the heavens' vault
and threw down the angels He found guilty,
and I believe Saint John held Him in his arms
and baptized Him in the river's water
and recognized Him before He was born
by moving within His mother's womb.[10]
And I believe in Rome, and in Saint Peter,
judge of penitence, good sense and folly.

But treacherous churchmen don't believe such things;
they love to take but skimp with their bounty,
they present charming faces but are horrible in sin,
they prohibit others from what they themselves enjoy,
and instead of matins they've invented a new office
which involves lying with a whore till sunrise
and then singing ballades and proses full of gaiety.
Caiaphas and Pilate will attain God long before them.

Monks used to be shut inside monasteries,
worshiping God before holy images, but now
if they are in a town beneath their sway
and find you with a lovely wife or mistress,
they'll take her (however much you may protest),
and when they're on top and her cunt is plugged
with those round balls hanging from their rod,
and when the letters are sealed and the hole closed,

from this will come forth heretics and Vaudois [11]
who promise and abjure and play with three dice:
that is what the Black Monks [12] consider charity.

My *estribot* is finished: its measure's right
and it's steeped in grammar and theology,
and may I be forgiven any errors it contains.
I dedicate it to God, that He may be more loved,
          and also to evil-seeking
             clergymen.

4

I   When they are blamed for something,
        women answer as would Isengrim: [13]
        one takes a lover to protect her patrimony,
        another because she's in direst poverty;
        one because her husband's old and she's still young,
        another because she's taller than her spouse;
        one because she needs a nice brown coat, while
        another has two and takes lovers in proportion.

II   A man with a woman on his land has war nearby,
        but nearer still he who has one on his pillow.
        When a husband is displeasing to a wife,
        then comes a war worse than that with neighbors.
        And I know a man who, were he beyond Toledo,
        there would be no wife, cousin or relation
        who would say, "May God bring him back to us";
        his departure only turns ire to laughter.

III   If a poor man steals a bedsheet,
        he's called a thief and bows his head,
        but if a rich man steals a treasure,
        he is honored in the court of Constantine.
        If some beggar steals a bridle,
        he'll be hung by a man who's stolen a horse.

There's no surer justice in the world than that
which makes the rich thief hang the poor one.

IV   A man who's stolen and slaughtered cattle and sheep
can make a splendid, though ill-gotten, feast,
and I know one who thus filled his cauldron
at Christmastime, but I won't divulge his name.
Meat so procured cannot but be unclean,
treacherous and against the laws of God,
and a man who thus thinks to honor the Christmas
meat has less sense than a babe in arms.

V   I sing and warble for myself alone,
since no one understands my language;
for people comprehend my words
as little as they do a nightingale.
Little matter that I know neither Frisian
nor Breton, nor can talk Flemish or Angevin,
for their wickedness clouds their brains
so they can't distinguish good from evil.

VI   What do I care if such crass men don't
heed my song, for they're all swine.

5

I   I have always despised fraud and treachery
and lived according to truth and justice;
and if this makes my fortunes vary, I don't
complain, for life seems fine and good to me.
I know that loyalty often causes ruination
while treachery and bad faith bring wealth,
but if a man rises through such fraud,
all the greater will be his fall.

II   Great barons feel as much pity for others
as did Cain for Abel;
they steal more readily than wolves

and lie more easily than whores.
If you pierce their bodies in several places,
don't think that truth will pour forth,
but only lies, of which they've such a fount
as will spill out like water from a spring.

III   I see many barons whose position is falser
than a glass stone in a ring, and whoever
thinks they're loyal is as mistaken
as a man who sells wolves for lambs.
They are like a counterfeit coin
(of neither proper weight or alloy)
designed with a crown and flower, but which
when melted is found to have no silver.

IV   From the Orient to the setting sun,
with anyone I'll strike a bargain:
to a loyal man I'll give a besant
if all disloyal men give me a nail;
and I'll give a mark of gold to courtly men
if ill-mannered men give me a tournois; [14]
to the truthful I'll give great heaps of gold
if I can have an egg from every liar.

V   All the laws such men observe
I could write on a tiny bit of parchment—
on half of the thumb of my glove.
All good men I could feed on a single cake,
for such people don't need rich food;
but if someone wanted to feed scoundrels,
he would only need to cry:
"Come eat, all you fine fellows!"

VI   He who has only a semblance of worthiness
should not be called upright and valiant,
nor righteous when he sneers at justice,
nor truthful when he pours forth lies.
For it is not right that sinners
should always reap the thanks and praise,

and thus the proverb: "A man who skins
a sheep will have no more wool to clip."

VII   In this *sirventes* I proclaim to one
and all that men who, in this world,
do not live by truth, justice and mercy
have no right to boast of worthiness.

VIII   Faidit, go and sing this *sirventes*
to En Guigon at Tournoël, for in worthiness
he has no equal in the world,
except milord En Eble of Clermont.[15]

6

There was once a city
in which fell such a rain
that everyone it touched
went mad; everybody,
that is, except one
who escaped by being
asleep in his house
when it happened.

He got up after sleeping,
when the rain had stopped,
and went out among the others
all of whom were acting mad.
One was in robes, another naked,
and another spat up in the air;
one threw a stone, another a stick,
and another tore apart his tunic;
one hit, another pushed, and yet
another thought he was a king
and took a stance with hands on hips,
and another leaped on shop counters; [16]
one uttered threats, another cursed,
one swore and another laughed,

one talked about nothing at all,
grimacing horribly all the while.

And the man who was still in his
right mind was much astonished
at seeing everyone so mad.
He looked up and down and saw
no one sane, for indeed
all sanity had fled. He was much amazed at them,
but they much more so at him.
On seeing him so calm, they thought
it was he who had lost his mind,
for he was not acting like them.
They were all certain that they
were sane and sound in mind
and that he was completely mad.
One hit him on the cheek, another
on the neck and knocked him down.
One pushed, another kicked—
he thought he could escape,
but one pulled, another tugged,
and he went down, got up and fell again.
Falling, stumbling and running as fast
as he could, he fled to his house.
He arrived mud-stained, bruised and half-dead,
yet happy to have escaped.

This fable represents the world
and the people who live therein.
The earth is the city
which is full of madmen.
For the greatest wisdom
is to love and fear God
and keep His commandments,
but now this wisdom has been lost.
The rain which has fallen is that
of Covetousness, bringing
great pride and wickedness
to all the people of the world.

And if God spared one man,
others consider him mad
and maltreat him because
his wisdom is not theirs.
For the spirit of God to them is folly,
but the friend of God, wherever
he may be, knows that they are mad
for they have lost God's wisdom,
but they think he is mad,
for abandoning worldly wisdom.

Sordello

Sordello came from the region of Mantua, from a castle called Got.[1] He was a noble chatelain, and handsome as a person. And he was a good singer and a good poet, and also a great lover; but he was very treacherous and false towards women and towards the barons with whom he stayed. And he fell in love with My Lady Cunizza, sister of Ser Ezzelino and Alberico da Romano, and wife of the Count of San Bonifacio, with whom he was staying.[2] And at the command of My Lord Ezzelino, he took My Lady Cunizza and made off with her.

Later he went to the region of Onedo, to the castle of the lords of Strasso, Ser Enrico and Ser Guglielmo and En Valpertino, who were very good friends of his.[3] And he secretly married a sister of theirs called Otha, and he then went to Treviso. And when the lord of Strasso found out about it, he wanted to do him harm, as well as to all the friends of the Count of San Bonifacio. Sordello therefore remained in the house of My Lord Ezzelino, always armed; and when he went out, he rode on a good war horse and had himself accompanied by a great number of knights.

And for fear of those who wanted to do him harm, he left and went to Provence, where he stayed with the Count of Provence.[4] And he fell in love with a noblewoman from Provence who was very beautiful; and in the songs he wrote for her he called her "Sweet Enemy," for he wrote many fine songs for this lady.[5]

Through a combination of fortunate circumstances, Sordello is one of the troubadours whose life we can trace in some detail. He was born around 1200, and his early career, including the celebrated rape of Cunizza da Romano, is outlined in the above biography. He probably left Italy around 1228 and,

* Notes accompanying this section begin on p. 302.

after wandering through many parts of Occitania and Spain, finally settled in Provence some time in the 1230s. There he became attached to the court of Ramon Berenguer IV and after his death in 1245, to that of his son-in-law, Charles of Anjou. We know too that he reached a position of considerable importance in these courts.

After more than thirty-five years of exile he finally returned to his homeland in 1265, accompanying his overlord, Charles of Anjou, on his expedition to Italy. We don't know whether or not he took part in the battles of Benevento (1266) or Tagliacozzo (1268); but he must have rendered Charles great services, for in the spring of 1269 he was awarded extensive lands in the Abruzzo. In August of that same year, however, someone else was already in possession of these lands, and because of this and the fact that his name is mentioned in no later documents, scholars have assumed that he died that summer, having had only a few months to enjoy his new wealth. We have reason to suspect that he came to a violent end, but we have no way of knowing the truth of the matter nor the manner in which it might have happened.

As a literary (and historical) figure, however, there is a considerable mystery connected with Sordello, and that is his extraordinary fame. One could answer that it was due to Dante, but this merely begs the question, because we don't really know why Dante picked him for a position of such eminence in the *Divine Comedy*. Only a small part of his fame can have come from his poetry. Even his best known poem, the *planh* on the death of Blacatz (Poem 3 below), was not nearly as widely read in the Middle Ages as were hundreds of other troubadour poems. One contributing factor may have been a certain air of scandal about his early life. There was apparently a tavern brawl, the rape of Cunizza, the secret marriage with Otha and finally the flight to escape vendettas. Even as late as 1266 we find him jailed at Novara (near Milan) for an unknown cause. There was also Sordello's political importance: he seems to have become part of the inner circle of Charles of Anjou's court, and Charles was a man of boundless ambition, who made his weight felt over much of Europe and the Near East.

In Dante's work Sordello is the shade that guides him and Virgil through much of the Ante-Purgatory (*Purgatorio,* VI–VIII). Yet nothing could be more enigmatic than the way Sordello is presented in these Cantos. He is indeed impressive ("Michelangelesque," as one critic put it), "seated by himself apart," "lofty and disdainful." There is a touching scene when he and Virgil realize they are both from the region of Mantua, followed by Dante's famous lament for his native land:

> *Ahi serva Italia, di dolore ostello,*
> *nave sanza nocchiere in gran tempesta,*
> *non donna di provincie, ma bordello!*

> (Ah, enslaved Italy, hostel of grief,
> ship without pilot in great tempest,
> no lady among provinces, but a brothel!)

So obviously Dante considered Sordello a great patriot. Could he have felt this merely on the basis of the Blacatz poem, or did he know much more about his political career than we do? Our knowledge would never lead us to think of him as a patriot, and it is even more puzzling that Dante considered him so when we remember that Sordello worked for Charles of Anjou, who was a member of the Capetian clan Dante so excoriated.

In English-speaking countries, of course, Sordello's fame rests on Robert Browning's poem. But it was not so much the historical figure that interested Browning; he merely used it (or at least Dante's version of it) to project his own ideas on the poet's dilemma when forced to choose between his art and the good of mankind.

We therefore find ourselves in the peculiar situation of seeing Sordello's image both enlarged and distorted by two other poets who bent it to fit their own personal needs. When considering him as a troubadour, therefore, we must try to wipe the slate clean of all these later accretions to his reputation and look at him merely as a poet. Regarded in this light, we can see him as one of the best troubadours in a period of decadence, and certainly one of the finest to come out of Italy. He is very much in the classic vein (and therefore cannot be compared to his contemporary Peire Cardenal or the slightly later Cerverí), and as such his poetry is always controlled and elegant. Yet in a certain sense his qualities are negative: he never makes aesthetic errors nor falls into the emptiness and vapidity of so many other troubadours of the decadent years. But by his day the molds had worn thin, and he could no longer suffuse his *chansos* with the same poetic vitality as the great classic troubadours, and only once, in the famous *planh* on the death of Blacatz, do we feel the need to "make it new."

1

I A man only lives when he lives joyfully;
to live another way is not to be alive.
Thus do I try to live and conduct myself
with joy, the better to serve the one I love,
for a man who lives in grief cannot perform
pleasant worthy deeds; and I shall be
thankful if this gracious lady makes my life
joyful, for any other life is worthless.

II I think of her so much and love her so truly
that night and day I tremble at my thoughts,
for her beauty and worth are unequaled,
and thus should the most honored ladies
obey her and let her lead them,
guiding, through her perfection, the worthiest
towards worth, just as ships at sea are guided
by the north star, the compass and the loadstone.

III And just as this fixed shining star
guides ships in danger on the high seas,
so should she, who resembles it, guide me
who am, through her, so hopelessly
lost at sea and in such distress
that I shall die and perish here
unless she help me, for I can find
no shore or port, no ford or bridge.[6]

IV   Harsh mercy and pity too long awaited
      make me perish with desire, for I cannot
      endure life without joy; I plead with her,
      serving and loving with such torment
      that a thousand times a day I wish my life
      would end, so much is my heart wounded
      by Love's darts; death would bring relief,
      for her pain is not as grave as mine.

V   Alas! Whence comes her desire to kill me
      since she can find me guilty of nothing?
      For, however ill she may treat me in deed
      or word, I shall never cease to love her.
      Why, therefore, am I so maltreated when I
      have pledged myself to her, and when,
      rather than leave her, I would prefer to have
      my soul parted from my body, so loyal is my love?

VI   N'Agradiva, my lady,[7] root of all merit,
      in my heart, body, word and deed
      I am yours, for you are faultless,
      pure and pleasing, gentle and perfect.

VII   May God grant, my lady, that you have pity,
      for in your hands lie my death and my life.

2

I   *Guilhem*   A lover and his lady, Sordello,
      de la Tor are so united in their love
                   that neither feels he could
                   have joy without the other;
                   but then if the lady dies
                   and the lover continues living
                   and cannot forget her,
                   what would be best for him:
                   to live on after her or die?
                   Tell me your opinion.

II   *Sordello*   Guilhem, I so faithfully love
the one who has me in her power
that without her I would not want
to live for any amount of wealth,
since it seems to me that if death
takes from a lover that in which
he has placed his every thought,
he had best go there with her
rather than remain here suffering
endless grief and anguish.

III   *Guilhem*   But I cannot see, Sordello,
what profit it would bring the lady
to have the lover die for her;
he would only be considered mad,
for life is preferable by far.
What did Andreus [8] accomplish
when he killed himself?
You're wrong in your opinion:
one should not choose a course
that causes only harm.

IV   *Sordello*   Guilhem de la Tor, I feel
you're on the side of madness.
How can you say life
is preferable to death
to one who has no joy
and is forever languishing?
Rather than suffer such a fate
a man should kill himself
without a thought if he can't
find some other way to die.

V   *Guilhem*   Sordello, I could find more
people to support my argument
than you could yours, for you
should realize that in death
there is no sport or laughter;
but life brings many benefits

to those who know where to seek,
and so the lover should abandon
whatever brings him no more joy
and look elsewhere for happiness.

VI   *Sordello*   But he'd have little joy,
Guilhem, for with the memory
of the pleasure he once had,
he could not avoid being
overcome by grief and tears;
but if he died with his lady,
other lovers would praise him
for having loved so truly,
and his sorrows would be over,
as would his tears and sighs.

VII   *Guilhem*   Sordello, since N'Azalais
of Vizalaina [9] has such true
and perfect merit, I feel that she
should be the judge of this debate;
for surely nobody could be
displeased by her decision.

VIII   *Sordello*   Since every worthy man is pleased
with Na Cunizza [10] and feels grateful,
Guilhem, for her rare, noble merit,
let us choose her together with
Azalais to decide and judge
and thus earn our gratitude.

3

I   With a sad, dejected heart I want to mourn Blacatz [11]
in this light melody, and it's only right I do so,
for in him I've lost both a lord and good friend,
and with his death all qualities of merit vanish.
So fatal is the harm therefrom that I don't see
how it can ever be repaired, unless someone

take out his heart and let the barons, who are so
easily disheartened, eat it so they may take heart.

II   The first to eat some of the heart will be the Emperor
        of Rome—he needs it badly if he wishes to conquer
        the Milanese, for they have humbled him and he lives
        disinherited, in spite of all his German soldiers.[12]
        And afterwards let the French king eat a bit, so he can
        recover Castile, which he lost through sheer stupidity,
        but if his mother is against it, he won't eat a thing,
        for it's clear that he does nothing against her will.[13]

III   I'd like to see the squeamish English king eat a large
        portion of the heart, and thus be valiant and good
        and recover the lands (whose loss covers him with
           shame),
        which the French king took knowing he was indolent.[14]
        As for the Castilian king, he would best eat for two,
        since he has two realms and cannot even manage one;
        but if he does, it will have to be in secret, for if
        his mother found out, she'd beat him black and blue.[15]

IV   I also want the King of Aragon to eat a bit
        of the heart, and thus be rid of the shame
        he receives there by Marseille and Millau,
        for no word or deed could now revive his honor.[16]
        And the King of Navarre should be given some,
        for he was, they say, a better count than king;
        it's a pity God makes men rise in power who
        through lack of valor then descend in merit.[17]

V   The Count of Toulouse must eat a lot if he
        compares his former with his present holdings,
        for if with another heart he can't repair his loss,
        he surely will not with the one he has.[18]
        And the Count of Provence should eat some too
        if he realizes that a man dispossessed is worthless;
        and although he defends himself as best he can,
        he must eat of the heart to help sustain the burden.[19]

VI   The barons will wish me ill because I speak the truth,
       but they should know I prize them as little as they do me.

VII   Belh Restaur,[20] since I know with you I can find mercy,
       I care little for those who don't consider me their friend.

Cerverí

Not too long ago this poet was known only as Cerverí de Girona, some sixteen poems were ascribed to him, and he was considered a very minor figure. But now all this has changed drastically. Thanks to the researches of a Spanish scholar, Martín de Riquer, we know that he also called himself Guilhem de Cervera [1] and that he wrote 120 works, five of them long narrative poems and one a set of proverbs. And since we now have more poems by him than by any other troubadour, he has recently shot into considerable prominence among Provençal scholars.

We have no medieval biography of Cerverí, yet we know a certain amount about his life thanks to the fact that he was attached to the royal court of Aragon. He wrote from 1250 to 1280 under the patronage first of James the Conqueror (1213–1276) and then of his son, Peter the Great (1276–1285). His services were rewarded by the granting of lands in a place called Santa Seglina, ten miles south of Gerona. His other patrons were the Cardonas, an immensely powerful and wealthy noble family of Catalonia, and chiefly Ramón Folch IV (1233–1276) who was in almost continual rebellion against James the Conqueror, and Ramón Folch's second wife, Sibila of Empuries, who outlived her husband by more than forty years, dying in 1317. (Cerverí refers to her as *la domn'als Cartz*, partly because of the word play of *Cartz-domna* with *Cardona* and also because *cartz*—"thistles"—were the heraldic emblem of the Cardona family.)

Now before discussing Cerverí as a poet, we have to understand one thing. The fact that we have such a mass of works by him is no reflection of how widely read his poetry was in the Middle Ages; it is merely the result of the chance preservation of one manuscript dedicated almost entirely to him.

* Notes accompanying this section begin on p. 304.

(Nearly all the rest of troubadour poetry has come down to us in manuscripts that are in fact medieval anthologies.) So with Cerverí we're in the unusual position of having what may be the complete works of a minor troubadour, and one very late in time. But at least this gives us the chance to see the great variety of Cerverí's output: he was a poet who would try his hand at anything, from light popular poetry to the most intricate and recondite endeavors in the realm of *trobar clus*. He had great facility and technical resources, and suffered from no fears at all about "making it new."

Yet he lived in an age in which, as Guiraut Riquier said (see his Poem 3), "men prefer to hear and see frivolity." But, as opposed to Guiraut Riquier, Cerverí seems to have had no compunctions whatsoever about being frivolous. To be sure, he tried writing serious poetry, but it suffers from an empty quality—one feels there is the facility and nothing else. He is at his best when doing light verse, or verse based on some poetic device (gimmick, if you will). Then his cleverness or his ability to entertain is allowed to come to the fore, and in this realm he is a master.

Apparently, like Guiraut Riquier, he thought of himself as a "troubadour" and objected to being called a "jongleur," yet in documents from the royal chancery we find him referred to as *joculatorus*. And this describes him perfectly—Cerverí the jongleur, the gifted juggler with words.

1

If you wish me to stop loving
(which is in fact impossible),
cease your gentle way of speaking,
my sweet and lovely lady.

I   And cease your sweet glances,
if you wish me to stop loving,
and your fine manners,
(which is in fact impossible)
and your gentle courtliness;

for your enchanting presence
bewitches those who see you,
so how could I not love you?
If you wish . . .

II   And cease your charm and grace,
        my sweet and lovely lady,
        if you want me to part from you;
        cease your gentle way of speaking,
        and leave that rich fount of merit
        which makes you without equal,
        and the youth in which you're clothed,
        and your gentle gratitude and honor.
        If you wish . . .

III   Don't show me your dear sweet body,
        (*if you wish me to stop loving*)
        so naturally lovely that to adorn it
        would be in fact impossible.
        Could I find another (saying yes would be
        a lie) through whom I might forget you?
        I doubt it, since my love for you
        makes all others turn away.
        If you wish . . .

IV   Enfan Pere,[2] every day
        you cause your merit to ascend,
        for your courtliness and valor
        preserve you from all error.

V   Noble Viscountess of Cardona,[3]
        there's nothing to praise in your
        sweet body that could not be praised
        a thousand times more in you.

2

I   It is hard for a man to find his way
        at sea, even when boats and ships pass by;

and even though the sea is flat and calm,
it is hard to measure it precisely;
yet even less can one see and know
the artifice and evil of false women.

II   And it is hard, upon seeing a bird fly,
to know where it goes or will come to rest;
and the leaves on a pine or on two beeches
are hard to count, as are the stars in heaven;
yet even less can a man escape harm
when he invites a vile woman inside his tent.

III   And for him who sees a serpent crawl
among rocks (if he dares tell the truth)
it will be hard to find a path or way
through which to crawl as did the serpent;
yet even less—and this is no joking matter—
can he escape the curses of a base woman.

IV   It is hard for a man to bind the four winds
and hold them locked within his house;
and it is hard to bridle a wild
ferocious lion as if it were a horse;
yet even less will it serve a man to share
his drinking cup with a wicked woman.

V   It is hard to stop the sun, or turn
blame into praise, or bears into sheep,
or chickens into cranes or turkeys,
or to make the waxing moon wane;
yet even less can a man come to a good end
by having a vile woman in bed with him.

VI   The Lady of Cartz and Sobrepretz (I say without
flattery) deserve all praise and discretion.

VII   There's no king the equal of King Peter,
towards whom God has shown such favor.[4]

3

I

I
go
sing-
ing,
think-
ing,
fix-
ing,
rhym-
ing,
hon-
ing,
prais-
ing,
loving
commands
of
af-
fec-
tion
with-
out
pleas-
ure.

II

Then
cur-
ing
harm
— — — —
— — — —
— — — — [5]

they'll
laugh
and

lan-
guish;
thin-
king
will show
the rich
that
af-
fec-
tion
is
one
with
joy.

III

I
sing
songs,
yet
grieve
to
see
the
might-
y
so
eas-
'ly
fooled,
saying
blankly
a-
ny
sen-
ti-
ment
is
shame-
ful.

IV

In
vain
I
go
pray-
ing,
beg-
ging,
seek-
ing;
they'll
say
with
nerve
one can
do much
to
make
oth-
ers
des-
pise
one
less.

V

Be-
neath
such
ills,
I
con-
ti-
nue
as
com-
man-
ded,
ris-
ing,

sinking,

leaving

ev'-

ry-

thing

to

seek

in-

dul-

gence.

VI   Prais-

                ing,

            waiting,

            singing;

                my

                life

                is

                ig-

                no-

                min-

                i-

                ous.

VII   Neither Sobrepretz, nor Cartz nor the King
            can I possibly fit into this song.[6]

4

I   Iflimit iflimis haflamard foflomor meflemen toflomo
            eflemerr aflamamioflomong goofloomood
            peofleomeople
    aflamand eafleameasyflymy aflarramoflomong thoflomose
            whoflomo haflamave noflomo
            loflomoyaflamaltyflymy,
      oflomor soflomo thefleme woflomorld
            coflomonsiflimidetlemers.

II   Ifirri difirrislifirrike afarra houfourrouse wheferrere
boforroth lafarradyfyrry afarrand
seferrervafarrant
laufaurraugh wheferren theferre loforrord
referretufurrurns toforro seefeerree whafarrat
bafarrad woforrork
theyfeyrrey've doforrone (Iflirri dafarrare sayfayrray
noforro moyorrore).

III   Howpowpow fipipine woupoupould bepepe apapa
wopoporld ipipin whipipich sipipilvepeper
wepepere lepepess pripipized thapapan apapa
wopoporthypypy waypaypay opopof lipipife,
apapas ipipin lepepent apapand capaparnipipivapapal.

IV   Imimi woumoumould bememe gaymaymay amamand
hamamappymymy imimin amama
romomoyamamal coumoumourt
imimif amamall thememe vamamaliamamant
peomeomeople thememere gomomot
pleameameasumumure
fromomom thememe womomorks Imimi wrimimite.

V   Forrovor jurruvust orrovone Chrirrivistmarravas Irrivi
wourrouvould lirrivike torrovo rurruvule
therreve grearreaveat barravarorrovons, arravand
errevextrarravact arrava toorroovooth frorrovom
earreaveach
marravan whorrovo worrovon't gorrovo
orrovoverreversearreaveas.

VI   Soforrobreferrepreferretz, wifirrith goofoorrood
jufurrudgmeferrent afarrand noforro
flafarratteferreryfyrry,
Ifirri praifairraise boforroth youfourrou afarrand
heferrer oforrof Cafarrartz.[7]

VII   Iflimi woufloumould thaflamat fiflimive kiflimings
         weflement wheflemere Goflomod
         peflemeriflimished,
         leflemed byflymy oufloumours, whoflomo
         oufloumoutshiflimines theflemem aflamall.[8]

Guiraut Riquier

With Guiraut Riquier we come to the last of the troubadours,[1] a man whose life was spent in an increasingly desperate and ultimately tragic attempt to maintain not only the forms but also the entire way of life represented by troubadour poetry.

Concerning our information about him, there is much in common with Cerverí. For neither poet do we have a Provençal biography; and for both the fact that so many poems have been preserved is a matter of chance rather than a reflection of how widely read they were. But with Guiraut Riquier we find something unusual: his artistic self-consciousness made him carefully date each of his poems and sometimes even accompany them with a little prose commentary explaining the poetical and musical form of the piece.

As a result, we can outline his life in some detail. He was born in Narbonne between 1230 and 1235. His first poems date from 1254, and for the next sixteen years he was to stay put in his native town, dedicating his songs to the Viscount of Narbonne, Aimeric IV (1239–1270). After his patron died, he went to Spain to the court of Alfonso X the Wise. Now this monarch (aside from being an abysmal politician) was not only a poet and scholar himself, but was also one of the most enlightened patrons of his time. Yet although Guiraut Riquier remained at his court ten years, and although his poems contain many eulogies of the king, he never seems to have been entirely happy there. In 1274, for instance, he addressed a famous *supplicatio* to Alfonso in which he strongly protested against the frequent confusion between the words "jongleur" and "troubadour" (insisting that the former should be reserved for the performer or entertainer, and the latter for

* Notes accompanying this section begin on p. 307.

the poet). Cerverí had made the same protest, but with considerably less insistence; for he *was* a jongleur, one who was gifted and apparently appreciated. But Guiraut Riquier ingenuously reveals that he felt himself to be a great troubadour whose talent and labors were not sufficiently rewarded. Yet even though we can see that he was not a great poet, but merely a competent one, he's to be pitied rather than laughed at, for there is something too embarrassing about the simplicity with which he gives away his hand, and something too melancholy about the obstinacy with which he tried to avoid the consequences of having been born in the wrong place at the wrong time.

In any case, after 1280 he returned to southern France, and once more began to search for understanding patronage. He tried various courts, and for a time was connected with that of Henry II of Rodez (as was Cerverí), but then he finally returned to his native Narbonne. As he grew older he wrote less and less, and his poetry became more and more religious. Then finally in 1292 he wrote his last work (Poem 3 below), which is a tragic admission of defeat

> *Mas trop suy vengutz als derriers*
> (But I was born too late)

and of despair, for which he could find consolation only in God.

1

I   The other day while walking
along a riverbank,
alone and joyful
(for Love had brought me
a desire to sing),
I suddenly saw
a gay shepherdess,
lovely and charming,
guarding her sheep;

I went to her
and found her proud
but yet polite,
and she seemed to welcome
my first question.

II   For I asked her:
"Were you ever loved?
Do you know how to love?"
She replied guilelessly:
"The truth is, Sir,
that I'm already promised."
"Young girl, I'm happy
to have found you; that is,
if I can give you pleasure."
"Have you searched high and low
for me? Only a madwoman
would believe a tale like that."
"Can't you see it's true?"
"No Sir, I can't."

III   "My charming young girl,
if you want my love,
I indeed want yours."
"Sir, that cannot be:
you have a mistress
and I a suitor."
"But since I love you
I don't see why
we shouldn't lie together."
"Sir, try some other course,
one that will bring you
greater benefit."
"There's none I desire more."
"Sir, this is sheer folly!"

IV   "I'm not being foolish;
you are so charming
that Love gives his consent."

"Sir, I'll be only
too glad to see
this discussion end."
"What stubbornness,
after I plead
with you so humbly!"
"Sir, think of my
dishonor if I took
you at your word."
"I could use force."
"What a thing to say!"

V   "Have no fear
of what I say, for I
will do you no dishonor."
"Then since you
promise to abstain,
I'll be your friend."
"When I'm about to err,
I'm helped by thoughts
of Belh Deport." [2]
"Sir, I can enjoy your
friendship now that
you're so amiable."
"What's that I hear?"
"That I desire you."

VI   "Young girl, what makes
you suddenly say
such pleasant things?"
"Sir, wherever I go
I hear gay songs
by En Guiraut Riquier."
"But as yet you haven't
uttered the one word
I await from you."
"Sir, does not
Belh Deport keep you
from committing wrongs?"

"No, she is no help."
"Aren't you entirely hers?"

VII   "Everything brings me
grief except the noble
Bertran d'Opian." [3]
"Your sorrow doesn't show;
but you must go now,
thus leaving me to grieve."
"Young girl, I'll often
take this path again."

2

I   To Sant Pos de Tomeiras [4]
    I came the other day,
soaked from rain, and entered
an inn whose hostesses
    I didn't know;
and thus I was surprised
to see the old lady laugh
as she told the young girl
some amusing tale;
and each one was as kind
as possible to me until
my lodgings were arranged.
And then I recalled
times gone by,
and to my joy remembered
who this old lady was.

II   And I said, "You are
    that former shepherdess
who pulled such tricks on me."
And she said good-naturedly:
    "I'll cease my sport
of waging war on you."

"As far as I can see
your attitude still
deserves chastisement."
"Had I been easygoing
it would not have taken long
to find a purchaser."
"To a man seeking lodgings
you have to say such things."
"But Sir, I am a neighbor
of that lover I don't love."

III   "Worthy woman, how
       a lover must desire
a young girl like you!"
"Good Heavens! He wants
       me as his wife,
but my mind's not yet made up."
"This might be your chance
to leave a life of poverty,
if he's a man of means."
"Sir, we could be well off,
except that I know him to be
the father of seven children."
"Then you'll be well served
by his oldest sons."
"No Sir, for none is more
than ten years old."

IV   "Foolish woman, you're
       giving up a lesser
evil for one yet worse."
"But it's still wiser than
       letting the heart
lead one into trouble."
"You're making a mistake,
and I'm sure that you'll
be dead within a year."
"Sir, you see before you
her who is my only comfort,

my only source of joy."
"Worthy woman, it would
seem she is your daughter."
"Sir, near La Ilha
you met us both before." [5]

V   "Then perhaps she could make
       amends for all
the wrongs you've done me."
"Before you make any plans,
    let's wait and see
how her husband feels."
"Worthy woman, I see
that your tricks are
just the same as ever."
"En Guiraut Riquier, I am
annoyed that you continue
writing such light songs."
"As for you, old age has
turned your singing bitter."
"Sir, do you think that age
has left you unaffected!"

VI   "Worthy woman, I did not
       think you'd curse me so.
Or are you making fun of me?"
"Sir, how can you think
    I would harbor
any ill intent towards you?"
"Since I'm in your house,
you must be kind
and tolerant with me."
"Sir, I have no desire
to reproach
or annoy you."
"Lady, how could you, if I
cannot stop loving you?"
"Sir, however that may be,
I shall always honor you."

VII   "May our discussion please
         the noble Count of Astarac [6]
     whom all should praise."
     "Sir, his boundless merit
         makes everyone speak
     of him with great affection."
     "Lady, if he comes here, will
     you give him a proper welcome?"
     "Sir, you'll doubtless hear
     what I intend to do."

3

I   I should refrain from singing,
     for songs must spring from joy,
     and I am so besieged by sorrow
     that pain assails me on every side.
     And when I think upon my grievous
     past, look to the harsh present,
     and worry for the future,
     I see only cause for tears.

II   Thus my songs can have for me
     no flavor, for they are joyless;
     God has so fashioned me that
     in singing I retrace my folly,
     good sense, gaiety or displeasure,
     what harms me or does me good—
     only thus can I speak well; yet
     even then I was born too late.

III   In noble courts no calling is now
     less appreciated than the fine art
     of poetry, since men prefer
     to hear and see frivolity,
     and cries uttered amid dishonor;
     for that which should be praised

has sunk into oblivion,
and we're surrounded by deceit.

IV   Through ill will and pride of so-called
Christians, who know not love
nor follow the commands of God,
we've been expelled from His Holy Place
and been disgraced in other ways;
thus are we punished
for our immoderate desires
and our excessive pride.

V   We should fear the grave peril
of the double death awaiting us:
that of defeat by Saracens
and of abandonment by God;
yet because of the hatred arisen
in our midst, we'll soon be conquered.
It would seem that our leaders
take their duties all too lightly.

VI   May He in whom we believe exists
unity, power, wisdom and good
give light to His works
by which sinners may be purified.

VII   Lady, Mother of charity,
obtain for us, through pity
of your Son, our Redeemer,
grace, pardon and love.

General Bibliography

Bibliographical Guides

The standard list of Provençal poets and poems and all the books thereon is Pillet and Carstens, *Bibliographie der Troubadours,* Halle, 1933. This has been brought up to date by the lists in Vol. II of Frank's *Répertoire Métrique* (see below under Metrics). To complete Frank's bibliography, the reader can consult pages 55–69 of Lommatzsch's *Leben und Lieder der provenzalischen Troubadours,* Vol. I, Berlin, 1957 (this is an anthology whose main usefulness is its bibliography).

Histories of Troubadour Poetry

The standard work on this subject is Alfred Jeanroy's *La Poésie lyrique des Troubadours,* 2 vols, Toulouse and Paris, 1934. But a word or two must be said about this book because of its enormous influence on almost all subsequent troubadour scholarship. It is complete, entirely reliable (factually speaking) and absolutely indispensable to anyone wanting to study the subject seriously. On the debit side, however, is the sad fact that Jeanroy, who spent the better part of his lifetime studying the troubadours, not only misunderstood but intensely disliked an important (and perhaps the most important) part of their poetry. (If such a statement should seem surprising, I suggest the reader look at what so eminent a scholar as Leo Spitzer has said on the subject in his *L'Amour lointain de Jaufré Rudel et le sens de la poésie des troubadours,* Chapel Hill, N.C., 1944, pp. 40–44.) It is a tragic situation, not only that a man's lifetime work should have been so misdirected, but also because Jeanroy's vast reputation (which in so many ways is justified) has done such an effective job of reburying Provençal literature.

In addition, several shorter literary histories are useful:

E. Hoepffner, *Les Troubadours,* Paris, 1955. This covers only the major figures.

J. Anglade, *Histoire sommaire de la littérature méridionale au moyen âge,* Paris, 1921. Covers *all* of medieval Provençal literature.

A. Jeanroy, *Histoire sommaire de la poésie occitane des origines a la fin du XVIIIᵉ siècle,* Toulouse-Paris, 1945. Covers all forms of poetry to 1800.

R. Briffault, *Les Troubadours et le sentiment romanesque,* Paris, 1945. Biased and not altogether reliable, but stimulating.

In many ways the best scholarly outline of troubadour poetry is that found in the introduction to Riquer's *Lírica* (see below under Anthologies).

For the English reader, Ezra Pound's writings on the subject have a special interest. There are three essays in *The Spirit of Romance* ("Il Miglior Fabbro," "Provença," and "Psychology and Troubadours"), his translations of Arnaut Daniel in *The Translations of Ezra Pound,* other renderings sprinkled through *Personae,* and finally the innumerable references to the troubadours in the *Cantos.* As with so many of Pound's multifarious activities, these writings vary enormously in quality. Generally he is best when interpreting the troubadours in the light of his personal and remarkable poetic insight, and weakest when he tries to be scientific and objective. But however great this variance may be, there is no justification whatever for scholars having so totally ignored his writings till now.

Origins

Trying to orient the reader among the enormous mass of literature that has grown up around this aspect of Provençal literature is an almost hopeless task. If, however, he is mad enough to want to go into it, the *only* objective book I have read on the subject is Le Gentil, *Le Virelai et le villancico. Le problème des origines arabes,* Paris, 1954. But let the reader be warned: the author has very wisely chosen to limit severely his field of operation, so much so that he only tackles a small specific portion of the problem, and although excellently written, this book is dense and difficult to read. Yet it is a model of what such a book should be, and furthermore its very complete bibliographies are the best guide I know in this distressingly complicated subject.

Metrics

Although not a book *on* metrics, but rather a catalogue of all
the forms used by the troubadours, there is the remarkable and
indispensable work by the late István Frank, *Répertoire Métrique
de la poésie des troubadours,* 2 vols., Paris, 1953–1957.

Language

The standard dictionary that everybody uses is the excellent
Petit dictionnaire Provençal-Français by Emil Levy, which (I
think) has recently been reissued by Carl Winter in Heidelberg
(it is undoubtedly inexpensive). For more detailed scholarship
there are the two monumental works by Raynouard, *Lexique
Roman,* 6 vols., Paris, 1838–1844 (available in a modern reprint)
and Emil Levy, *Provenzalisches Supplement-Wörterbuch,* 8 vols.,
Leipzig, 1894–1924 (so named because it was designed as a sup-
plement to Raynouard's dictionary).

As for grammars, the most complete is Joseph Anglade's *Gram-
maire d l'Ancien Provençal,* Paris, 1921 (still available and cheap).
Although briefer and harder to come by, O. Schultz-Gora's *Altpro-
venzalisches Elementarbuch,* 5th ed., Heidelberg, 1936, is somewhat clearer and more manageable. Also excellent and widely used
by students are the grammars contained in the anthologies of
Bartsch-Koschwitz, Appel, and Crescini (see below under Anthologies). Appel's is completed by his *Provenzalische Lautlehre,* Leipzig, 1918.

Anyone interested in studying the present-day language will find
an excellent list of books on the subject in P. L. Berthaud and J.
Lesaffre, *Guide des études occitanes,* Paris, 1953.

Anthologies

Among the dozens and dozens of anthologies that have appeared,
I will give only the most important.

First of all there are those intended primarily for philology students—that is, with good grammars and glossaries, variant readings,

few notes and no translations. Of these, the three classic works
are:

Bartsch & Koschwitz, *Chrestomathie provençale*, 6th ed., Mar-
burg, 1904;

Appel, *Provenzalische Chrestomathie*, 6th ed., Leipzig, 1930;

Crescini, *Manuale per l'avviamento agli studi provenzali*, 3rd ed.,
Milan, 1926.

For the more general public, the two anthologies that, from a
critical point of view, stand head and shoulders above the other
are:

André Berry, *Florilège des Troubadours*, Paris, 1930 (seventy-
six poems with French translations and notes).

Martín de Riquer, *La Lírica de los trovadores*, Barcelona, 1948
(113 poems with Spanish translations and notes). Unfortunately
only Vol. 1 has appeared, covering the twelfth-century poets, but
I have been told that the entire work is to be reissued in a single
volume covering all the troubadours.

Of these two, the first is more popular in tone and focussed on
troubadour verse more purely from an aesthetic point of view; the
second is more scholarly and, for the ground it covers, more
complete.

Other anthologies I can recommend are:

Jean Audiau, *Nouvelle anthologie des troubadours*, Paris, 1928
(eighty poems with French translations). This book, however, is
somewhat marred by Lavaud's not too reliable notes in the back
(he was entrusted with completing the book after Audiau's tragic
death at the age of twenty-nine).

A. Serra-Baldó, *Els Trobadors*, Barcelona, 1934. A small anthology (forty poems) with translations and notes in Catalan (which
is liable to be of little help to the English-speaking reader), but
very intelligent and reliable.

Cavaliere, *Cento liriche provenzali*, Bologna, 1938. I have not
been able to see this book, but I know that it is highly regarded.

Piccolo, *Primavera e fiore della lirica provenzale*, Florence, 1948
(eighty-five poems with Italian translations and notes). Accurate
and reliable.

Roncaglia, *Venticinque poesie dei primi trovatori*, Modena, 1949.
Covers only the early poets. No translations, but excellent vocabulary and bibliographies.

Gennrich, *Lo Gai Saber*, Darmstadt, 1959. No translations, some
notes and German glossary—but with a good selection of music.

Nelli and Lavaud, *Les Troubadours*, 2 vols., Paris-Brussels, 1961–
1966. Useful because it covers *all* of medieval Provençal literature,

including the epic and didactic poems. But the portion containing the lyric poetry (in Vol. II) is taken over lock, stock and barrel from the above-mentioned edition of J. Audiau and is thus more than somewhat out of date.

For the English-speaking reader there is:

H. J. Chaytor, *The Troubadours of Dante*, Oxford, 1902 (forty-six poems). No translations, but extensive notes, vocabulary and even a small grammar of the language. Although perhaps now a bit outdated, this superb little book is still the best thing to have appeared in English.

R. T. Hill and T. G. Bergin, *Anthology of the Provençal Troubadours*, New Haven, 1941 (and since reprinted). A huge selection (154 pieces) with no translations, a few strangely desultory notes and a complete glossary. Although not as reliable as its appearance would suggest, it is useful chiefly because it covers so much ground.

Music

All the troubadour melodies have been edited by F. Gennrich in *Der Musikalische Nachlass der Troubadours*, 3 vols., Darmstadt, 1958–1965. In spite of being the last word in thorough, up-to-date scholarship with exhaustive bibliographies, the music is transcribed according to the "modal" method (see Introduction, p. 26), with the same often awkward results that are beginning to disturb scholars more and more.

For reference purposes, the reader can consult the two standard histories of medieval music in English whose bibliographies will lead them to other works: Dom Anselm Hughes, *Early Medieval Music up to 1300*, London and New York, 1954 (this is Vol. II of the *New Oxford History of Music*); and Gustave Reese, *Music in the Middle Ages*, New York, 1940.

A good glimpse of what scholars are now thinking on the subject of how to transcribe these troubadour melodies is provided by J. Chailley's article in the review called *Romania*, Vol. LXXVIII (1957), pp. 533–538.

Biographies

For years the standard edition of the *vidas* and *razos* was that published by Chabaneau in Vol. X of the *Histoire Générale de*

Languedoc (see below under History). Then in 1950 new editions began coming thick and fast. In that year there was the first edition of J. Boutière and A.-H. Schutz's *Biographies des Troubadours.* Then came Favati, *Le biografie trovadoriche,* Bologna, 1961, which I haven't seen but which was roundly criticized by other scholars. Now finally we have the second edition of the above-mentioned Boutière and Schutz (Paris, 1964) with French translations and extensive notes, which I'm sure will be the standard edition for years to come.

History

Trying to orient the reader in this maze is a task at which I quite frankly throw up my hands. The main problem is that there is no general history of southern France in this period; it's all too often treated as a mere adjunct of French, English or Spanish history, or we get limited regional histories of specific areas of Occitania. As for the "adjunct" histories, the best I know (and they are really excellent) are in Catalan. Both are by Jordi Ventura: *Alfons el Cast,* Barcelona, 1961, and *Pere el Catòlic i Simó de Montfort,* Barcelona, 1960. In English there is also Amy Kelly's very readable *Eleanor of Aquitaine and the Four Kings.* As for the regional histories, there is Devic and Vaissète's monumental *Histoire générale de Languedoc,* 16 vols., Toulouse, 1872–1904, but this is not a connected history in the modern sense; it is more a vast compilation of documents and miscellaneous facts to be dipped into for reference purposes.

The best I can do, therefore, is to suggest that the reader consult the bibliographies in the back of Ventura's two books and those sprinkled about in two works by Joseph Calmette: *Le monde féodal,* Paris, 1951, and *L'élaboration du monde moderne,* Paris, 1949 (Volumes IV & V in a collection called Clio).

For the important subject of the Catharist heresy and the Albigensian Crusade, there is a complete booklist in P. de Berne-Lagarde, *Bibliographie du Catharisme Languedocien,* Toulouse, 1957.

Notes

The notes are, I hope, self-explanatory, except perhaps those on the poems themselves. For reference purposes, with each poem I give the first line and then a number preceded by the word "Pillet." This number refers to a very handy cataloguing system by which one can instantly find the poem in Pillet and Carsten's *Bibliographie* and in Vol. II of Frank's *Répertoire Métrique* (see above under Bibliographical Guides), and thereby find out where else it has been edited. After this, for those poems to which we have music, appears a Gennrich number by which the reader can find the transcription in Vol. I and the notes and bibliography in Vol. II of his *Nachlass* (see above under Music).

Introduction

1. I am here referring to critics whose aim was to reach the general literate public, and not to Provençal scholars (of which there have been a good many) whose works were directed to other specialists. For Chaytor and Pound, see pages 236 and 233.

2. This is the kind of generalization that sets musicologists' teeth on edge. To be sure, we have polyphonic music from earlier periods, but it consists of examples from theoretical treatises in which the authors seem to be speculating about possibilities rather than discussing music actually performed. The first extensive manuscript we have of music in this latter category is the Winchester Troper, which dates from the middle of the eleventh century. Then towards the end of the century we start getting the remarkable tropers from Saint-Martial of Limoges.

3. We must not forget that one of the leaders of the First Crusade was the Count of Toulouse, Raymond of Saint-Gilles.

4. Even though geographically and historically it is safe to call the Languedoc the heart of Occitania, we must not forget that many of the greatest troubadours came from Aquitaine, and spe-

cifically from the Limousin (Arnaut Daniel, Giraut de Bornelh, Bertran de Born, Bernart de Ventadorn and others).

5. Raymond Berenguer IV had become Count of Barcelona in 1131, and then annexed Aragon by marrying Peronella, the daughter and heiress of the last king, Ramiro the Monk. Through her mother, incidentally, Peronella was the granddaughter of the first troubadour, William IX of Aquitaine.

6. Agde and Nîmes were ruled by a collateral branch: Bernard-Aton V (1129–1159) and his son, Bernard-Aton VI (1159–1214).

7. For anyone who wants to check on all these brothers and nephews, there is a good genealogy with dates of rule in Jeanroy's *Poésie Lyrique,* Vol. 1, p. 189.

I should also, perhaps, give a brief outline of what happened in Montpellier between 1202 and 1204, since it might look a bit confusing on the chart. William VIII died in 1202 leaving an only daughter, Maria, as heiress. Two years later she divorced her husband (the Count of Comminges) and married Peter II, thereby bringing Montpellier to the house of Aragon.

8. This is, of course, only part of the story. Perhaps more important was the fact that now, with the rise of the fairs of Champagne, that great cradle of later medieval commerce, France could begin to compete economically with the English crown and with Occitania.

9. The great Saint Bernard of Clairvaux, for instance, had tried, with notable lack of success, to preach among them.

10. During his siege of Toulouse, a woman on the walls threw a stone that struck him on the head—an act of divine justice if there ever was one.

11. One scholar, Jean Mouzat, has conjectured that four poems attributed to other troubadours, and one anonymous poem, might actually be by Eble of Ventadorn (*Cultura Neolatina,* XVIII (1958), pp. 111–120).

12. It is interesting to note how all these patrons died within the short space of ten years. Barral of Marseille in 1192, Raymond V of Toulouse in 1194, Ermengarde of Narbonne in 1194 or 1197 (she had resigned her rule in 1192), Alfonso of Aragon in 1196, Richard the Lionhearted in 1199 and William VIII of Montpellier in 1202. Roger II of Albi-Béziers-Carcassonne, although not such a patron of troubadours, also died in 1194; his wife, Adelaide of Toulouse (whom the troubadours referred to as the Countess of Burlatz), died in 1199 or 1200.

13. One of the greatest of troubadour scholars, Stronski, said on this question: "Ne cherchez pas de femme. These songs are dis-

sertations on love, not expressions of love. It is high time we abandoned fantastic ideas on the role of 'free love' or of more or less idealistic 'love cults' among southern French society in the troubadour period. Ordinary common sense played about the same role then as it has in any other epoch, and a body of poetry with such overtones would not have been patronized, or even tolerated." (Page XI of his edition of Folquet de Marseille—see the bibliography under that poet.)

In a different vein, an amusing story is told about the painter Matisse which could serve as a nice little parable on this subject. One lady, horrified by a painting of his of a woman with a green face, said to him, "Wouldn't it be horrible to see a woman walking down the street with a green face?" "It certainly would," Matisse replied. "Thank God it's only a painting!"

14. But keep in mind what I said on p. 17 and in the previous note about this adultery being essentially a poetic fiction.

15. A very handy dictionary of *senhals*—and in general of all the women who appear in troubadour verse—is Fritz Bergert's *Die von den Trobadors genannten oder gefeierten Damen*, Halle, 1913.

16. This is the end of Cercamon's Poem 1, p. 43.

17. At this point I can imagine someone already familiar with troubadour verse saying, "Yes, but what about Bernart de Ventadorn?" Here was a poet who said:

> Singing is worthless unless
> it arises from within the heart.

Now the first thing we must realize is that Bernart de Ventadorn is an exception among troubadours, and a strong one; it is not, as romantic critics tried to maintain, that all the other troubadours are out of step with him. Secondly, we must realize that this sincerity is, perhaps to a large extent, a part of the literary framework of a highly conscious artist and therefore somewhat on the same order as Arnaut Daniel's "games" with words, sounds and rhymes. It is, if you will, a device—his device; and the greatness of his poetry resides in his having found words adequate to this intensity of feeling, and thus ultimately, like Arnaut Daniel, rests on language. Thirdly, we must remember that Stronski's dictum (see note 13 above) applies equally to Bernart de Ventadorn; even his poems are not expressions of personal love but dissertations on love. And lastly, we mustn't forget that even he had moments of being fed up with the whole machinery of courtly love (see his Poem 8, p. 98).

18. Perhaps these notions would have withered of their own accord had it not been for the vast influence of Jeanroy (see p.

232), who at the inexcusably late date of 1934 gave them a new lease on life. One result has been that as recently as 1952, an otherwise intelligent and meticulous scholar, Walter Pattison (see the bibliography under Raimbaut d'Orange), could criticize that poet for lacking "sincerity" and being "artificial."

This situation is all the more surprising when one realizes that the first critic to break the ice was Berry (see p. 235), four years *before* Jeanroy's great work! But perhaps because of the "popular" nature of this anthology, it has been too long in being recognized for the important work it was.

Winds of change, however, have been blowing quite strongly in the last twenty years or so, and especially from Italy, to the pleasant point where judgments such as Jeanroy's are now considered in that country as little more than historical curiosities.

19. In discussing variety of techniques, we should mention the two schools of *trobar leu* (literally "easy poetry") and *trobar clus* ("closed or hermetic poetry"). The first is self-explanatory; the second (also called *trobar ric*) is that in which verbal (or conceptual) girations made the poetry difficult to understand. The classic example of *trobar leu* is Bernart de Ventadorn; that of *trobar clus* is Arnaut Daniel. For an interesting debate between Giraut de Bornelh and Raimbaut d'Orange on the subject of these two styles, see p. 104.

20. Anyone curious to see how these "modal" transcriptions sometimes differ from one another will find three scholars' versions of the same piece (Giraut de Bornelh's "Reis Glorios"—p. 126 of this anthology) printed together in Archibald T. Davison and Willi Apel's *Historical Anthology of Music*, Harvard, 1949, p. 15. If the reader's thirst for variety is still not quenched, he can find yet a fourth version in Gennrich's *Musikalische Nachlass* (see the General Bibliography under Music), Vol. I, p. 65.

William of Aquitaine

Bibliography

We possess eleven poems of William of Aquitaine, but the music only to part of one of them. The standard edition is Jeanroy, *Les Chansons de Guillaume IX, Duc d'Aquitaine*, 2nd ed., Paris, 1927 (in a series called "Classiques Français du Moyen Age"). It is cheap and still available; its only disadvantage is that the more ribald (and hence amusing) passages are left untranslated.

In addition, a large bibliography has grown up around William of Aquitaine, and the reader can find a list of the more important works in Riquer's *Lírica de los Trovadores,* pp. 4–5.

1. The Provençal biography adds another sentence about William's descendants, but it is so confused and full of misinformation that it is best left out.

2. This passage occurs towards the end of Canto VIII.

Poem 1: *Companho, faray un vers tot covinen* (Pillet 183, 3; Gennrich 287)

This poem is based on a *double entendre* apparently quite common in the Middle Ages. Jeanroy (in his *Origines de la Poésie Lyrique en France,* p. 52) quotes another poem in which a certain Jean de la Tournelle complains that a rich man stole from him a horse he used to ride night and day.

3. Confolens (as it is now spelled) is a town about thirty miles northwest of Limoges.

4. *En* for men and *Na* for women (both of which contracted to *N'* before a name beginning with a vowel) were titles of distinction very much like the modern Spanish *Don.*

5. Gimel is five miles northeast of Tulle, in the foothills of the Massif Central—hence the "highland" breed. Nieul (in its modern spelling) is the village "down there below" (thirteen miles southwest of) Confolens.

Poem 2: *Farai un vers, pos mi sonelh* (Pillet 183, 12)

6. In the interest of truth, it is only fair to mention that two of the four manuscripts in which this poem is preserved give the figure as a mere eighty-eight. These two lines, incidentally, turn up in the Pound *Cantos,* at the beginning of Canto VI.

7. In one manuscript, in place of the last two lines there is another stanza which at least has the advantage of satisfying one's sense of justice. (The Monet of the first line, by the way, is undoubtedly the name of a jongleur.)

> Monet, ride off in the morning,
> and take my poem in your satchel
> straight to the wives of En Garin
>   and En Bernart,
> and tell them, for the love of God,
>   to kill that cat.

Poem 3: *Farai un vers de dreyt nien* (Pillet 183, 7)

This is the first example we have of a type of poem called a *devinalh,* or "riddle." The last two lines are undoubtedly a request for the friend in Anjou to send (presumably also in verse) the key to the riddle. One critic (Scheludko) has suggested that the key might be "dreams."

8. One of the two manuscripts in which this poem is preserved inserts another stanza between VI and VII. Not only is it dull and banal, but Jeanroy considers it apocryphal.

Poem 4: *Ab la dolchor del temps novel* (Pillet 183, 1)

Here we have William of Aquitaine in a more serious vein (but even then he can't repress a slight leer—see the end of Stanza IV). In any case, this is by far his loveliest poem, and the image in Stanza III is justifiably famous.

9. Bon Vezi ("Good Neighbor") is a *senhal,* or pseudonym, for the lady in question.
10. This is apparently a set phrase meaning "we have everything we need."

Poem 5: *Pos de chantar m'es pres talentz* (Pillet 183, 10; Gennrich 7)

Scholars have concluded that this poem was probably written in 1117, just before the excommunication on William (the "burden" of Stanza VIII) was lifted. The "exile" to which he refers in Stanza II is probably a trip to Spain to fight the Moors and/or to go on a pilgrimage to Santiago.

11. The son is the future William X, born in 1099.
12. This is Foulque V the Younger, Count of Anjou from 1109 to 1129, and later King of Jerusalem (1131–1144). He was a "relative" in that he was the brother of William IX's first wife and therefore step-uncle of William X.
13. These various furs were a symbol of the noble, courtly life.

Cercamon

Bibliography

We possess only seven poems definitely ascribable to Cercamon, and none of them with music. The best edition is by Jeanroy, *Les Poésies de Cercamon,* Paris, 1922 (in the "Classiques Français du Moyen Age"), a book that is inexpensive and still available.

1. For *pastorelas* see p. 22 of the Introduction, as well as the note on Poem 5 of Marcabru (p. 247). The second sentence of the biography is a taking apart of his name—*cercar,* "to go about, to search" and *mon,* "world."

2. Another poem of his, however—*Quant l'aura doussa s'amarzis* ("When the gentle breeze turns bitter")—is better known and appears in many anthologies. Its opening stanza with a description of autumn is charming, but the rest of the poem is somewhat of a bore. In any case, Pound translated it among a group of poems called "Langue d'Oc" in *Poems from Lustra* (reprinted in *The Translations of Ezra Pound*).

Poem 1: *Ab lo temps qe fai refreschar* (Pillet 112, 1b)

This poem is preserved in only one manuscript, and the scribe who copied it must have been suffering from indigestion, for there are a dozen or so places that don't quite make sense, have a syllable missing or something else wrong. Jeanroy tried to "emend" the text, and I have chosen the alternate course of trying to make do with what we have. The latter method has the advantage of avoiding some pitfalls merely to fall into others.

Marcabru

Bibliography

We have forty-one poems of Marcabru, and four of them with music. For years the standard edition has been that of Dejeanne, *Poésies complètes du Troubadour Marcabru,* Toulouse, 1909. But now a new edition is being prepared by the Italian scholar, Roncaglia, who has already published a good many individual poems in two periodicals called *Studi medievali* and *Cultura neolatina* (which I haven't been able to see). What we know about his life and the chronology of his poems is summed up in an article by P. Boissonnade in *Romania,* Vol. XLVIII (1922), pp. 207–242.

But this is only a fraction of the bibliography that has grown up around Marcabru; a good summary of the rest can be found in Roncaglia's little anthology, p. 27.

1. Audric del Vilar (probably from Auvillar, on the south bank of the Garonne, halfway between Montaubon and Agen) was a man who exchanged a biting *tenso* with Marcabru.

2. Panperdut: literally "Lost Bread." As in present-day Rousillon, this epithet probably meant "a simple-minded or useless person," the implication being that even the bread you might give him would be wasted.

3. See Poem 3, Stanza VIII, where he bemoans his death.

4. A word more about Marcabru's language. He is probably the most difficult of all the troubadours. Jeanroy says in his *Poésie Lyrique,* "Diez admitted that of his poems he understood scarcely a quarter; Suchier, forty-six years later, confessed to similar ignorance; and although today we have all the elements of a critical edition and excellent interpreters have applied to this poetry all the resources of their intellects, we cannot boast of having made any appreciable conquest into this unknown territory." But even Marcabru himself seems to have had some difficulties along these lines, for he says in one poem:

> It will be a wise man
> who can understand my song,
> what each word means
> and how the argument unfolds,
> for I myself have trouble
> clearing up obscure passages.

5. This is the opening stanza of our Poem 2.

6. And minor poets such as Bernart Marti.

Poem 1: *Dirai vos en mon lati* (Pillet 293, 17)

This poem (and the same can be said of the next one too), with its strong and somewhat crude language, with its peasant wisdom, its complaints about the world's going to pot, and its derisive sneers at cuckolded husbands, is typical of Marcabru's output.

Poem 2: *Dirai vos senes duptansa* (Pillet 293, 18; Gennrich 9)

7. That is to say, if its evil consequences were removed.

8. For some reason beyond my comprehension, scholars always leave out this stanza, even though it is found in five of the eight manuscripts containing the poem.

9. This stanza is singularly frustrating. It might well contain the key to Marcabru's misogyny, yet we know no more than what he

states here. (For a similarly tantalizing mystery, see Jaufre Rudel, Poem 4, Stanza VI and the note pertaining to it.)

Poem 3: *Pax in nomine Domini* (Pillet 293, 35; Gennrich 11)

This is Marcabru's famous crusading song, usually called the "Vers del Lavador" because of the refrain word which ends the sixth line of every stanza. It was written (probably in 1137—see note 15 below) to incite Christians to fight the Saracens in Spain and to persuade them that this was as worthy an enterprise as that of fighting Saracens in the Holy Land.

Since the music to this poem has also become well known, I will give it along with the words of the first stanza:

10. This line appears in Ezra Pound's Canto XXVIII.

11. *Lavador* means literally "washing place." The idea being, of course, that in fighting the Saracens (and avenging God) one's sins will be washed away.

12. The companion being Liberality.

13. The "adversary" is the devil (as also in the next-to-last line of Stanza VI).

14. The Emperor is Alfonso VII of Spain (1126–1157).

15. The marquis is Raymond-Berenguer IV of Barcelona, who was also Marquis of Provence. The next phrase is a reference to the Knights Templars.

16. The count is William X of Aquitaine (1127–1137), son of a troubadour and father of Eleanor. He is mourned in Antioch because his brother Raymond was Prince of Antioch.

Poem 4: *A la fontana del vergier* (Pillet 293, 1)

This lovely and touching work is very unlike Marcabru's usual poetic mood. Here he depicts the grief of a young girl whose lover has left for the Holy Land. It was undoubtedly written around the time of the Second Crusade (1146 or 1147).

17. This is Louis VII of France, leader of the Second Crusade.

Poem 5: *L'autrier jost' una sebissa* (Pillet 293, 30; Gennrich 10)

Since none of Cercamon's *pastorelas* "in the old style" (see his biography) have come down to us, this is the oldest *pastorela* we have. It has considerable spice and charm, particularly in the peasant girl's sharp-tongued answers. Pound, incidentally, translated most of the poem in *The Spirit of Romance* (in the chapter called "Proença").

The fourth line of each stanza in the original ends with the word *vilana,* and I have therefore used a similar device in the translation.

Poem 6a: *Estornel, cueill ta volada* (Pillet 293, 25)

Poem 6b: *Ges l'estornels non s'oblida* (Pillet 293, 26)

This pair of poems served as a model for Peire d'Alvernhe's similar pair about the nightingale (see p. 70). But here, instead of the delicacy and restraint of the later version, the language is often harsh and the sense of realism strong. With a remarkable disregard of courtly conventions, we see the lover as distrustful and suspicious and the woman as a sort of courtesan full of wiles and charms.

The mention of Lérida (in Stanza III of the second poem) shows that it was written after that city was captured in 1149, and thus near the end of Marcabru's career.

18. Unfortunately we know nothing about this not too celibate and undoubtedly colorful abbot of Saint Privat.

19. Namely, the good abbot.

Jaufre Rudel

Bibliography

We only possess six poems definitely ascribable to Jaufre Rudel, and four of them with music. The standard edition is that of Jeanroy, *Les Chansons de Jaufré Rudel*, 2nd ed., Paris, 1924 (in the "Classiques français du moyen âge"). It is inexpensive and still available. Two other editions (which I haven't been able to see) have since appeared: M. Casella, *Jaufré Rudel, Liriche* (in Il Melagrano), Florence, 1945, and S. Battaglia, *Jaufre Rudel e Bernardo di Ventadorn, Canzoni* (in Coll. Speculum), Naples, 1949.

For further bibliography the reader can consult page 48 of Roncaglia's anthology.

1. For Blaye, see further on. As for the title of Prince, it was common in that region simply as a synonym for "lord" (of a castle or town).

2. This biography has been the principal source of Jaufre Rudel's fame outside the world of Provençal letters; it was used by many of the romantic poets—Uhland, Heine, Carducci and Swinburne among others.

3. This question has been the subject of endless discussion on the part of specialists, discussion that, in my opinion, is fruitless and inconclusive. But it still sputters on, in spite of one critic's having stated over fifty years ago that "we are floating in a sea of uncertainty." Even if this biography's only value were its psychological and spiritual truth, which is undeniable, that would suffice to make it an important document.

4. A propos of these *paubres motz*, see what I say under Bernart de Ventadorn, p. 84.

5. The arguments about this aspect of Rudel far exceed in quantity those over his biography. But here too "we are floating in a sea of uncertainty."

Poem 1: *Lanquan li jorn son lonc en may* (Pillet 262, 2; Gennrich 12)

In the original of this poem, the word *lonh* ("far away") comes at the end of lines 2 and 4 of each stanza, and I have therefore done the equivalent in the translation. Because this is Jaufre Rudel's most famous poem, I shall give the music (along with the words to the first stanza).

Lan - quan li jorn son lonc en may

M'es belhs dous chans d'au-zelhs de lonh,

E quan mi suy par - titz de lay

Re - mem-bra·m d'un' a - mor de lonh;

Vau de ta - lan em - broncx e clis

Si que chans ni flors d'al - bes - pis

No·m platz plus que l'y - verns ge_____ latz.

Poem 2: *Quan lo rius de la fontana* (Pillet 262, 5; Gennrich 14)

Yet another poem about Rudel's distant love; less vague and elusive than Poem 1, and rather more down to earth. In fact,

Appel, who tried to maintain that this distant love was the Virgin Mary, was slightly embarrassed as to how to interpret the end of Stanza II.

6. Filhol (literally "Godson") is the name—or nickname—of a jongleur. Hugo Bru—Hugh the Swarthy—is probably Hugues VII of Lusignan, who took part in the Second Crusade. Envoys such as this, having no visible connection with the rest of the poem but passing out compliments to patrons, were common in troubadour verse. Incidentally, the word "romance" in line 3 of this stanza simply refers to the Provençal language (as opposed to Latin).

Poem 3: *Belhs m'es l'estius e·l temps floritz* (Pillet 262, 1)

Commentators have understandably shied away from this poem because it is by far the most enigmatic of Rudel's works; in spite of this, it is perhaps his greatest poem. It is obviously written as the result of some personal tragedy (the biggest enigma of all—that of Stanza VI—I have already discussed above), and perhaps because he is now "rid of his mad burden" as he says in the last line, his verse takes on a solemnity and a coherence of language and imagery previously lacking. But its meaning is still unfathomable in certain places: aside from the major mystery of Stanza VI, Jeanroy himself was not sure what lines 3 and 4 of Stanza V meant, and he admitted to being totally baffled by Stanza VII. So rather than indulging in personal conjectures as to what these obscure passages are all about, I have preferred translating them fairly literally and letting the reader judge for himself.

Peire d'Alvernhe

Bibliography

We possess about twenty poems of Peire d'Alvernhe, and only one of them with music. They have recently been carefully and intelligently edited by A. del Monte, *Peire d'Alvernhe, Liriche,* Torino, 1955.

1. That is, Clermont-Ferrand, the capital of the Auvergne (hence the poet's name).

2. Or in other words, beyond the Pyrenees, into Spain.

3. This is the opening line of our Poem 3.

4. For Giraut de Bornelh, see p. 114. For the distinction between

canso and *vers,* see p. 21 of the introduction and also the biography of Marcabru (p. 44).

5. This is, with considerable variants, Stanza XIV of our Poem 4.

6. The Dauphin of Auvergne was both a celebrated patron of the troubadours and a poet in his own right. As for this biography as a whole, it is interesting to note that it appears at the head of five important troubadour manuscripts.

7. It is only fair to warn the reader that these dates are a surmise on my part, based on the following: we know he was a client of Spanish monarchs in 1158, and it seems reasonable to assume that he could only have achieved such a status if he had already become well known; or in other words that his poetic career began about ten years earlier. This is also supported by the biographer's statement that he died old. In addition there are some documents in Montpellier dating from the 1140s mentioning a Peire d'Alvernhe, who could well be our poet. (For a discussion of these, see Pattison's *Raimbaut d'Orange,* p. 24, note 50. As he rightly points out, the whole matter is in considerable need of further investigation.) I have mentioned all this since, because of Peire d'Alvernhe's innovating role, it is important to try to fix the beginnings of his poetic career.

8. Pillet 323, 24. This poem can be read either in the del Monte edition (p. 108) or in Riquer's *Lírica de los Trovadores* (p. 204). This boasting on Peire d'Alvernhe's part brought on a strong counterattack by a rather embittered minor poet, Bernart Marti, a disciple of Marcabru. (See E. Hoepffner, *Les Poésies de Bernart Marti* in the "Classiques français du moyen âge," Paris, 1929. The poem is printed on p. 14.)

9. Concerning his technical mastery, one detail must be pointed out, and that is his extraordinary control of syntax, of using long sentences as a device for giving unity to his poetic form. An outstanding example of this is our Poem 5, in which Stanzas IV through XIII are all one sentence—thereby converting most of the work into one long arc or breath. This same poem is also an example of another way in which Peire d'Alvernhe was important as an innovator. He was the first troubadour to write religious poetry, a vein in which he seems to have been quite as capable as in his love poetry.

10. This lack of appreciation of Peire d'Alvernhe's greatness and importance has surely been one of the major blunders of Provençal scholarship. The first one to break the ice, if somewhat timidly and with evident concern about stepping on others' toes, has been del Monte in his edition. He takes the all-important step of trying

to understand what the Middle Ages was all about and judging Peire d'Alvernhe in his proper milieu. To the intelligent reader such an approach might seem rudimentary, but it was precisely this step that Jeanroy and his followers never bothered to take. In short, for anyone who wants to understand Provençal poetry and get it in its proper perspective, there would be nothing better than getting del Monte's edition of Peire d'Alvernhe and carefully digesting the whole thing, poetry, introduction, notes and all.

Poem 1: *Rossinhol, el seu repaire* (Pillet 323, 23)

In form and framework this poem is an imitation of Marcabru's about the starling (see p. 56), but in tone it is very different; instead of the realism and strong language of the older poet, here everything is grace and delicacy.

Poem 2: *Chantarai pus vey qu'a far m'er* (Pillet 323, 12)

Now for the first time we come to the pure poetry characteristic of the great troubadours and of which Peire d'Alvernhe was such a master. Here the content is largely conventional, and everything hangs on the poet's diction and sensibility.

11. This opening stanza is famous for its statement of the poet's beliefs, of the struggle between the need for singing and the painful labor of "making it new" as Ezra Pound put it.

In the original some variation of the word "song" (*chantarai, chant,* etc.) appears in each line of this stanza, and I have therefore attempted a similar device in English.

12. This beautiful lark image resembles the opening of Bernart de Ventadorn's famous poem *Quan vei la lauzeta mover* (see p. 91), but it is here used to express a kind of fluttering ecstasy (note the movement: the trembling leaves, and the falling sunbeams contrasted with the rising bird) as opposed to the longing and nostalgia of the other poem.

Poem 3: *Dejosta·ls breus jorns e·ls loncs sers* (Pillet 323, 15; Gennrich 36)

This, along with the next one, is the most famous of Peire d'Alvernhe's poems (note its mention in the biography), and Jeanroy states that for a long time it remained one of the classic specimens of the courtly lyric.

But its beauty almost completely defies transposition into another language. Even more than the previous poem, it relies

on a marvelously controlled and restrained diction combined
with a lovely interweaving of sound (using such devices as
alliteration and related rhymes) and meaning. Perhaps the
reader can get some glimpse of this from the first stanza
printed under the music below.

But here too, there are difficulties. This is the only music
we have of Peire d'Alvernhe (and of a man whose melodies,
the biography states, were the finest ever written), and yet it
has come down to us in quite garbled form. It is contained in
only two manuscripts and these two versions differ so widely
as to present scarcely the same melody. The only solution is to
flip a coin and write down one of them.

De - jo - sta·ls breus jorns
e·ls loncs sers, Quan la
blanc' au - ra bru - ne - zis, Vuoill
que branc e bruoill mos sa - bers
D'un nou joi qe·m fruich' e·m flo - ris;
Car del doutz fuoill vei clar-zir los gar-rics,
Per qe·s re-trai en-tre·ls e - nois e·ls freis
Lo ros - si-gnols e·l tortz e·l gais e·l pics.

13. In the Middle Ages green was the symbol of youth (as it still is), and white that of being in love (also, of course, of purity).

14. There are two mysteries here. Firstly, is this the Aldric del Vilar mentioned in Marcabru's biography (see p. 44) and with whom Marcabru exchanged poems? And secondly, is Audric the villain (as I have translated it), or is he merely the recipient of the poem (in which case the line should read, "Audric, let that villain know . . .")? Unless some historian succeeds in investing the phantom of Audric with flesh and blood, this line will always remain more than somewhat of a puzzle.

Poem 4: *Cantarai d'aqestz trobadors* (Pillet 323, 11)

Here we have Peire d'Alvernhe in a very different vein. This poem, however, was as famous as the previous one (it is also mentioned in the biography), and it was done the honor of being imitated by the Monk of Montaudon (see p. 185). After considerable discussion by scholars, it now seems fairly well-established that it was not only written, as the poet states, in Puivert (for which see note 21 below), but also in the autumn of 1170.

In addition, it was probably written to be recited in the presence of the poets and jongleurs mentioned, and is therefore not to be taken as a piece of literary criticism but rather as a kind of gentle spoofing—a poetic parlor game. And anything is grist for the mill, whether it be the physical, biographical or literary idiosyncrasies of the people in question.

I haven't given the whole poem because the interest of such a work lies in references to people we know something about. Those in the omitted verses are people whose literary or historical profiles are either nonexistent or so dim as to be of interest only to the specialist.

15. Like Peire d'Alvernhe, Peire Rogier was from the Auvergne and also gave up a church career to become a troubadour—a change which Peire d'Alvernhe seems to think was a mistake. He wrote between 1160 and 1176, and frequented the courts of Ermengarde of Narbonne, Raimbaut d'Orange (see note 19 below) and Alfonso of Aragon.

16. This stanza on Giraut de Bornelh (for whom see p. 114) seems to be a parody of various passages of his poetry, as for instance:

I worry so
that I grow thin and dried out.

Or when he doesn't want his poetry to be obscure, but simple, so that it can be sung by everyone, and he says:

> I like to have my sonnet sung
> by raucous, clear voices,
> or hear it carried to the well [i.e. by women watercarriers].

17. For Bernart de Ventadorn, see the biography on p. 82, and especially note 2 where this stanza is discussed.

18. The Limousin from Brive is probably the jongleur connected with Bernart de Ventadorn. They exchanged a *tenso*, and he is mentioned again at the end of another of Bernart's poems—see Appel's big edition of Bernart de Ventadorn, Poems 15 and 45.

19. This Raimbaut is undoubtedly Raimbaut d'Orange, for whom see p. 100.

20. This line about the frog in the well only appears in one group of manuscripts; another group has

> is such that he sings high and low

which, according to many scholars, is the preferable reading. Preferable or not, it is distinctly more banal.

21. Puivert is a little village about thirty miles southwest of Carcassonne, dominated by the still imposing ruins of the medieval castle in which this group probably gathered.

Poem 5: *Dieus, vera vida, verais* (Pillet 323, 16)

> This is Peire d'Alvernhe's finest religious lyric and, with its alliteration and remarkable syntax (for which see note 9 above), an excellent example of how he could control poetic diction.

22. The story of the Centurion and his servant is in Matthew 8: 5–13 and also in Luke 7: 1–10.

23. Archetriclinus, which in the King James Bible is properly translated as governor or ruler of the feast, was thought to be a proper name in the Middle Ages, that of the husband in the marriage of Cana (John 2: 8–9).

24. According to the legendary lives of the saints, Luke painted the Virgin's portrait.

25. An allusion to the story of Moses and Aaron before Pharaoh. Aaron cast down his rod and it turned into a serpent. Then Pharaoh's wisemen and sorcerers did the same and their rods also

turned into serpents, "but Aaron's rod swallowed up their rods." (See Exodus 7: 8–13.)

26. This is apparently a reference to the miracle of the quail in Exodus 16: 13.

27. The story of Saint Peter's deliverance is told in the Acts of the Apostles 12: 7. The last two lines are an allusion to Christ's prophecy of Peter's crucifixion (see John 21: 18–19).

Bernart de Ventadorn

Bibliography

We possess forty-one poems definitely attributable to Bernart de Ventadorn (eighteen of them with melodies), all of which were splendidly edited by Carl Appel in *Bernart von Ventadorn, Seine Lieder,* Halle, 1915. Appel later edited a selection of twenty poems (*Bernart von Ventadorn, Ausgewählte Lieder,* Halle, 1926)—a volume that is rather useless, but which has the advantage of being cheap and still available. Since then two other selections have been published, one by Battaglia with twenty-seven pieces (see the bibliography under Jaufre Rudel), and another by Ghezzi with twenty-five pieces (*La personalità e la poesia de Bernart de Ventadorn,* Genoa, 1948). In addition, an excellent selection of twenty pieces can be found in Riquer's *Lírica de los Trovadores.* (Of these last three works, I have only been able to use the Riquer.)

1. One can still see the ruins of this castle near the town of Egletons, twenty miles northwest of Tulle.

2. This information, as a version of the biography contained in another manuscript admits, is gleaned from Stanza IV of Peire d'Alvernhe's famous satire (see p. 77). And one can't escape the dreadful suspicion that Peire wasn't as interested in facts as he was in trying to find rhymes to go with Ventadorn—no easy stunt—and lit on *dorn* ("palm"), *arc d'alborn* ("laburnum bow") and *forn* ("oven"), two of which Bernart had already used in another poem where he was up against the same problem (No. 12 in the big Appel edition).

3. In this sentence and the next one the biographer has undoubtedly confused two viscounts of Ventadorn—Eble II (who lived at least until 1147) and Eble III (who ruled from then to 1169). The first of these—the friend and contemporary of William

of Aquitaine (see p. 15 of the Introduction)—was referred to by Latin chroniclers as Ebolus Cantator (Eble the Singer), and they said of him that "he loved poetry to a ripe old age." Now if Appel's calculations are correct, Bernart must have been about twenty years old when he died, and therefore would have been brought up and trained under him. (In this connection, see Stanza IV of Poem 1 where Bernart refers to the "school of Eble.")

4. But this Viscount and wife must be of the next generation, because the older Viscountess could scarcely have been of an age to excite a young poet's amorous feelings. So here we undoubtedly have Eble III; but which of his two wives the biographer had in mind—Marguerite of Turenne or Alais of Montpellier—it is impossible to know.

5. There is a lovely reminiscence of this in the Pound *Cantos* (VI).

> 'My Lady of Ventadour
> 'Is shut by Eblis in
> 'And will not hawk nor hunt
>   nor get her free in the air
> 'Nor watch fish rise to bait
> 'Nor the glare-wing'd flies alight in the creek's edge
> 'Save in my absence, Madame.

6. Further confusion. This is undoubtedly Eleanor of Aquitaine, but she did not become Duchess of Normandy until she married Henry Plantaganet in 1152.

7. This is Henry of Anjou (and Normandy), who was crowned king of England in 1154. In spite of what the biographer says in the next sentence about Bernart staying behind, we can gather from his poetry that he accompanied the pair to England.

8. This is Raymond V of Toulouse, who died in 1194.

9. A Cistercian monastery about five miles northwest of Hautefort, the castle of Bertran de Born, who also retired there before dying (see p. 137).

10. Uc de Saint-Circ was a well-known thirteenth-century troubadour who apparently wrote several of these biographies. But here too there is a snag: the son of the Viscountess whom Bernart loved could only be Eble IV, whose death (around 1200) must have coincided quite closely with Uc's birth, thus making the latter a man with prenatal memory. However, he could have been exaggerating for effect and actually gotten the story from the grandson, Eble V. But by that time the information—at least that about Bernart's early life—was not exactly hot off the presses; it

was in fact about seventy years old. So all in all, it is difficult to know what to believe about what.

11. These are the opening lines of *Chantars no pot gaire valer* (Poem No. 15 in the big Appel edition).

12. This is why Bernart de Ventadorn is one of the few love poets among the troubadours appreciated by nineteenth-century scholars (and those whose existence in the twentieth century is more chronological than spiritual). For further remarks along these lines, see note 17 to the General Introduction (p. 240).

Concerning this aspect of his poetry, it's worth noting that Bernart's entire production is love poetry (or at least as much of it as has been preserved). Even his two extant *tensos,* or debates, are concerned with love.

13. Stanza V of Poem No. 27 in the big Appel edition (*Lonc tems a qu'eu no chantei mai*).

14. This is the opening of our Poem 4.

Poem 1: *Lo tems vai e ven e vire* (Pillet 70, 30)

> Appel, on the rather slim evidence of Stanza IV, believed this to be an early work written at Ventadorn; but it is difficult to believe that Bernart, at the beginning of his career, could have achieved such effortless mastery.

15. Undoubtedly a reference to Eble II "The Singer," for whom see note 3 above.

16. This is probably a reference to Psalm 84:10 (83:11 in the Latin Vulgate): "For a day in thy courts is better than a thousand."

17. In the preceding line, the word *arma* in the original can mean not only "grain, kernel" as I have translated it, but also "soul," and the idea behind this wordplay is that the body's existence, once deprived of the soul (here, the poet's love), becomes aimless and meaningless.

Poem 2: *Tant ai mo cor ple de joya* (Pillet 70, 44; Gennrich 291)

> It was formerly assumed that this poem was written in the early 1150s in praise of Eleanor of Aquitaine, after her departure to England. But recently a lot of dust has been kicked up over this (see note 19 below), and some scholars now favor a date some twenty years later.
>
> Concerning Bernart de Ventadorn's juxtaposing of joy and grief, notice how beautifully in this poem he makes the transition from one to the other at the end of Stanza III.

18. In the Middle Ages, Pisa was the stock symbol for wealth (like Croesus before and the Rockefellers since). For another example, see Peire d'Alvernhe's Poem 2, Stanza IV.

19. This may be the first reference in all of literature to the Tristan legend, but there is no way of being certain (much depends on whether we date this poem from the 1150s or the 1170s). In any case, in the last ten years an argument of occasionally startling violence has been raging over this and other possible first references. The last four lines of this stanza, incidentally, are quoted twice in Pound's *Rock-Drill*, Canto 93.

20. The *domna jauzionda* ("joyful lady") of the original is also quoted by Pound, in Canto VI.

Poem 3: *Pois preyatz me, senhor* (Pillet 70, 36; Gennrich 29)

This is yet another of the poems which Appel connected with the earlier English period of Bernart's production.

21. The thought behind these lines is that what others see is only a shadow of the poet, his real self being with his loved one.

22. "My Squire" is a *senhal*, or pseudonym, for a friend or fellow-troubadour.

23. *Aziman* (literally "diamond" or "magnet") was formerly assumed—on the basis of the biography—to be a *senhal* for Eleanor of Aquitaine. But as Appel pointed out, it's a little difficult to imagine a poet whose father was an archer and his mother an oven tender, addressing a queen as he does in Stanza IV of this poem, or as in another poem in which the same *senhal* appears:

> She would do wrong not to have me
> come there where she undresses.

Possible but unlikely. So all we can say is that this pseudonym must refer to some lady attached to the English court.

Poem 4: *Can vei la lauzeta mover* (Pillet 70, 43; Gennrich 33)

This is the most famous single poem in all of Provençal literature. As Jeanroy pointed out, it was admired even in faroff lands, where the language was scarcely understood. And the melody, which we give below, was as famous as the words; it has been found tacked on to French, Latin, German and Catalan poems.

Can vei la lau - ze - ta mo - ver
De joi sas a - las con - tral rai, Que s'o - bli - d'e·s
lais - sa cha - zer Per la dous- sor
c'al cor li vai, Ai! tan grans en- ve - ya m'en ve
De cui qu'eu ve - ya jau - zi - on,
Me - ra - vi - lhas ai, car des - se
Lo cor de de - zi - rer no·m fon.

24. Isolated lines from this first stanza (occasionally altered) turn up in various places in the Pound *Cantos*. Line 1 in Canto VI, line 3 in Canto LXXIV (*Pisan Cantos*), and line 4 at the opening of Canto 91 (*Rock-Drill*).

In a slightly less serious vein, one of the Provençal biographies contains an "interpretation" of this opening stanza which is, in its own way, a masterpiece of what can be produced by the literal, unpoetic and dirty mind. Discussing the poet's relations with the Duchess of Normandy (presumably Eleanor of Aquitaine), it says:

And Bernart called her "Lark" for love of a knight who was in love with her [sic!], and she called him "Sunbeam." And one day the knight came to the duchess and entered her room. When she saw him, she raised up the hem of her cloak, lifted it over her

*neck and threw herself back on the bed. And Bernart saw every-
thing, for one of the duchess' ladies-in-waiting had shown it all to
him in secret. And that was why he wrote the song which says,
"When I see the lark move."*

25. A reference to the myth of Narcissus, who fell in love with
his own image in a pool and vainly tried to embrace it.

26. This is an allusion to a medieval proverb about the fool who,
instead of dismounting and leading his horse over the bridge by
the bridle, stays on and topples into the water (bridges presumably being rickety affairs in those days).

27. Appel said it was impossible to know who lay behind the
senhal of Tristan: it could be a protector, protectress or friend.
Pattison has recently made a very intriguing case for its referring
to Raimbaut d'Orange (see the bibliography under that poet);
but to me his arguments aren't too convincing, and I still feel that
Appel's original scepticism is as far as we can go.

Poem 5: *Can par la flors josta·l vert folh* (Pillet 70, 41; Gennrich 31)

This poem and the one following, judging from the number
of manuscripts in which they are preserved, were almost as
popular in the Middle Ages as the preceding one. As Riquer
points out, however, this fact is in sharp contrast with their
almost total neglect in modern anthologies.

28. Pound quotes the last two lines of this stanza at the opening
of Canto XX.

29. This line would seem to indicate that Bel Vezer ("Lovely
Vision") and the lady of the poem are not the same person. All we
can gather about the former is that she must have been a patroness
of Bernart.

Poem 6: *Ab joi mou lo vers e·l comens* (Pillet 70, 1; Gennrich 16)

For a commentary on this poem, see the remarks above
under Poem 5.

30. These lines refer to the story in the *Iliad* and in Ovid's
Remedio Amoris of the lance given by the centaur Chiron to
Peleus, father of Achilles: its wound could only be cured by an-
other wound from the same lance.

31. For Bel Vezer, see note 29 above.

32. One out of the twenty-one manuscripts containing this poem

adds another envoy of four lines; but since it might well be apocryphal, and in any case is very banal indeed, I have omitted it.

Poem 7: *Non es meravelha s'eu chan* (Pillet 70, 31; Gennrich 28)

In spite of a few rather silly passages (the horns in Stanza V and the bears and lions in Stanza VII), I give this work because of its importance in understanding Bernart's position as a poet. It is interesting to see Dante use rather similar terms in explaining how he was able to forge the *dolce stil novo:*

> . . . . I am one who, when
> inspired by love takes note
> and sets down the words it speaks within me.
> *Purgatorio,* XXIV, 52–54

33. This *senhal* (literally "My Courtly One") does not refer to the lady of the poem, but rather to some unknown patroness.

Poem 8: *Amics Bernartz de Ventadorn* (Pillet 323, 4 = 70, 2; Gennrich 35)

A *tenso,* or debate, between Bernart de Ventadorn and a certain Peire, who could be Peire d'Alvernhe, although this is by no means certain. It is entertaining because it shows Bernart in such a completely different light from that exhibited in the rest of his poems—so different, in fact, that some scholars have tried to deny his part authorship. But his name is there in the text itself, and we can only assume that he had moments of feeling rather fed up with the whole business of courtly love.

Raimbaut d'Orange

Bibliography

We possess forty poems definitely attributable to Raimbaut d'Orange (only one with music), all of which have been recently edited by Walter T. Pattison, *The Life and Works of the Troubadour Raimbaut d'Orange,* Minneapolis and London, 1952.

1. Orange is a town west of the Rhône, fourteen miles due north of Avignon, famous for its Roman ruins. It contains a triumphal arch and the best preserved Roman theater in the world.

Courthézon is five miles southwest of Orange, and it seems to have been Raimbaut's favorite place of residence.

2. The *senhal* "Jongleur" indeed does turn up in Raimbaut's poems, but no one knows who Maria de Vertfuoil is, or if this information concerning her can be trusted.

3. The Marquis of Busca belonged to the house of Montferrat (in northwestern Italy), but no one has been able to trace a daughter who became countess of Urgell (a town in the Pyrenees, just south of Andorra).

4. This and another poem (No. XVII in the Pattison edition) prove beyond a doubt that Raimbaut had relations with someone in Urgell, but who it was we don't know (Pattison avoids the whole question).

5. I can only sympathize with the reader who is a little puzzled by the phrase "with the back of his hand," but that indeed seems to be what the original says.

6. There follows another sentence about Raimbaut's descendants, but since it is dull and full of mistakes I have left it out. The fact of the matter is that he had no legitimate children, and his estates were inherited by his two sisters. As Pattison points out, however, he might well have had two illegitimate daughters, but we know nothing about them.

7. Omelas, fifteen miles due west of Montpellier, was a town of some importance in the Middle Ages, but today, as Pattison says, nothing remains but ruins, and its church is used as a sheepfold.

8. One's usual idea of a nobleman in the Middle Ages—one who, let us say, was lord of the town of X—is that of a man who owned everything and everybody in X and ruled it capriciously and autocratically. But the reality of the situation was often very different indeed. The only thing Raimbaut d'Orange held outright, for example, was Courthézon; but he held no more than bits and pieces of the other towns of which he was lord, and even these bits and pieces were either in pawn or had to be shared with some relative. For the reader interested in how this sort of thing actually operated in Raimbaut's case (and a specific case is often far more illuminating than a welter of generalizations), I highly recommend Pattison's chapter on Raimbaut's economic position.

9. We know at least that he was in relations with the slightly older troubadours Peire d'Alvernhe and Peire Rogier and with his contemporary Giraut de Bornelh. He must also have known Bernart de Ventadorn.

10. In the *planh* (lament), *S'anc jorn agui joi ni solatz* (Pillet 242, 65).

Poem 1: *Pois tals sabers mi sortz e·m creis* (Pillet 389, 36; Gennrich 37)

Like Bernart de Ventadorn's Poems 5 and 6, the popularity of this poem in the Middle Ages is in sharp contrast with its almost total neglect in modern anthologies.

In the original, the fifth line of each stanza ends in the word *lenga* ("tongue"), and I've therefore used the same device in the translation.

11. There is another four-line envoy which I've omitted because it is in only two of the eighteen manuscripts (and unreliable ones at that), is corrupt in its text and is not particularly interesting.

Poem 2: *Ara·m platz, Giraut de Borneill* (Pillet 389, 10a = 242, 14)

This is not only, as Jeanroy said, undoubtedly the oldest example of a literary controversy in a modern European language, but it touches on a subject that has been smoldering ever since then: should art be for the many or for the few?

But in order to explain Giraut de Bornelh's sudden surrender in Stanza VI, and Raimbaut's subsequent willingness to change the subject, it must be understood that the two men weren't arguing on an equal footing. Though Giraut de Bornelh was by then probably already more famous as a poet than Raimbaut d'Orange, he was nevertheless a professional troubadour and therefore dependent on the patronage of such men as Raimbaut; the latter, on the other hand, although a nobleman and a poet himself, was to a great extent dependent on the former to maintain his reputation as a patron. And this interdependence undoubtedly explains why they both carefully avoid letting the discussion degenerate into the insults which often accompanied such debates.

12. For *trobar clus,* which more or less means "obscure poetry," see the discussion in note 19 to the Introduction.

13. Years ago Kolsen, the editor of Giraut de Bornelh, advanced the theory (now generally accepted) that Linhaure was a literary nickname for Raimbaut d'Orange. It is based on a word-play between *aur* ("gold") and *Aurenga* ("Orange") and means literally "of golden lineage." The *Senh'en* preceding it is a title compounded of *Senher* and *En*, its nearest equivalent being the form of address used in Spanish letters, Señor Don.

14. There have been almost as many interpretations of this stanza as there have been editions of the poem. The manuscripts

present different versions and none of them are clear. The most sensible interpretation seems to be that of Jeanroy (followed by Riquer in his *Lírica de los Trovadores*), in spite of the fact that I have used Pattison's readings for the rest of the poem.

15. The red side of the shield was that shown to the enemy in combat.

16. This is undoubtedly the court of Alfonso II of Aragon.

Poem 3: *Escotatz, mas no say que s'es* (Pillet 389, 28)

An amusing nonsense poem—Raimbaut himself calls it a *No-say-que-s'es* ("Don't-know-what-it-is")—similar in tone to William of Aquitaine's Poem 3. But Raimbaut goes one step further; he throws a final monkey wrench in the works by making the last line of each stanza prose.

17. The words *vers* and *sirventes* are explained in the general introduction (p. 21). Of the *estribot* there are only two examples preserved in Provençal, and the reader will find one of them in Peire Cardenal's Poem 3 (p. 197).

18. "Jongleur" was a reciprocal *senhal* used by Raimbaut d'Orange, designating himself as well as a lady who was his confidante. If we are to believe the biography (a dubious enterprise) the lady in question was called Maria de Vertfuoil. As for the prose line, the original has *espatla* ("shoulder") instead of *espaza* ("sword"). The change was suggested by Riquer, and it must be admitted that it fits in far better with the obviously dirty meaning intended.

19. By this point it should be evident to the reader that the "deeds" referred to are not those performed on the field of battle.

Poem 4: *Assatz sai d'amor ben parlar* (Pillet 389, 18)

Another humorous poem, this one full of dubious advice as to how to get along with women.

20. Ie. without women.

21. Mon Anel ("My Ring") is a *senhal* for an unknown lady.

22. For the *senhal* "Jongleur," see note 18 above.

23. But Raimbaut was not a native of Rodez. This might be a hyperbole meaning that since his Ring Lady lives there, he too lives there in spirit; or it may be a sign of deference to the Countess of Rodez (for whom see note 25 below), a well-known patroness of the troubadours.

Poem 5: *Lonc temps ai estat cubertz* (Pillet 389, 31)

Anybody who has seen or read Wycherley's *The Country Wife* will be amused to see the same joke turning up here five centuries earlier.

24. As opposed to Raimbaut's body, which is not whole (*entier*).
25. Monrozier was one of the residences of the Counts of Rodez, and therefore the lady mentioned here is probably Agnes, wife of Hugues II of Rodez. The last line is ironic; his joy is by no means perfect (*entier*).

The Countess of Die

Bibliography

The Countess of Die's poems were first edited by Schultz-Gora in *Die provenzalischen Dichterinnen,* Leipzig, 1888, and then by Kussler-Ratyé in *Archivum Romanicum,* Vol. I (1917), pp. 161–182. All of them are also printed in Riquer's *Lírica de los Trovadores.*

1. Die is a town twenty-five miles southwest of Valence, in the foothills of the Alps.
2. Two of them belonged to a younger branch of the family of the Counts of Poitiers (and Dukes of Aquitaine) and had become Counts of Valentinois (the area around Valence): one died around 1188 and the other, his grandson, in 1226. Of the other three, one held lands around Narbonne and must have died around 1177; the remaining two are no more than names in documents— mere historical shadows.
3. There was not only the poet (Raimbaut III), but also his grand-nephew (Raimbaut IV) who died in 1218 and who, Pattison believes, also wrote poetry.

A good summary of what we know (or, to put it more accurately, what we don't know) about the Countess of Die and which of the various Williams of Poitiers and Raimbauts d'Orange the biographer might have had in mind, can be found in Pattison's edition of Raimbaut d'Orange (see the bibliography under that poet), pp. 27–30.
4. A fifth one—a dialogue with Raimbaut d'Orange—is usually

ascribed to her, but her participation in this poem is at best extremely doubtful.

Poem 1: *Estat ai en greu cossirier* (Pillet 46, 4)

This poem, with its frank passion and sensuality, is probably the Countess of Die's most striking work.

5. "In bed or dressed" is merely an epithetical way of saying "night and day."

6. *Flore and Blanchefleur* is a medieval romance, versions of which have turned up in almost every country in Europe, from Iceland to Hungary and Spain. It concerns two children whose attachment to one another blossoms into love, and how, as they grow up, they overcome the endless obstacles put in the way of their love.

Poem 2: *A chantar m'er de so qu'ieu no volria* (Pillet 46, 2; Gennrich 38)

A very touching poem, more or less in the form of a letter to her lover, in which the Countess pleads with him to treat her less harshly.

7. Heroes of a lost medieval romance also cited by Arnaut de Mareuil.

Giraut de Bornelh

Bibliography

We possess seventy-seven or seventy-eight poems ascribable to Giraut de Bornelh, and only four of them with music. They were all edited by Adolf Kolsen in his *Sämtliche Lieder des Trobadors Giraut de Bornelh,* Halle, Vol. I, 1910; Vol. II, 1935. There are valuable notes on the text and its interpretation in Kurt Lewent, *Zum Text der Lieder des Giraut de Bornelh,* Florence, 1938. His biography was done earlier by Kolsen in *Guiraut von Bornelh, der Meister der Trobadors,* Berlin, 1894. More recent is Bruno Panvini's *Giraldo de Bornelh, Trovatore del sec. XII,* Catania, 1949, which, in spite of a few interesting points here and there, is on the whole a remarkably useless book.

At last reckoning, all these works (except the Kolsen of 1894) were still available.

1. Excideuil is a town almost twenty miles northeast of Périgueux, and very near Bertran de Born's castle of Hautefort. Bornelh is very probably the modern hamlet of Bourney, about six miles northwest of Excideuil. As for the Viscount of Limoges, he was Ademar V who ruled from 1148 to 1199 and whom Giraut accompanied on the Third Crusade.

2. This repetition of three variations of the word "understand" in three lines is in the original, and perhaps not ·without reason: his poetry was as difficult for his contemporaries as it is for modern scholars.

3. The verb here, *aprendre,* could also mean "teaching." It's tantalizing that this passage is so ambiguous because it gives one of the few glimpses we have into how troubadours acquired their craft.

4. Ezra Pound had a somewhat different complaint about Giraut de Bornelh. In *The Spirit of Romance* he said, "Yeats gives me to understand that there comes a time in the career of a great poet when he ceases to take pleasure in riming 'mountain' with 'fountain' and 'beauty' with 'duty.' Giraut de Bornelh seldom reached the point where he ceased to take pleasure in the corresponding banalities. But one must not go too far to the other extreme in estimating him; allowance is to be made for the hostility of our time toward anything savoring of the didactic in verse; and long-windedness was no such crime in the Twelfth or Thirteenth Century as it is today."

Poem 1: *Ailas, com mor!—Quez as, amis?* (Pillet 242, 3)

A dialogue between Giraut de Bornelh and a friend (whom Kolsen suggested might be Raimbaut d'Orange) who tries to help him overcome his timidity. Note that Giraut de Bornelh was fond of using dialogue in his poetry, a device which reappears in several other poems printed here.

Poem 2: *Can lo glatz e·l frechs e la neus* (Pillet 242, 60)

This poem—which seems to have enjoyed a considerable reputation in the Middle Ages, judging from the number of manuscripts containing it—is rather unusual for Giraut de Bornelh in that it is an endless chain of similes.

5. Saying that someone was from Béziers seems to have been equivalent to calling him a dolt. See also note 6 below.

Poem 3: *Er'auziretz enchabalitz chantars* (Pillet 242, 17)

This poem also seems to have been well-known in the Middle Ages. Not only were its metric scheme and rhymes imitated by three other poets, but Dante in his *De Vulgari Eloquentia* cites it as a model of versification.

6. Here the people of Béziers are taken as a symbol of ingratitude (see also note 5 above). Note that if Panvini is right in dating this and the previous poem from 1171 and 1169 respectively, these sentiments about Bézierites could have some basis in fact. For (as I mentioned in the Introduction, p. 4) in 1167 the burghers of Béziers rose up and killed the Viscount, and then two years later Alfonso of Aragon helped the Viscount's son get his revenge by perpetrating a general massacre of the bourgeoisie.

7. I must confess to being rather perplexed by this passage. Could Giraut's looking out to sea, and saying four lines later that his lady is far from him, mean that this poem was written while he was "overseas"? If so, where and why? No other commentator has mentioned this possibility.

8. Lay brothers, those who took a simple vow instead of being ordained, were the ones given the more menial work in monasteries and therefore undoubtedly a somewhat downtrodden, dejected lot.

9. Linhaure, as we have already seen in note 13 on p. 264, was a nickname for Raimbaut d'Orange. Lers (or l'Hers as it is spelled nowadays) is a place on the banks of the Rhône just south of Orange which still contains the ruins of its medieval castle.

10. Joios was the name of Giraut de Bornelh's jongleur.

Poem 4: *Un sonet fatz malvatz e bo* (Pillet 242, 80)

This is a sort of *devinalh* (see William of Aquitaine, Poem 3, and Raimbaut d'Orange, Poem 3) in which the poet claims that unrequited love has driven him mad. This poem, along with another by Raimbaut de Vaqueiras, apparently inspired Petrarch's famous *Pace non trovo, e non ho da far guerra*.

11. We don't know who this Jaufré is; we can only suppose he was some contemporary character of dubious reputation.

12. The Cato mentioned here was a third- or fourth-century

Roman poet who wrote a book of maxims called *Disticha de Moribus ad Filium*. In the Middle Ages it was thought to be the work of the famous early Roman statesman, Cato the Elder, and was very widely read.

13. This line is so garbled in the manuscripts that, like Appel in his *Chrestomathie*, I have thought best to omit it.

Poem 5: *L'altrer, lo primer jorn d'aost* (Pillet 242, 44)

This is a *pastorela*, but a rather unusual one, in that here the peasant girl wants them to "lie together in the shade" and the poet will have none of it. Yet in spite of this somewhat unlikely situation, it is a poem of great charm and elegance.

14. Alès (as it is now spelled) is a town about twenty-five miles northwest of Nîmes.

15. The "yes" is that of consent in marriage.

16. La Louvière (in its modern spelling) is a village about twenty-five miles southeast of Toulouse, halfway between Castelnaudry and Saverdun.

17. Escaronha was probably the wife of Bernard, Lord of Isle-Jourdain.

Poem 6: *Reis glorios, verais lums e clartatz* (Pillet 242, 64; Gennrich 58)

This *alba*, or dawn song, is, in modern times at least, by far the most famous of Giraut de Bornelh's poems, and Riquer quite rightly calls it one of the loveliest gems in all of Provençal literature.

The first six stanzas are spoken by a friend who has spent all night guarding the lovers against surprise and is now warning them of the approaching dawn, and the last stanza (whose authenticity, by the way, some critics have questioned) is spoken by the lover himself.

Ezra Pound translated this poem twice, once quite literally in *The Spirit of Romance* (in the essay called "Proença"), and more freely but rhymed in *Personae* (as the first poem in "Langue d'Oc" in *Poems from Lustra*).

Since the music to this poem has gained almost as much fame as the poem itself, I will give it below:

Reis glo-ri-os, ve-rais lums e clar___ tatz,

Deus po-de-ros, Sen-her, si a vos platz

al meu com-panh si-atz fi-zels a-iu-da;

Qu'eu no lo vi, pos la nochs fo ven-gu-da,

Et a-des se-ra l'al - ba.

Poem 7: *Ges aissi del tot no·m lais* (Pillet 242, 36)

In spite of this being Giraut de Bornelh's best known poem in the Middle Ages (judging again from the number of manuscripts containing it, and also by the fact that its metric scheme and rhymes were imitated by three other poets), it has been totally neglected by modern scholars, and, to the best of my knowledge, it has never been printed except in Kolsen's edition of the complete works.

18. We know absolutely nothing about this Alamanda d'Estancs.
19. Hence the poet, like the robber, needs the company of a friend (the one mentioned at the beginning of the stanza).

Poem 8: *Per solatz revelhar* (Pillet 242, 55)

This poem is quoted by Dante to support his qualification of Giraut de Bornelh as an artist of "rectitude."
A word about the translation. The text relies on two words for which there are no exact English equivalents: *solatz* (which I have feebly rendered as "solace," but which actually means

a whole range of things—"diversion, amusement, joy, conversation, and companionship"); and *pretz* (which appears as "worth" in my translation, and which not only means that but also "value, merit and distinction").

20. This is Gui V (1199–1230), son of the Ademar of Limoges whom Giraut accompanied on the Third Crusade. Gui retook the castle of Excideuil in December 1211, and it is probably this event to which the *razo* refers. But Stanza VIII of the poem, in which Giraut states that his house was spared, directly contradicts the statement here about his books and clothes being robbed. This discrepancy has led most critics to dismiss the whole *razo* as nonsense. But its author, who was after all much closer to the events than we, must have had something in mind; but what in fact it was we don't know.

21. I have reestablished the stanza order clearly indicated in the manuscripts. Kolsen reverses IV and V.

22. This is a reference to the custom of remunerating jongleurs not only in money, but also in clothing and other accoutrements.

23. We know nothing about the story of the Goose of Bremar, except what Giraut de Bornelh and one other poet imply—namely that it was a pretty simple-minded tale.

24. This is the Dauphin of Auvergne, who was not only a patron of troubadours, but also a poet himself. His biography says that he was "one of the wisest, most courtly and most generous men in the world . . . and who knew more about love, gallantry and war" and so on.

In connection with this poem, it is interesting to note that Jeanroy says that towards the end of his long life (ca. 1150–1235) the Dauphin became the representative of an epoch that was gone forever.

Arnaut de Maruelh

Bibliography

We have thirty-one lyric poems definitely attributable to Arnaut de Maruelh, six of them with music. The standard edition is that of R. C. Johnston, *Les Poésies lyriques du troubadour Arnaut de Mareuil*, Paris, 1935; as the title of this book implies, it does not include the nonlyric poems such as the *ensenhamen* and the five *saluts d'amour*.

1. This is the modern Mareuil-sur-Belle, about halfway along the main road from Périgueux to Angoulême.

2. The Countess of Burlatz (so called because she was raised in the castle of that name about five miles northwest of Castres) was Adelaide of Toulouse, daughter of Count Raymond V. She married Roger II Taillefer, Viscount of Béziers and Carcassonne, in 1171, and died in 1199 or 1200. (See note 12 to the Introduction.)

3. In the one poem given here he cites the Marquis of Montferrat, and in several other poems he mentions a mysterious "Sir Genoese."

Poem 1: *Si·m destreignetz, dompna, vos et Amors* (Pillet 30, 23; Gennrich 54)

So that the reader can judge the gentle beauty and controlled diction of Arnaut's verse, I give below the first stanza of this poem. (I would give the music too, but the only manuscript in which it is preserved gives an incomplete version.)

> Si·m destreignetz, dompna, vos et Amors,
> c'amar no·us aus ni no m'en puosc estraire:
> l'us m'encaussa, l'autre·m fai remaner,
> l'us m'enardis e l'autre·m fai temer,
> preiar no·us aus per enten de jauzir;
> mas, si cum cel qu'es nafratz per morir,
> sap que mortz es e pero si·s combat,
> vos clam merce ab cor desesperat.

4. There is considerable confusion and mystery about this envoy. In the first place, like many envoys it varies from manuscript to manuscript, and the version given here is only one of several possibilities. In the second place we not only don't know who this "Precious Jewel" is, but we don't even know whether this *senhal* refers to the lady of the poem or to someone else—in which case it could even refer to a man. (In the original it is Belh Carboncle, which literally means "Lovely Carbuncle" in the sense of a precious stone.) The only reasonably certain thing in these three lines is that the Marquis of Montferrat was Bonifacio I (1188–1207).

Bertran de Born

Bibliography

Besides the thirty-nine poems we can definitely ascribe to Bertran de Born, there are five of doubtful attribution. Out of this total of forty-four, there is only one with music.

There have been five separate editions of his works. Three of them were done by Albert Stimming, in 1879, 1892 and 1913. The last of these, entitled merely *Bertran von Born,* appeared in the Romanische Bibliothek published by Max Niemeyer, Halle; it has a long historical introduction and good notes, all of which are very helpful. (At last reckoning it was, strangely enough, still available and very inexpensive.) Antoine Thomas, the French scholar who unearthed most of the contemporary documents concerning the poet, put out an edition called *Poèsies Complètes de Bertran de Born,* Toulouse, 1888. And lastly, Carl Appel published his *Die Lieder Bertrans von Born* in 1932, in a series called Sammlung Romanischer Übungstexte, also put out by Max Niemeyer, Halle. For the text this is the best edition, but unfortunately there are no notes, merely a glossary at the back. (It is also still available and cheap.) In addition the reader can consult L. E. Kastner's "Notes on the Poems of Bertran de Born" which appeared in *The Modern Language Review,* in the issues of 1932, 1933 and 1934.

The best general work on his life and historical role is Carl Appel, *Bertran von Born,* Halle, 1931 (not to be confused with his other book, above). For a mine of detailed and accurate information about the noble families in immediate contact with Bertran de Born, there is Stanislaw Stronski, *La légende amoureuse de Bertran de Born,* Paris, 1914 (the title is somewhat misleading).

In spite of this large bibliography (and this is only a fraction of what has been written on Bertran de Born), a great deal of work remains to be done. In the first place, none of the five editions listed above has translations, and in the second place the history of southwestern France during the later twelfth century is still very murky—both English and French historians treat it merely as an adjunct to their own histories.

1. Hautefort, as it is now spelled, is a castle about twenty-one

miles northeast of Périgueux, and very near Excideuil (see p. 268, note 1). Although completely rebuilt in the sixteenth and seventeenth centuries, it is still standing and commands a splendid view of the surrounding countryside.

2. The Count of Périgord was Helias VI Talairan (1158/66–1203), and the Viscount of Limoges was Ademar V (1148–1199). For the latter see also p. 268, note 1. Before becoming King of England in 1189, Richard the Lionhearted was made Count of Poitiers and Duke of Aquitaine in 1169 (although he was not formally installed in this position till 1172).

3. For Dalon, see note 9 on p. 257.

4. This is part of Stanza II of Poem 9.

5. These lines are from Stanza III of Poem 4.

6. These are the last two lines of Poem 3.

7. *Inferno*, Canto XXVIII, lines 118–142.

Poem 1: *Rassa, tan creis e monta e poia* (Pillet 80, 37; Gennrich 39)

8. These are the three oldest sons of Henry II and Eleanor of Aquitaine: Henry the Young King, Richard the Lionhearted and Geoffrey of Brittany. Rassa is one of the many examples in Provençal literature of a reciprocal *senhal* or nickname.

9. Concerning this lady, see note 17 below.

10. I have omitted a large section of this *razo* because it does little but summarize the last half of the poem.

11. These four names are explained in the *razo* at the head of the poem.

12. A vavasor was one of the lower grades of feudal nobility.

13. This is a sneer, first of all at those who spend their time hunting instead of fighting, and secondly at those cheapskates who use buzzards for their falconry.

14. Aigar and Maurin were the heroes of a Provençal epic poem, only fragments of which have come down to us. The Viscount and Count whom Bertran de Born is here trying to embroil are, respectively, Ademar V of Limoges and Richard the Lionhearted.

15. One of the biographies states that Marinier ("Sailor") is a *senhal* for Henry the Young King, but since Bertran de Born also uses it in two other poems clearly written after Henry's death in 1183, it seems likely that the biographer was mistaken. As for Golfier de las Tors (or de Lastours in modern French) he was the brother-in-law of Bertran's brother Constantin. For those who find that sentence confusing, here is a little genealogy:

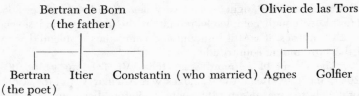

16. Papiol was the name of Bertran de Born's jongleur. The pseudonym Bel Senhor is a bit of a mystery. Most critics state that it refers to Maeut de Montagnac, but 1) this lady is herself somewhat of a mystery (see note 17 below), and 2) it is a little difficult to understand how this *senhal* could apply to the lady of the poem—or in other words why, after praising her to the skies, Bertran would call her wicked (*mal*).

Poem 2: *Domna, puois de me no·us chal* (Pillet 80, 12)

> This poem about the "borrowed" lady was imitated by two other troubadours (Elias de Barjols and Cerverí) and in our day was translated by Ezra Pound (in *Lustra*) after he had already written an earlier poem on the same theme ("Na Audiart").

17. There is considerable confusion concerning this Maeut of Montagnac. The author of the *razo* has either invented her out of whole cloth or confused her with Raymonda of Montagnac, who was a distant cousin (not sister) of Maria de Ventadorn and Aelis de Montfort and who married Helias Talairan, Count (not brother of the count) of Périgord. For this whole involved question see Stronski's *La légende amoureuse* cited above in the bibliography.

18. Here is what we know—or don't know—about this name and those in the rest of the poem:

Bel Cembeli ("Beautiful lure") is a *senhal* for an unknown lady.

Aelis is undoubtedly the Aelis de Montfort mentioned in the previous note.

The Viscountess of Chalais is Guiborc de Montausier, wife of Olivier de Chalais.

There was, to be sure, a viscounty of Rochechouart in the Limousin, but unfortunately we know of no Viscountess by the name of Agnes.

Audiart may be Audiart de Malamort, a companion of the Maria de Ventadorn mentioned in note 17 above.

Mielhs-de-Be ("Better than good") was a *senhal* for Guischarda de Beaujeu (from the Beaujolais wine region of Burgundy), wife of Archambaud VI of Comborn.

We have no idea to whom Faidida and Bel Miralh refer.

For Bel Senher and Papiol, see note 16 above.

Aziman ("Magnet") is probably a reciprocal *senhal* between Bertran de Born and the equally famous troubadour Folquet de Marseille. (See note 8 under Folquet de Marseille.)

Poem 3: *Lo coms m'a mandat e mogut* (Pillet 80, 23)

Recent research has pretty well proven that this poem was written in 1184 or 1185. The circumstances were these: in 1184 Alfonso of Aragon's brother, Sancho, who was Count of Provence, signed a treaty with Alfonso's enemies, the Genoese, thereby allying himself with Raymond V of Toulouse. This bit of treachery was soon cut short, however, when Alfonso in the spring of the following year removed Sancho from the government of Provence and made a pact with Richard the Lionhearted against Raymond of Toulouse. Sometime during all these troubles he undoubtedly attacked, or intended to attack Toulouse—and this military campaign was accompanied by another of propaganda almost equally intense. Alfonso got Peire Vidal (see his Poem 1) and Folquet of Marseille to write for him, while Raymond of Toulouse "urged and commanded" Bertran de Born to write this magnificent poem.

19. The Count is Raymond V of Toulouse, and Aramon Luc d'Esparro is apparently his messenger.

20. Hauberks were coats of chain mail, and actons were quilted jackets worn beneath the hauberks as padding.

21. There are three Montaigus (modern spelling) near Toulouse; it is unclear (and unimportant) which one Bertran de Born had in mind. The Prat Comtal ("Count's Field") and the Peiro ("Stone Step") were places in the immediate vicinity of Toulouse.

22. Cendal, ciclatoun and samite were expensive silk fabrics (the second often interwoven with gold) used in those days by the upper classes throughout Europe.

23. The various people and places in this stanza are:

The king is Alfonso of Aragon. Tarascon is here a symbol of Provence, which he had lost in 1184 (see the introduction to the poem above).

Mont Albeo is apparently the present-day farm of Montauberon, near Montpellier, the lord of which would therefore be William VIII of Montpellier.

In the next line we have Roger II, Viscount of Béziers, Carcassonne and Albi, and his cousin Bernard-Aton VI, Viscount of Nîmes and Agde.

Then comes Peter of Lara, Viscount of Narbonne (nephew of the great troubadour patroness, Ermengarde).

The Count of Foix is Roger-Bernard I; Bernardo is Bernard IV of Comminges.

Sancho is the brother of King Alfonso mentioned above in the introduction to the poem.

Poem 4: *Un sirventes on motz no falh* (Pillet 80, 44)

An extraordinary poem for its vividness and sense of immediacy, and a marvelous example of how Bertran de Born can get us interested even in his own petty squabbles.

24. The Viscount of Limoges was Ademar V. Since most critics agree in dating this poem from 1182 or 1183, the biographer has made a mistake in calling Richard king; he did not come to the throne till 1189.

I have omitted the second half of this *razo* because it is neither particularly interesting or informative.

25. The Viscount of Limoges and Richard the Lionhearted (see previous note).

26. Poetically this is a marvelous stanza, but what it's all about is a bit of a mystery. Guilhem de Gordo was lord of the castle of Gourdon, about twenty miles north of Cahors. As for the two viscounts, they might be Ademar of Limoges and Raymond of Turenne, but that is little more than a guess.

27. For Helias Talairan, Count of Périgord, see note 2 above. Lombards, the north Italian merchants established in towns throughout France in the Middle Ages, were the subject of continual sneers in the literature of the time.

28. Baiart is Bertran's horse (the name means "bay-colored").

29. A reference to the fable in which the peacock says, "Give me back my feathers."

Poem 5: *Si tuit li dol e·lh plor e·lh marrimen* (Pillet 80, 41)

This is a *planh* (or lament) for Henry the Young King, the oldest son of Henry II and Eleanor of Aquitaine, who died at Martel on June 11, 1183.

Unfortunately, however, there is no way of being sure that Bertran de Born wrote this poem. To state the problem briefly, it's preserved in three manuscripts, one of which attributes it

to him, another to Peire Vidal and a third to Richard de Ber-
bezill. And to confuse matters even more, we have another
lament on the death of Henry the Young King (*Mon chan
fenisc ab dol et ab maltraire*) which is definitely by Bertran de
Born.

But whoever wrote this one, it is surely one of the finest
planhs in all of Provençal literature. Pound translated it early
in his career (in *Personae*), and the first line turns up towards
the end of Canto LXXX and again at the beginning of Canto
LXXXIV.

One word about the form: in the original, the first, fifth and
last line of each stanza end respectively with the words *marri-
men, jove rei engles* and *ira*, hence the similar repetitions in
the translation.

Poem 6: *Puois lo gens terminis floritz* (Pillet 80, 32)

This poem, interesting enough in itself for its calumnies of
the King of Aragon, is almost more interesting because of the
razo that precedes it, with its famous (though perhaps apocryphal) account of an interview between Bertran de Born and
Henry II. The poem dates from 1184.

30. The people mentioned here are Henry II of England, his
eldest son whose death Bertran mourned in the previous poem, and
Alfonso II of Aragon.

31. A long and wildly inaccurate genealogy follows, attempting
to prove that the King of Aragon was descended in male line from
a mere lord of Carlat (a village in the southern Auvergne, seven
miles southeast of Aurillac). The only kernel of truth in this whole
matter was that Alfonso's grandmother was daughter and heiress
of the Viscount of Carlat and Milhau. But this kernel seems to have
been expanded into a fable that must have had considerable cur-
rency in southwestern France, for not only does Bertran de Born
seem to have believed it (see Stanza II of this poem), but a contemporary and otherwise reliable chronicler, Geoffroy de Vigeois,
also makes the same mistake.

32. A *lai* is a kind of poem which, formally speaking, ends the
way it begins. Hence the implication that the same thing will happen to King Alfonso's lineage. For its supposed origins in Milhau
and Carladès, see the previous note.

33. Tyre is here taken to mean the Holy Land, which in those
days was infested with adventurers and swindlers of all sorts.

34. For Sancho and the loss of Provence, see the introduction to
Poem 3 above. As far as we know, Jaufré III, Count of Roussillon,

was not dispossessed (this seems to be nothing but a smear on Bertran's part), but rather died a natural death in 1164, leaving his possessions to his son Guirard II, who died without heirs in 1172 and bequeathed all his lands to Alfonso of Aragon.

35. Vilamur (the modern Villemur) is a town about twenty miles north of Toulouse, but what events these lines refer to, nobody seems to know.

36. The King of Castrojeriz (a town in Spain about twenty miles west of Burgos) was Alfonso VIII of Castille (1158–1214). These lines allude to the homage done him by the King of Aragon for Saragossa.

37. The Roi Tafur ("the Brigand King") was the leader of a band of notoriously lawless Armenian soldiers who participated in the First Crusade, particularly in the siege of Antioch.

38. To understand these lines one must go back a way in Aragonese history. When Alfonso I the Battler, the last king of united Aragon and Navarre, died in 1134, his possessions were divided up. Aragon went to his brother, Ramiro II "the Monk" (1134–1137) (hence line 3 of this stanza), the maternal grandfather of Alfonso II; and Navarre went to a distant cousin, García Ramírez V (1134–1150) (the gentleman in line 1), who passed it on to his son Sancho VI "the Wise" (1150–1194) (the good King of Navarre in line 4). At no point was there any question of usurpation—this is just another smear on Bertran's part.

39. The good queen is Sancha, wife of Alfonso of Aragon and sister of Alfonso VIII of Castille mentioned in note 36 above.

40. Berenguer de Besalú was Raymond-Berenguer III of Provence, a brother of Alfonso of Aragon who was killed in an ambush near Montpellier in 1181. But saying that Alfonso was responsible for his death seems to be yet another smear without basis in fact.

41. In 1173 Alfonso II asked the Greek Emperor Manuel for the hand of his daughter Eudoxia, but by the time she arrived in Montpellier the following year, she found (undoubtedly to her vast surprise) that Alfonso had, in the meanwhile, married Sancha of Castille. Eudoxia was not sent packing, as Bertran says in one final nasty crack, but stayed and married William VIII of Montpellier.

Poem 7: *No puosc mudar un chantar non esparja* (Pillet 80, 29)

This poem, written in 1188, on the renewal of hostilities between Richard the Lionhearted and Philippe Auguste, is one of Bertran de Born's rare ventures into complex rhymes. In form it is an exact imitation of Arnaut Daniel's *Si·m fos Amors*

de joi donar tant larga and uses the same rhymes in *-arga,
-anc, -arc, -omba, -om, -er, -ens* and *-esta*. But Bertran de
Born, who was not so practiced a hand at such intricacies, admits defeat in the last line. Dante in his *De Vulgari Eloquentia*
nevertheless cites this work as a model of war poetry.

42. A mistake similar to the one pointed out in note 24 above;
if, as critics maintain, this poem dates from 1188, Richard did not
become king till the following year.

43. Pommels were the knobs or balls affixed to the tops of tent
poles.

44. Cahors is a city on the river Lot, and Cajarc is a town about
twenty miles upstream. Chinon is the famous castle twenty-seven
miles southwest of Tours in which Henry II apparently kept his
treasury. It was here that he was to die so miserably a year later.

45. Lusignan is a town about fifteen miles southwest of Poitiers,
seat of a noble family famous in the Middle Ages, members of
which became Kings of Cyprus. Bertran is here obviously comparing himself to wealthier and more powerful noblemen; but for
what noble family Rancon stands, I don't know. Today it is a mere
village twenty miles north of Limoges.

46. Gisors was an important castle forty miles northwest of
Paris. Because of its strategic position on the border between
France and Normandy, it was a continual bone of contention between the French and English Kings (the latter being also Dukes
of Normandy). Concerning the burning of the ship, Appel points
out that since the various streams converging at Gisors are all too
small to float anything much bigger than a rowboat, this whole
passage is probably to be taken ironically.

47. This abrupt change to a discussion of the difficulties Bertran
has suffered at the hands of his lady, is somewhat of a mystery.
All the critics I have been able to consult have kept a deathly, and
probably embarrassed, silence on this point. Could it be intended
humorously—as a preview of the defeat by Arnaut Daniel's rhyme
scheme to which Bertran admits at the end of the poem?

48. Treignac is a town on the Vézère, thirty miles southeast of
Limoges, whose castle belonged to the Viscounts of Comborn, a
family mentioned in several other poems of Bertran de Born. Papiol,
as we've seen before, was Bertran's jongleur.

49. Who this Rotgier was, nobody knows. For an explanation of
the last line, see the introduction to the poem above.

Poem 8: *Ar ve la coindeta sazos* (Pillet 80, 5)

The best introduction to this work is the *razo* preceding another poem, *Be·m platz quar trega ni fis* written in the same
year of 1194.

> When King Richard had made peace with Bertran de Born
> and had given him back his castle of Altafort, he took the cross
> and went overseas. And Bertran remained fighting with Aimar,
> the Viscount of Limoges, with the Count of Périgord and with
> all the other barons of the region. And . . . when Richard
> was on his way back [from the Crusade], he was captured in
> Germany, where he spent two years in prison and then finally
> bought his way out.
> And when Bertran de Born heard that the king was to be
> released from prison, he was overjoyed at the thought of the
> benefits he would receive from the king, as well as of the harm
> that would be brought to his enemies . . .

50. This line is missing in all four manuscripts in which the
poem is preserved.

51. The kings and great noblemen of this epoch had begun em-
ploying bands of mercenary soldiers, since what troops they could
collect by the usual means of feudal military service no longer
sufficed for their continual wars. Aside from the pillaging and destruction these mercenaries wreaked wherever they went (hence
the "highwaymen" in the first line of this stanza), men like Bertran
de Born also looked down on them because they fought for money.
(In addition, of course, the state of feudal anarchy which favored
smaller noblemen like him could easily be upset—and was soon to
be—by greater lords with enough resources to have paid troops.)

52. This, of course, is a reference to Richard the Lionhearted.

Poem 9: *Miei-sirventes vuolh far dels reis amdos* (Pillet 80, 25)

Most scholars date this poem from 1195, even though it's
not at all clear to what historical events concerning Richard
the Lionhearted (died 1199) or Alfonso VIII of Castille
(1154–1214) Bertran de Born is alluding. In any case, this
and the following work are by far the most remarkable war
poems I have ever read—they're perhaps unique in all of literature. And I say this in spite of Ezra Pound's understandably
wry crack that "this kind of thing was much more impressive
before 1914 than it has been since 1920."

Poem 10: *Be·m platz lo gais temps de pascor* (Pillet 80, 8a)

As extraordinary as this poem is (see my remarks above),

there is unfortunately no way of being certain that it is by Bertran de Born. To state matters succinctly, out of the fifteen manuscripts containing the poem, only five attribute it to him, and the other ten manuscripts divide their attributions among five other poets, thereby making the confusing nearly hopeless.

53. As we've seen before, Papiol is Bertran's jongleur, and Yes-and-No is Richard the Lionhearted.

Arnaut Daniel

Bibliography

We possess nineteen poems by Arnaut Daniel (the eighteen traditional ones plus one—of somewhat dubious authenticity—brought to light about twenty years ago), and only two of them with music. Two editions of his poems came out around the turn of the century: one in Italian—Ugo Angelo Canello, *La Vita e le opere del trovatore Arnaldo Daniello,* Halle, 1883; and a reworking of this edition in French by R. Lavaud—*Les Poésies d'Arnaut Daniel, reédition critique d'après Canello,* Toulouse, 1910. These have now been replaced by an up-to-date Italian edition—Gianluigi Toja, *Arnaut Daniel, Canzoni,* Florence, 1960.

For the English-speaking reader, there is a large selection (ten poems with the originals on facing pages) available in *The Translations of Ezra Pound.* But one should keep in mind what Pound himself said about these translations: "I have proved that the Provençal rhyme schemes are not *impossible* in English. They are probably *inadvisable.*" And unfortunately, these are among his least successful translations; preferable are those in prose contained in his essay on Arnaut Daniel called "Il Miglior Fabbro" (reprinted in *The Spirit of Romance*). They give a better feeling of the original and are occasionally even more poetic in their own way.

1. This is the modern Ribérac, nineteen miles west of Périgueux. For Arnaut de Maruelh, see p. 133.

2. That is, he received an education preparing him for an ecclesiastical career (cf. Peire d'Alvernhe and Arnaut de Maruelh).

3. The identity of these two people, in spite of considerable research on the part of scholars, remains a complete mystery.

4. This is the envoy of Poem 3, the original of which appears on p. 159.

5. For his friendship with Bertran de Born, see note 22 below. As for his attendance at the coronation of Philippe Auguste, see the envoy of Poem 1 and the corresponding note.

6. *Purgatorio,* Canto XXVI.

7. This is the line T. S. Eliot quotes in his dedication to *The Waste Land:* "For Ezra Pound, *il miglior fabbro.*"

8. Ie. Giraut de Bornelh.

9. A more or less literal translation of these lines is: "The bitter breeze clears the forked (or branched) copses, which (breeze), when gentle, thickens (them) with leaves, and keeps the joyous beaks of the branched birds (ie. the birds sitting on the branches) stammering and mute, (whether they are) in pairs or alone." Notice how this tortuous wording is so controlled and flowing in the original.

10. This is why I have only included three poems of his in this anthology. His finest poetry—like the lines quoted above—is literally untranslatable, and I have therefore limited myself to those poems of his which lose least of their charm when transposed into another language.

11. The poem originated in an argument over a delicate point of courtly love. Apparently a lady called Aja told a certain knight of Cornil that she wouldn't love him *si el no la cornava el cul,* where *cornar* means "to blow, as a trumpet," and *cul* is the same word as in French or Spanish. Being of a somewhat finicky nature, the gentleman from Cornil refused, whereupon two troubadours, Raimon de Durfort and Turc Malec, wrote poems accusing him of having transgressed the code of courtly love (according to which one had to do whatever one's lady demanded). Arnaut Daniel in his poem comes to the gentleman's defense, going into considerable physiological detail over the unpleasantnesses and dangers involved in carrying out such a command.

12. These are the lines quoted before, at the end of the Provençal biography. They form the envoy of our Poem 3.

Poem 1: *Doutz brais e critz* (Pillet 29, 8)

Pound quite rightly said that this was "perhaps the most beautiful of all the surviving poems of 'the better craftsman' . . . at least it seems to lose less of its glamor in translation."

13. An allusion to Vivien, nephew of Guillaume au Court-Nez in the epic poem *La Chanson de Guillaume.* Apparently famine

plays a certain role in the story. The "yawn and stretch" in the next line probably means "yearn and pine."

14. A reference to the story of the centurion who pierced Jesus' side with his lance and was cured of his blindness by the blood that issued from the wound.

15. An altered version of this line turns up in the middle of Pound's Canto VII:

> Lamplight at Buovilla, e quel remir.

(for Buovilla, see the biography above and note 3).

After this, in the Toja edition there follows another stanza which is clearly (from repeated rhyme words, from the context and from the manuscript tradition) an *alternate* to our Stanza V, and therefore to print both of them together as he does is surely a mistake.

16. If this poem dates from shortly after Philippe Auguste's coronation in 1180, as the envoy seems to state (see note 18), then the Byzantine Emperor would be Alexius II (1180–1183), the lord of Rouen, Henry II of England, and the King of Tyre and Jerusalem, Gui de Lusignan.

17. A rather mysterious stanza, both in the sudden change to politics and in meaning. The lord of Galicia is presumably the same as the Fernando in line 7 of this stanza, and would therefore be King Fernando II of Leon (1157–1180). The count's son, Raymond, could either be the future Raymond VI of Toulouse (son of Raymond V) or Raymond-Berenguer III of Provence (son of Raymond-Berenguer IV, Count of Barcelona). It would help if we knew which of these had gone on a pilgrimage (presumably to Santiago de Compostela in Galicia) and had a scrape with King Fernando en route.

18. Étampes is a town just south of Paris, and the "good king" would therefore be Philippe Auguste, who was crowned in 1180.

Poem 2: *Lo ferm voler qu'el cor m'intra* (Pillet 29, 14; Gennrich 91)

This is Arnaut Daniel's famous *sestina*, a form which he seems to have invented and which was to be copied by later troubadours and by Dante and other Italian poets.

This form involves a stanza of six (hence the name) lines ending in six refrain words which alternate in strict succession, capped by an envoy containing all six refrain words in the space of three lines. To make this clearer, here are the refrain words of the poem, written out under their respective stanzas:

I	II	III	IV	V	VI	Envoy
intra (enters)	cambra	arma	oncle	verga	ongla	
ongla (nail)	intra	cambra	arma	oncle	verga	
arma (soul)	oncle	verga	ongla	intra	cambra	
verga (rod)	ongla	intra	cambra	arma	oncle	ongla-oncle
oncle (uncle)	verga	ongla	intra	cambra	arma	verga-arma
cambra (chamber)	arma	oncle	verga	ongla	intra	cambra-intra

Note how this succession works. The refrain word in the first line of any given stanza goes to the second line in the following stanza, that of the second line to the fourth, that of the third line to the sixth, the fourth to the fifth, the fifth to the third, and the sixth to the first. Mathematicians will recognize a permutation group, and even the layman will notice that six is the maximum number of stanzas possible, since a seventh would mean a return to the first. A compressed envoy is therefore substituted.

A propos of what I said about Arnaut Daniel's humor, notice that the choice of refrain words (aside from their interesting sound relationships, *ongla-oncle, arma-cambra*) borders on the absurd in a love poem; notice also the first line of Stanza IV and the dirty second line of the envoy.

Because of its fame, I will give the first stanza of this poem along with the music.

Lo ferm vo - ler qu'el cor m'in - tra

No·m pot jes becs es - cois - sen - dre ni on - gla

De lau - sen - gier qui pert per mal dir s'ar - ma;

E car non l'aus batr' ab ram ni ab ver - ga,

Si - vals a frau, lai on non au - rai on - cle,

Jau - zi - rai joi, en ver - gier o dinz cam - bra.

19. As with the Spanish *carne y uña*, this expression is roughly equivalent to our "hand in glove."

20. That is, of course, his mother.

21. Among the many interpretations suggested for this line, the most likely seems to be that it refers to Aaron's rod, which was also a symbol of the Virgin Mary.

22. An Italian Rennaissance scholar, Giovanni-Maria Barbieri, quotes a commentary from a now lost Provençal manuscript which said that "Bertran de Born and Arnaut Daniel were such close friends that they called each other *Desirat* ('Desired')." One never knows how much one can rely on such scraps of information, but since there is nothing improbable about it, we can assume that Arnaut Daniel dedicated this poem to his great contemporary.

Poem 3: *En cest sonet coind'e leri* (Pillet 29, 10)

23. A city famous in the Epic Legends. According to one (*Anseïs de Cartage*) it was besieged by Charlemagne for seven years, finally captured and then retaken by the Saracens, who burned it to the ground and rebuilt it. Charlemagne once more besieged it, and as a result of his prayers to God and to Saint James, the walls crumbled and the city fell. From then on the city was deserted and pilgrims (at the time of *Anseïs*) could still see the ruins on their way to Santiago de Compostela. Another version (*Gui de Bourgogne*) tells much the same story, except that after its destruction by divine agency there formed in its place a lake full of large black fish (which probably represented the Saracens transformed by Charlemagne's curse). Modern scholars have identified it with a place near Ponferrada in northwest Spain.

24. "That makes it drown" is a very free rendering. The original has "that will not evaporate."

25. An allusion to lovers from an unknown romance or popular legend.

26. These are the lines quoted twice in the introduction; they are probably the most famous three lines in all of Provençal literature. Arnaut Daniel himself refers to them jokingly in another poem (*Ans qe·l cim*):

> I know so much that I can stop the incoming tide,
> And my ox is faster than a hare.

The Monk of Montaudon also refers to them in his satire against other troubadours (see p. 186). Even the words Dante puts in

Arnaut Daniel's mouth—*Ieu sui Arnaut* . . .—seem reminiscent of
this passage.

Peire Vidal

Bibliography

Of Peire Vidal we have some forty-seven poems (thirteen
of them with music). There have been three editions of his
complete works: the first by KarlBartsch, *Peire Vidal's Lieder,*
Berlin, 1857; then a reworking of this by J. Anglade, *Les
poésies de Peire Vidal,* Paris, 1913 (2d edition 1923, in "Les
classiques français du moyen âge"); and replacing both of
these, the recent edition by Avalle, *Peire Vidal, Poesie,* Milan
and Naples, 1960. On the poet and his works there is a useful
book by E. Hoepffner, *Le troubadour Peire Vidal, sa vie et son
oeuvre,* Paris, 1961. But a word of warning: the Avalle edition
is not only expensive, but has no translations. So for the student
merely interested in familiarizing himself with the poetry,
Anglade's edition might be preferable, in spite of its occasional
lapses.

1. Uc de Baux was not only nephew of the troubadour, Raimbaut d'Orange, but also son-in-law of Barral, Viscount of Marseille,
who was Peire Vidal's principal patron.

2. "To go overseas" was the usual medieval expression for going
on a crusade to the Holy Land.

3. The original is somewhat garbled here and could also be in-
terpreted to mean "sat on an imperial throne."

4. This is the Barral mentioned in note 1 above (he ruled Mar-
seilles from 1178 to 1192) and his first wife Adelaide (to mod-
ernize her name) of Roquemartine.

5. A reference to Richard the Lionhearted and his departure for
the Third Crusade (1190).

6. Raymond V, who died in 1194.

7. Pennautier (as it is now spelled) is a town just three miles
northwest of Carcassonne.But who this Loba is we don't really
know. The biographer of another troubadour, Raimon de Miraval,
says she was the daughter of Raimon de Pennautier and the wife

of one of the lords of Cabaret, but there are difficulties in the way of this identification as well as others that have been proposed. The Cabaret is a region just north of Carcassonne, the center of which is a group of three castles whose splendid ruins can still be seen near the modern village of Lastours. This region, incidentally, was a hotbed of Catharist heresy at the beginning of the thirteenth century.

8. It is because of this legend that Pound (in Canto IV) compares Peire Vidal to Actaeon, who having accidentally seen the goddess Diana while she was bathing, was changed by her into a stag and then pursued and killed by fifty hounds.

9. For Barral, see notes 1 and 4 above.

Poem 1: *Drogoman senher, s'ieu agues bon destrier* (Pillet 364, 18)

This poem is a companion piece to Bertran de Born's Poem 3 (the notes to which see for the details of the campaign which motivated these poems). Here Peire Vidal is turning out propaganda for Alfonso of Aragon (as opposed to Bertran's for the Count of Toulouse). First of all there is the element of *gap* or boasting with its marvelously absurd exaggerations. But even more important is the fact that the poet is apparently badly in need of a new horse.

10. *Drogoman*, which, like its English equivalent, means "interpreter," is undoubtedly a pseudonym for William VIII of Montpellier.

11. This Gui might well be the brother of William VIII of Montpellier, Gui Burgundion, who died in 1182.

12. Bérard de Mondesdier was the hero of an epic legend; he was considered the very model of courtliness.

13. The king is Alfonso II of Aragon. Balaguer is a town in Spain, northeast of Lérida. Autavès and Crau are regions just east of the Rhône, between Tarascon and the mouth of the river. As for the "highwaymen," the original has *rocinier* which means literally "men mounted on nags" and is intended as an insulting reference to the mercenary soldiers in the pay of the Count of Toulouse.

14. The *gravier* ("strand") was the river-bank facing the western walls of Toulouse. Aspe and Ossau (as they are now spelled) are two river valleys in the western Pyrenees; this was apparently the war cry of the Basque and Béarnais troops in the hire of the Count of Toulouse.

15. The most likely candidate for Na Vierna, a woman whom

Peire Vidal addresses in many of his poems, is Vierna de Ganges (or de Porcellet), half-sister of the Adelaide de Roquemartine mentioned in note 4 above. "Thanks to Montpellier" means, literally, thanks to the Lord of Montpellier, William VIII, who, it is understood, will give him the good horse, thereby permitting him to appear in battle as a knight, thereby permitting him to win his lady's favor, etc., etc.

Poem 2: *Ab l'alen tir vas me l'aire* (Pillet 364, 1)

A touching poem of yearning and homesickness—emotions somewhat unusual in twelfth-century poetry.

16. These were almost exactly the limits of the part of Provence ruled by the house of Aragon. Vence is a town on the Côte d'Azur, halfway between Nice and Antibes, and somewhat inland. The Durance is a river that flows into the Rhône just south of Avignon.

Poem 3: *Anc no mori per amor ni per al* (Pillet 364, 4; Gennrich 60)

A remarkable poem that starts off as a quite exceptionally beautiful love song, shifts to a crusading song and ends in an attack on Richard the Lionhearted for not yet having carried out his vow of going to the Holy Land (he took the cross in 1187 but didn't leave till 1190—which means that the poem was written some time in that interval) and for not having paid Peire Vidal the money he owed him! The reader should also keep in mind that the last envoy (Stanza VIII) is in only one of the twenty-three manuscripts containing the poem, and therefore was probably added later to thank Richard for finally carrying out his promises.

I must also warn the reader that this poem has come down to us in a good many different versions. For complicated reasons I have chosen one (closer to Anglade than Avalle) that seems to correspond to an older state of the poem (with the exception of the above-mentioned last envoy). It has a different order for Stanzas II–IV, omits a stanza before V, and omits a line in VII.

In any case, this marvelous tour-de-force seems to have enjoyed great popularity in the Middle Ages; not only is it contained in a large number of manuscripts, but its metrical scheme and rhymes were copied by ten other poets.

Since the melody to this poem is also very lovely, I will give it along with the first stanza.

Anc no mo - ri per a - mor ni per al,

Mas ma vi - da pot be va - ler mo - rir,

Quan vei la ren qu'eu plus am e de - zir

E re nom fai mas quan do - lor e mal,

No·m val be mortz, et an-car m'es plus greu,

Qu'en breu se - rem ja velh et ilh et eu

E s'ais-si pert lo meu e·l seu jo - ven,

Mal m'es del meu, e del seu per un cen.

17. This seems to be a reference to Darius III Codomannus, Alexander's opponent, who was abandoned by most of his men and was finally killed by those closest to him.

18. It was apparently an ancient belief that certain snow crystals when exposed to the sun's rays could produce fire.

19. A reference to the capture of Jerusalem by Saladin in 1187.

20. Before becoming King of England in 1189, Richard the Lion-hearted was Count of Poitiers.

Folquet de Marseille

Bibliography

The nineteen poems of Folquet de Marseille (along with ten others of doubtful authorship) were superbly edited by the Polish scholar (writing, thank God, in French), Stanislaw Stronski in *Le Troubadour Folquet de Marseille,* Cracow, 1910. This has recently been reprinted by offset (Geneva, 1968) at a ghastly price close to $20. But since this edition still remains a model of troubadour scholarship, since the poet is one of the greatest in the Provençal Pantheon, and since so few of his poems appear in modern anthologies (with the ridiculous exception of a rather lovely religious *alba* that Stronski proved quite conclusively couldn't be by Folquet de Marseille), it is a price that the market will just be forced to bear.

We still have the music to thirteen of these poems—a very high percentage of the total.

1. These are Richard the Lionhearted, Raymond V of Toulouse and the same Barral of Marseille who was the protector of Peire Vidal. For him and his wife, Adelaide of Roquemartine, who is mentioned in the next paragraph, see notes 1 and 4 under Peire Vidal.

2. For these patrons who all died within such a short period of time, see note 12 to the general introduction (p. 239). Adelaide of Roquemartine was separated from her husband in 1191 and died in 1201.

3. Le Thoronet is a romanesque abbey just off the main road from Aix-en-Provence to Fréjus on the Côte d'Azur, five miles north of the town of Le Luc. It is still standing, completely intact, and it is one of the most beautiful Cistercian abbeys in France.

4. Grandselve was an important Cistercian abbey (not a trace of which remains) about twenty-five miles northwest of Toulouse, near the village of Bouillac.

5. In order to get a proper idea of the sound and rhythm of this stanza, the reader should realize that all its rhymes are masculine, or in other words he should be sure to accent all the rhyme words on the last syllable—*sové, avé, mercé, faissó* and *razó.*

6. Jeanroy, for instance, in his *Poésie lyrique des troubadours,*

Vol. II, pp. 148–151 does little but complain about what he considers to be Folquet's dry, logic-chopping verse.

7. *Paradiso*, IX, 37. It must be noted that Folquet de Marseille—although perhaps because of the role he played later in his life—is the only troubadour Dante places in Paradise.

Poem 1: *Amors, merce! no mueira tan soven!* (Pillet 155, 1; Gennrich 77)

This and another poem by Folquet de Marseille (*Per Deu, Amors*), judging by the number of manuscripts in which they appear, were among the best-known poems in all of Provençal literature, a fact which is in sharp contrast to their almost total neglect in modern times.

8. Stronski conjectured that Aziman ("Magnet") was a reciprocal *senhal* between Folquet and Bertran de Born (see note 18 under the latter poet). He also suggested, with considerable reservations, that Tostemps ("All-the-Time") might be a pseudonym for the troubadour Raimon de Miraval.

Poem 2: *Tant m'abellis l'amoros pessamens* (Pillet 155, 22; Gennrich 87)

This poem was also very famous in the Middle Ages, and it was quoted by Dante in his *De Vulgari Eloquentia*. Since its melody is particularly lovely, I will give it along with the first stanza of the poem.

9. Who these three patronesses from Nîmes are, is a bit of mystery. Stronski said they might be the mother, wife and perhaps sister of the last Viscount of Nîmes, Bernard-Aton VI.

Poem 3: *En chantan m'aven a membrar* (Pillet 155, 8; Gennrich 80)

This poem must have been known in far-off lands, for its melody and, to a certain extent, its contents were copied by the German minnesinger Friedrich von Hûsen.

10. For Aziman, see note 8 above.

11. This is William VIII of Montpellier (1172–1202) next to whom Folquet de Marseille was to be buried many years later (see p. 174). Folquet is here asking to be pardoned for remarks made in an earlier poem, where he had criticized William for repudiating his first wife, the daughter of the Greek Emperor, Manuel I Comnenus.

The Monk of Montaudon

Bibliography

We have only sixteen poems by the Monk of Montaudon (two of them with music), and they have been edited three separate times—first by E. Philippson, *Der Moench von Montaudon*, Halle, 1873; then by C. Klein, *Die Dichtungen des Moenchs von Montaudon;* and finally by R. Lavaud in the Duc de la Salle de Rochemaure's *Les Troubadours Cantaliens*, 2 vols., Aurillac, 1910. This last book is a strangely heterogeneous affair, a mixture of twelfth-century troubadours and nineteenth-century regionalist poets. The works of the Monk of Montaudon are in the second part of Vol. II, and the notes in Vol. I. Also the translations are in French, except for dirty passages, which have been rendered into Latin.

1. Orlac is the modern town of Aurillac in the southern Auvergne. Vic-sur-Cère (as it is now called) is ten miles to the northeast.

2. Nobody has yet been able to identify Montaudon with any degree of certainty. In any case, it must *not* be confused with Montauban, the town north of Toulouse.

3. These details are based more or less on information the biographer gleaned from Poem 1 below.

4. Puoi Santa Maria is the modern Le Puy, and the court mentioned in the next sentence was a kind of poetic society which gave a sparrow hawk as a prize.

5. This Villafranca has also not been identified (Spain is full of Villafrancas and, unfortunately, a good many of them seem to have had Benedictine monasteries).

Poem 1: *L'autrier fui en paradis* (Pillet 305, 12)

A little dialogue between the Monk and God, in which the two take sides somewhat different from those one might expect.

6. This Paris is not the French capital, but probably some obscure village in the southern Auvergne. The person referred to seems to be Guigue Meschin, lord of Randon and Châteauneuf which, although two separate castles at that time, now form the village of Châteauneuf-de-Randon, about thirty miles southwest of Le Puy.

7. Or in other words, Richard the Lionhearted. (Olairos is either the town of Oloron in the western Pyrenees or the island of Oléron off the west coast of France, both of which were within Richard's domains.)

8. A reference to Richard's captivity in Germany from late 1192 to early 1194.

Poem 2: *Autra vetz fui a parlamen* (Pillet 305, 7)

Another dialogue with God, this one prompted by the complaints of holy images (ie. statues) that their prerogatives in the matter of being painted are being infringed upon by women using so much make-up.

9. As one scholar (André Berry) said, "This is perhaps a reference to an ointment which served both as make-up and as an astringent. Doesn't the Monk further on complain of a certain excess breadth which spoils his fun?"

10. This is the same Aelis de Montfort mentioned under Bertran de Born, note 17.

Poem 3: *Pois Peire d'Alvernh' a chantat* (Pillet 305, 16; Gennrich 297)

This poem is modeled, both in form and content, on Peire d'Alvernhe's famous satire (see his Poem 4). It was written about twenty-five years later—1195—and the Monk could therefore benefit from a whole new generation of troubadours at which to poke fun and sling mud. As with the other poem, I have omitted the passages concerning lesser-known figures.

11. A poet from Saint-Didier-en-Velay (twenty-six miles northwest of Le Puy), who became lord of that town by 1165 and died between 1195 and 1200. The Monk of Montaudan is reproving him for the fact that (as the Provençal biographer says) he had to get the permission of his lady's husband in order to court her.

12. This is Raimon Jordan, Viscount of Saint-Antonin (twenty-two miles northeast of Montauban) who wrote towards the end of

the twelfth century. His biography states that when he went off to war and was wounded, his lady was mistakenly told that he had been killed. Out of grief she became a heretic, and thus the weeping mentioned here.

13. This is the troubadour Raimon de Miraval (from the town of that name twelve miles north of Carcassonne) who wrote between 1180 and 1213. In his poems he is always giving away his castle, but since he shared it with three brothers (and therefore only owned one quarter of it), and since in any case it seems to have been a rather dismal place, the gift involved little loss.

14. Peirol was a well-known troubadour from the Auvergne, who wrote between 1185 and 1221. About his taking up with whores, we know no more than what's stated here.

15. Gaucelm Faidit was from Uzerche (thirty-two miles southeast of Limoges) and was an almost exact contemporary of Peirol. The biographer says of him that he "dearly loved to eat and drink, and thus became exceedingly fat . . . . And he married a whore . . . . called Guilhelma Monja. She was lovely and well-educated, but she soon became as big and fat as he."

16. Guilhem Ademar was a poet from Meyrueis (twenty-five miles south of Mende). He was a knight turned jongleur who wrote towards the end of the twelfth century.

17. This is a reference to the famous lines of Arnaut Daniel, for which see his Poem 3 and note 26.

18. The Monk of Montaudon is poking fun at Arnaut de Maruelh's continual cries for mercy (one scholar counted twenty-one such passages in his poetry).

19. In a biography of Folquet de Marseille (which I did not give under that poet) the story is told of how upon being spurned by one lady he became very sad and "abandoned singing and laughter," but was soon revived by the attentions of another lady. It seems to be this abandonment to which the Monk of Montaudon is referring, although there does exist the possibility that he is referring to the taking of monastic vows.

20. This is a reference to the episode of his tongue being cut out (see the biography on p. 164). There is perhaps also a play on words, meaning that "he'll need a silver tongue to talk his way out of the trouble he's in."

21. For the "lard," see the biography in which King Alfonso commands him to eat meat. One gathers that the good Monk felt the lack of it to be one of the main hazards of monastic life.

22. Caussade is probably the town fourteen miles northeast of Montauban. Lobeo might be the modern Loupian, about halfway

between Agde and Montpellier. If so, En Bernart would be Bernart-Aton, Viscount of Nîmes and Agde.

Guilhem de Cabestanh

Bibliography

We have only nine poems of Guilhem de Cabestanh (none with music), and at that two of them are of doubtful attribution. They have been excellently edited by Arthur Långfors, *Les chansons de Guilhem de Cabestanh*, Paris, 1924 (in the series "Les Classiques francais du moyen âge"). This edition is still available and inexpensive.

1. Cabestany is a village just three miles southeast of Perpignan.
2. Of Castel-Roussillon there is nothing left but some medieval and Roman ruins three miles east of Perpignan. Raymond and his wife Seremonda are completely historical figures, and one of those strange accidents of fate has even preserved their marriage contract dating from 1197.
3. To be a killjoy about this whole lovely story, it must be stated that we have documentary evidence that Seremonda outlived her husband and even married again. And what's more, other versions of the story go on to tell how Guilhem's death was avenged by King Alfonso of Aragon, who died in 1196, a year before Seremonda and Raimond were married!
4. This passage is from Canto IV.
5. Boccaccio used it for one of the stories in the *Decameron*, and Stendhal translated it in *De l'amour*. (Both of these used different versions of the story from the one printed here.)

Poem 1: *Lo jorn qu'ie·us vi, dompna, primeiramen* (Pillet 213, 6)

Although this poem has no particularly outstanding qualities, it is all the same typical of the charm and delicacy of Guilhem de Cabestanh's verse.

Peire Cardenal

Bibliography

We have seventy-four poems definitely attributable to Peire Cardenal (only three of them with music), and twenty-two others which may well be by him. The long-awaited edition by René Lavaud finally appeared two years after his death: *Poésies complètes du troubadour Peire Cardenal,* Toulouse, 1957. One hates to carp at a man's lifetime work which he was never to see in print, yet this edition is somewhat of a disappointment: it is badly organized, excessively verbose and not altogether reliable. But it's the best we have, and I have followed it for the most part in my translations and notes.

1. This is the modern Le Puy. The Velay is the region around it.
2. That is, the canonry of the cathedral, as opposed to that of one of the lesser churches.
3. This is James I the Conqueror (ruled 1213–1276).
4. Miquel de la Tor was from Clermont-Ferrand. He was not only a poet himself, but he also, around 1300, compiled an anthology of troubadour verse (which is now lost but which we know about thanks to a sixteenth-century Italian critic).
5. This one short phrase, written in 1861 by the great Spanish critic, Milá y Fontanals, characterizes Peire Cardenal far better than most of the reams of verbiage turned out concerning him since then (see his *De los Trovadores en España,* p. 42).

Poem 1: *Ar me puesc ieu lauzar d'Amor* (Pillet 335, 7; Gennrich 185)

An amusing satire in which Peire Cardenal boasts of having freed himself from all the ridiculous bondage of courtly love.

6. I have omitted a fifth stanza and envoy in which Peire Cardenal suddenly dashes headlong into untranslatable alliteration. Here is a sample, just to set the reader's head properly swimming:

Pauc pres prim prec de pregador
can cre qu'il, cuy quer convertir,
vir vas vil voler sa valor,
don dreitz deu dar dan al partir.

Poem 2: *Li clerc si fan pastor* (Pillet 335, 31)

A particularly violent attack against the greed and treachery of the churchmen of the day.

7. Isengrim was the wolf in the very popular medieval fable of Reynard the Fox.

8. Probably a reference to Gregory IX's attempts to bring the Emperor Frederick II to heel, attempts which were reduced pretty much to nought by the Treaty of San Germano in 1230.

Poem 3: *Un estribot farai, que er mot maistratz* (Pillet 335, 64)

Another and even more virulent attack on the clergy.

9. An *estribot* is a verse form of which only two examples remain in all of Provençal literature. It is not a lyric form (ie. it is not divided into stanzas), but rather built on a long succession of alexandrines all on the same rhyme. (It was mentioned in Raimbaut d'Orange's Poem 3—see note 17 there.)

10. A reference to the story in Saint Luke (1:41) of how Mary, after the Annunciation, went to tell the news to her cousin Elisabeth, who was then already pregnant with the future Saint John. "And it came to pass, that, when Elisabeth heard the salutation of Mary, the babe leaped in her womb."

11. The original has *li'retge e li essabatatz,* or "the heretics and the shoed-ones." In those days "heretic" meant specifically a Catharist (or Albigensian); whereas *essabatatz* was a popular name for the Vaudois (or Waldenses, followers of Peter Waldo of Lyons), apparently because of a particular kind of shoe they wore in their ambulant life of Christian poverty.

12. The Black Monks were the Benedictines.

Poem 4: *Las amairitz, qui encolpar las vol* (Pillet 335, 30)

Another diatribe, this one directed against courtesans, and against the injustices committed by the rich against the poor.

13. For Isengrim, see note 7 above. "Women," by the way, is a feeble translation of *amairitz*, English amorous terminology being somewhat meager. In French it would be "amantes" or "amoureuses."

Poem 5: *Tostemps azir falsetat et enjan* (Pillet 335, 57)

This poem, in which the invective is directed more generally against fraud and falsehood among the rich, was—judging once more from the number of manuscripts containing it— Peire Cardenal's most widely read work during the Middle Ages.

14. A besant was a gold (or silver) coin of Byzantine origin. A tournois was a coin minted in the northern French town of Tours. As one can see from the context, the former was of considerable value and the latter of little value.

15. Faidit could be the troubadour Gaucelm Faidit (for whom see note 15 under the Monk of Montaudon), but there is no way of knowing. En Guigon is probably Gui II, Count of Auvergne (1194–1224), brother of the Eble of Clermont mentioned in the last line. Tournoël was a castle whose magnificent ruins are still standing eight miles north of Clermont-Ferrand.

Poem 6: *Una ciutatz fo, no sai cals* (cf. Pillet p. 299)

This extraordinary fable (or "sermon," as it is called in some manuscripts) with its allegory of the rain, is quite different from anything else in Provençal literature. The idea may have been invented by Peire Cardenal, but there is also some reason for believing it to be of popular origin.

In form this piece is not lyric (ie. not divided into stanzas), but is composed rather of rhymed couplets.

16. In the Middle Ages shops either consisted of outdoor wooden stalls (as in present-day European markets) or of a house whose front groundfloor window was covered at night by a solid wood shutter hinged at the bottom and which, during the day, was let down into a horizontal position to serve as a counter. It was these counters on which the madmen jumped.

Sordello

Bibliography

We have forty-three poems by Sordello, none of them with music. For years the standard edition was that of de Lollis (Halle, 1896), but this has recently been replaced by Marco Boni's excellent *Sordello, le poesie,* Bologna, 1954.

1. This is the modern Goito, nine miles northwest of Mantua. In Provençal, by the way, the poet's name is Sordel, but since he himself was Italian and since the Italian form of his name has become so much more familiar, I will use it throughout.

2. Ezzelino, lord of the March of Treviso (before dying in 1259, he succeeded in dominating not only Treviso, but also Verona, Vicenza and Padua), was a tyrant whose cruelties made Dante place him in Hell in the "red boiling" of Phlegeton. As for his sister, Cunizza, she was a woman who in her youth gained considerable notoriety by escapades of the sort described here. In her old age she finally settled down in Florence, as a guest of the Cavalcante family, dying when Dante was fifteen years old. He may well have met her there; in any case, by that time the mellowness of age seems to have made her a highly respected woman, for Dante places her in Paradise, in the same Canto (IX) as Folquet de Marseille. Her husband, Rizzardo de San Bonifacio, was lord of Verona until Ezzelino took over in 1226.

3. About these lords of Strasso we know almost nothing. In addition, the location of the "region of Onedo" (Onedes in the original) has more than somewhat mystified scholars.

4. This was Raimond Berenguer IV, who died in 1245.

5. We haven't the vaguest idea who this lady was.

Poem 1: *Aitant ses plus viu hom quan viu jauzens* (Pillet 437, 2)

This was Sordello's best-known *chanso* in the Middle Ages.

6. Sordello gets his metaphor a bit mixed here, with the sudden introduction of a ford and bridge.

7. N'Agradiva (the word means "agreeable, charming") is a *senhal* for Guida of Rodez, one of the best-known patronesses of

the thirteenth century. She was the daughter and sister of Counts of Rodez, and in about 1235 she married Pons of Montlaur, who was also lord of Vauvert and Castries (two towns between Montpellier and Saint-Gilles).

Poem 2: *Uns amics et un'amia* (Pillet 236, 12 = 437, 38)

I have included this poem so the reader can get some idea of what a *partimen* is like (see p. 22 of the introduction). This one is typical, with the small exception of the fact that in the end two judges are chosen instead of one. Guilhem de la Tor, with whom Sordello shares this poem, was a troubadour from the Perigord who spent most of his career in far-off Lombardy. His biography tells a touching tale of how when his wife died, he went mad and, after trying all sorts of devices to resuscitate her, finally died himself of despair.

8. A reference to André de France, who according to tradition died consumed with love for the Queen of France.

9. This Adelaide was the wife of Cavalcabò, lord of Viadana (as the town is now spelt—it is thirteen miles northeast of Parma), from whom she separated in 1234, apparently out of fear of being poisoned by him.

10. This, of course, is the famous Cunizza da Romano. But we're not at all sure it was she whom Sordello had in mind, for the two best manuscripts give a completely different name, Agneseta, which scholars haven't been able to identify.

Poem 3: *Planher vuelh en Blacatz en aquest leugier so* (Pillet 437, 24)

Although in theory this famous poem is a *planh* on the death of Blacatz, it is in fact a thinly disguised (and cleverly worked out) *sirventes* giving Sordello opportunity to fulminate against most of the reigning sovereigns of his day. Scholars now agree —after much discussion on the subject—that this poem was written towards the beginning of 1237 (or the end of 1236).

11. Blacatz was lord of Aups (in Provence, fourteen miles northwest of Draguignan). He was not only a highly regarded patron of troubadours (many of them praised him to the skies for his generosity), but also a poet himself.

12. The emperor is Frederick II, who had just been "humbled" by the Second Lombard League, of which Milan was the ringleader.

13. Louis IX (Saint Louis) of France, after a period of ten years beneath the tutelage of his mother, Blanche of Castile, had finally begun to rule personally in 1236; but even then she continued to have great influence over him. It was also through her that he could have claimed rights to the throne of Castile.

14. This is Henry III (1216–1272). For an account of how Philippe Auguste stripped his father of most of the English possessions in France, see p. 9 of the introduction.

15. Fernando III (San Fernando) became King of Castile in 1217 and of Leon in 1230—hence the "two realms." His mother was not only a sister of Blanche of Castile (see note 13 above), but seems to have shared with her the desire and ability to lead her son around by the nose.

16. This is James the Conqueror of Aragon (1213–1276). Marseille had rebelled against his cousin, Raimond Berenguer of Provence (see note 19 below) in 1230; and then, around 1237, he made a vain attempt to reconquer Millau, which had once been his.

17. This is Thibaut, Count of Champagne, who was crowned King of Navarre in 1234. He was also, incidentally, a fine poet—one of the best of the northern French trouvères.

18. Here we have Raymond VII of Toulouse who, with the treaty of Meaux in 1229, had lost two-thirds of his patrimony (see p. 13 of the introduction).

19. This is Raimond Berenguer IV of Provence, whom Sordello is here inciting to continue the struggle against his enemies, Raymond VII of Toulouse, the city of Marseille (see note 16 above) and their allies.

20. Belh Restaur (literally "Good Restorer") is probably another *senhal* for Guida of Rodez, for whom see note 7 above.

Cerverí

Bibliography

The complete works (except for the proverbs) have been superbly edited by Martín de Riquer, *Obras completas del trovador Cerverí de Girona*, Barcelona, 1947. The articles in which Riquer proved that Cerverí was identical with an author of proverbs called Guilhem de Cervera, and that he also called himself Cerverí de Girona appeared in Vol. XXIII (1950), p. 91 and Vol. XXVIII (1959–60), p. 257 of the *Boletín de la Real Academia de Buenas Letras de Barcelona*.

Until Riquer brings out his promised biography of Cerverí, the best general survey of his life and works I know is that in Hoepffner's little book, *Les Troubadours* (see p. 233 above).

1. In a way the two names are identical, for Cerverí also means "from Cervera." Since there are several towns by this name in Catalonia, there is no way of our knowing which one he (or his family) came from. As for the Girona, which could have been his place of residence, that is merely the Provençal (and Catalan) form of Gerona.

Poem 1: *Si volets que·m laix d'amar* (Pillet 434a, 65)

A charming *balada* (a kind of dance song) in which the refrain not only returns at the end of each stanza but is interwoven into the stanza itself.

2. This is Peter the Great of Aragon (for whom see the introduction) when he was still heir to the throne (*infante*).

3. This is Sibila of Cardona (for whom also see the introduction). The original of this last envoy is rather curious in that Cerverí splits the word *Cardona* over two lines for the sake of the rhyme and meter, and then in the last two lines he piles up a wonderful jumble of alliterated monosyllables:

> Prous vezcomtesa de Car-
> dona, tan dir no poria
> de be del vostre cors car
> qu'en vos mays mil tans no·n sia.

Poem 2: *Greu pot nuyl hom conoixer en la mar* (Pillet 434, 1)

This poem is a gloss on the following passage from Proverbs, 30: 18–20:

There be three things which are too wonderful for me, yea, four which I know not: The way of an eagle in the air; the way of a serpent upon a rock; the way of a ship in the midst of the sea; and the way of a man with a maid. Such is the way of an adulterous woman; she eateth, and wipeth her mouth, and saith, I have done no wickedness.

4. For the Lady of Cartz and King Peter, see the introduction. As for Sobrepretz (literally "High Merit"), it is a *senhal* which as far as I know has not yet been identified.

Poem 3: *Us an chan* (Pillet 434a, 80)

Here we have Cerverí the juggler with words at his trickiest: a poem in which every line is a monosyllable, except for two in each stanza and the envoy, where he admits defeat (like Bertran de Born, in his Poem 7).

5. Two of these lines are missing in the manuscript, and the third is a meaningless monosyllable.

6. For Sobrepretz, Cartz and King Peter, see note 4 above and the introduction.

Poem 4: *Taflamart faflama* (*Tart fa*) (Pillet 434a, 66 and 68)

In case the reader is a bit perplexed, let me assure him that this is a faithful translation of thirteenth-century pig Latin, which, as far as I can see, differs not in the slightest from that in fashion when I was a kid two-thirds of a millennium later. The interposed syllables are (the dashes stand for the vowel of the syllable being interposed upon):

Stanza I: –fl–m–
Stanza II: –f–rr–
Stanza III: –p–p–
Stanza IV: –m–m–
Stanza V: –rr–v–
Stanza VI: –f–rr– (like II)
Stanza VII: –fl–m– (like I)

So that the perhaps incredulous reader can see for himself, here are the opening words of the original, both in pig Latin and in deciphered form.

| Taflamart | faflama | hoflomom | maflamal . . . |
| Tart | fa | hom | mal . . . |

7. For Soforrobreferrepreferretz and Cafarrartz, see note 4 above and the introduction.

8. A reference to James the Conqueror's projects for a crusade to the Holy Land. The fiflimive kiflimings might be those of Aragon, Castile, Portugal, France and England.

Guiraut Riquier

Bibliography

We have 104 poems of Guiraut Riquier, and forty-eight of them with music (a tremendously high percentage of the total, but this again is due to chance). The standard edition of his works was done more than a hundred years ago by J. L. Pfaff as Vol. IV of Mahn's *Die Werke der Troubadours*, Berlin, 1853. For a study of his life and works, there is J. Anglade's *Le Troubadour Guiraut Riquier. Etude sur la décadence de l'ancienne poésie provençale*, Paris, 1905.

Unfortunately, I have been able to consult neither of these works, so I have had to select from the mere dozen or so poems that have appeared in other anthologies. Since this practice of making anthologies from other anthologies is one of the plagues of the modern world, I have consistently avoided it in the rest of this book—but here I had no choice.

1. Calling Guiraut Riquier the "last of the troubadours" is one of those sweeping statements that makes scholars shudder; but it is nevertheless substantially true.

Poem 1: *L'autre jorn m'anava* (Pillet 248, 49)

Written in 1260, this is the first in a series of six *pastorelas* which together form a little romance or novel. They all concern the same shepherdess whom Guiraut Riquier encounters at intervals of several years.

2. This *senhal* appears in many poems of Guiraut Riquier, poems stretching over a period of twenty years, yet we have no idea to whom it refers.

3. This Bertran d'Opian is also a mystery (he was probably from the modern Oupia fifteen miles northwest of Narbonne).

Poem 2: *A Sant Pos de Tomeiras* (Pillet 248, 15)

Written in 1282, this is the last in the same series of six *pastorelas*. Here—twenty-two years later—Guiraut Riquier enters an inn to find it is run by his former shepherdess. But his efforts are as fruitless as ever, even with the now grown daughter with whom he tries, so to speak, to get the consolation prize.

4. Saint-Pons-de-Thomières (as it is now spelled) is a town twenty-five miles northwest of Narbonne.

5. A reference to *Pastorela* No. 5, in which Guiraut Riquier had met the shepherdess with a baby near l'Isle-Jourdain (twenty miles west of Toulouse).

6. This is Bernard IV, Count of Astarac from 1249 to 1291.

Poem 3: *Be·m degra de chantar tener* (Pillet 248, 17)

A tragic, bitter and yet touching poem which is not only Guiraut Riquier's swan song, but in a certain sense that of all troubadour poetry. It was written in 1292, after almost forty years of wandering in search of sympathetic patronage, and finally we see the poet overwhelmed by the futility of his endeavors.

Index

NOTE: This index is limited to names and words which seemed important or which appear with some degree of frequency in the text. All medieval personages are listed under their first names. Modern forms of place names are given preference. Only spelling variants which might cause confusion are cross-indexed; for the rest, the reader should develop a certain tolerance for medieval indecisions such as Montagnac-Montanhac, Auvergne-Alvernhe, Maruelh-Maroill-(or the modern)Mareuil.

Numbers in boldface indicate the pages where a troubadour's poems (or the notes thereto) are presented, where a name is discussed or a word explained.